ESSAYS ON CAPITAL AND INTEREST

THE COLLECTED WORKS OF ISRAEL M. KIRZNER

ISRAEL M. KIRZNER

Essays on

Capital and Interest

An Austrian Perspective

Edited and with an Introduction by

PETER J. BOETTKE and FRÉDÉRIC SAUTET

LIBERTY FUND Indianapolis

This book is published by Liberty Fund, Inc., a foundation established to encourage study of the ideal of a society of free and responsible individuals.

Editors' introduction and index © 2010 by Liberty Fund, Inc.
Essays on Capital and Interest was first published by Edward Elgar Publishing in 1996.

Author's introduction to *Essays on Capital and Interest* © 1996 by Israel M. Kirzner. Reprinted by permission.
"An Essay on Capital" © 1966 by Israel M. Kirzner. Reprinted by permission.
"Ludwig von Mises and the Theory of Capital and Interest" is reprinted from *The Economics of Ludwig von Mises: Toward a Critical Reappraisal*, edited by Laurence S. Moss (Kansas City: Sheed & Ward; Arlington: Institute for Humane Studies, 1976), 51–65. Reprinted by permission of the Institute for Humane Studies.
"The Pure Time-Preference Theory of Capital and Interest" is reprinted from *The Meaning of Ludwig von Mises: Contributions in Economics, Sociology, Epistemology, and Political Philosophy*, edited by Jeffrey M. Herbener (Norwell, Mass.: Kluwer Academic, 1993), 166–92. Reprinted with kind permission of Springer Science and Business Media.
"The Theory of Capital" is reprinted from *The Foundations of Modern Austrian Economics*, edited by Edwin G. Dolan (Kansas City: Sheed & Ward; Arlington: Institute for Humane Studies, 1976), 133–44. Reprinted by permission of the Institute for Humane Studies.

Printed in the United States of America.

C 10 9 8 7 6 5 4 3 2 1
P 10 9 8 7 6 5 4 3 2 1

Library of Congress Cataloging-in-Publication Data

Kirzner, Israel M.
    Essays on capital and interest : an Austrian perspective / edited and with an introduction by Peter J. Boettke and Frédéric Sautet.
        p. cm. — (The collected works of Israel M. Kirzner)
    "Essays on Capital and Interest was first published by Edward Elgar Publishing in 1996."
    Includes bibliographical references and index.
    ISBN 978-0-86597-780-8 (hbk.: alk. paper)—
    ISBN 978-0-86597-781-5 (pbk.: alk. paper)
    1. Capital.   2. Interest.   3. Austrian school of economics.   4. Von Mises, Ludwig, 1881–1973.   I. Boettke, Peter J.   II. Sautet, Frédéric E.   III. Title.
    HB501 .K473 2012
    332'.041—dc23   2012000553

LIBERTY FUND, INC.
8335 Allison Pointe Trail, Suite 300
Indianapolis, Indiana 46250–1684

B'EZRAS HASHEM

CONTENTS

INTRODUCTION TO THE
LIBERTY FUND EDITION

Explaining the nature of capital and the phenomenon of interest has been one of Israel Kirzner's goals in his work on pure theory. These themes were already present in *Market Theory and the Price System*, but it was with the publication of *An Essay on Capital* (essay 2 in this volume) in 1966 that the author tackled the subject directly. Subsequently, Kirzner published two other essays continuing the exploration of the same theme. "Ludwig von Mises and the Theory of Capital and Interest," published in 1976 (essay 3 in this volume), reflects on Ludwig von Mises's theory of capital and interest. "The Pure Time-Preference Theory of Interest," published in 1993 (essay 4 in this volume), attempts to clarify the difficult issue of the pure time-preference theory of interest (e.g., explaining why the price of a tree does not equal the value of the total fruit output). We are using in this volume the 1996 edition of *Essays on Capital and Interest* published by Edward Elgar, which gathered those three essays and an introduction (essay 1 in this volume). We have included Kirzner's 1966 preface before the text of essay 2, as well as, at the end of this volume, an article entitled *The Theory of Capital*, which was published in 1976.

A constant theme in Kirzner's work is methodological subjectivism. As early as his doctoral work under the mentorship of Ludwig von Mises, Kirzner realized the importance of a subjective approach to understanding economic phenomena. Kirzner often cites Hayek's famous statement in *The Counter-revolution of Science:* "And it is probably no exaggeration to say that every important advance in economic theory during the last hundred years was a further step in the consistent application of subjectivism."[1] Kirzner's theoretical research on the nature of capital and interest is an early application of subjectivism in his work.

Austrian economists have always pursued a subjectivist approach to interest and its relationship to capital, going back to Carl Menger's emphasis that resources could not be intrinsically productive. Menger saw interest as the result of subjective valuations rather than an intrinsic property concerning the physical nature of capital. Kirzner put it in a thoroughly subjectivist manner: "In exactly the same way as Austrian value theory had no

---

1. See Friedrich A. Hayek (1979), *The Counter-revolution of Science: Studies on the Abuse of Reason,* 2d ed. (Indianapolis: Liberty Fund), p. 51.

place for 'cost of production' as an independent explanatory element . . . in the causation of economic value, a Mengerian capital and interest theory could have no place for the productivity of capital as an independent explanatory element in accounting for the structure of prices. . . . All prices, including interest, are brought about strictly by the actions expressing the valuations of purposeful human beings."[2] Austrian economists view the phenomenon of interest as the result of time preference and not as some intrinsic property of capital goods. The interest rate is merely a price, albeit one "particular kind of price—the intertemporal price—that is determined, along with all the other market phenomena, by the multiperiod plans that are being made by market participants."[3]

Mark Blaug concisely summarized the contribution of Kirzner's original *Essay on Capital* as follows: "Capital theory should never lose touch with its microeconomic foundations in acts of individual choice and must be viewed as consisting essentially of the economics of multi-period production planning."[4] If *Market Theory and the Price System* examines how relative prices adjust to changing circumstances to guide production and consumption decisions so that the coordination of economic activity results, then *An Essay on Capital* focuses on the concept of the "plan": the multiperiod production plans that actors initiate, revise in the wake of new knowledge, and sometimes leave unfinished. It is this notion of the "plan" that opens up the intellectual space for Kirzner's later work on entrepreneurship and his more mature understanding of the entrepreneurial market process.

One can find parallels between Kirzner's work on entrepreneurship (after 1973) and his work on capital and the existence of interest. Kirzner's work on interest builds on Eugen von Böhm-Bawerk's and Mises's views in the same way that his work on entrepreneurship builds on Hayek's and Mises's research. Just as he sought to enrich Mises's view of the entrepreneur, he sought to clarify the work of Mises on interest. In doing so, Kirzner emphasized the following points: (a) future streams of output do not automatically flow from present resources (i.e., capital does not possess a productivity of its own), (b) capital goods at a given time are the results of past plans because all production is planned production (i.e., human purpose gives value to capital goods), and (c) production plans

---

2. See p. 4, below.
3. See p. 49, below.
4. See Mark Blaug (1969), "An Essay on Capital," *Econometrica* 37 (1), p. 158.

imply the sacrifice of present resources in order to obtain future ones (i.e., the value that this sacrifice represents to the individual gives rise to the phenomenon of interest).

The original 1966 *Essay* contains only one reference to entrepreneurship.[5] A literal reading of Kirzner's original work on capital and interest would conclude that it does not have much to do with his work on entrepreneurship. This is because his work on capital and interest was published before entrepreneurship became the focus in his career and he probably did not see any reason to develop an entrepreneurial theory of the phenomenon of interest and the capital structure. At another level, however, Kirzner's theory of capital and interest is about decision-making, plans, and projects of many individuals in a multiperiod context. In other words, it covers ground similar to that covered by market process theory. So while the two subjects of capital and entrepreneurship are analytically distinct, Kirzner's research on capital theory gave him the raw material for his future work on the issue of coordination and entrepreneurship in market process theory.

In 1966 Kirzner thought of the market as a system of interlocking individual plans using capital goods over multiple periods. Some of these plans "interlock" well with others and some do not. At any given time, some plans are finished, others are being revised, and new ones are emerging. A theory of capital based on purposeful human decisions is a key element in understanding the market process. In this sense, Kirzner realized that capital theory was much more than simply a "mere adjunct to the theory of interest." The idea of the market as a process, which became the focus of his work at the end of the 1960s, was already present in Kirzner's 1966 work on capital and interest.

In addition, Kirzner's theory of capital and interest further elaborates the bridge between the logic of choice in microeconomics and the emerging structure of the macroeconomy. In his review of the 1996 *Essays on Capital and Interest*, Roger Garrison went so far as to offer a warning to all economists of the Austrian persuasion:

> No Austrian economist who takes his subjectivism seriously should draw a Hayekian triangle until he has read Professor Kirzner's *Essays!* There is no inherent clash between the macroeconomic theorizing that the Hayekian triangles facilitate (including the Austrian theory of the business cycle) and the Kirznerian perspective that keeps the triangle

5. See pp. 41–42, below.

adequately subjectivized. Quite to the contrary, it is precisely our understanding of the process that Professor Kirzner elucidates, the ongoing attempts on the part of many entrepreneurs to carry out their individual multiperiod plans (as guided by market rates of interest or as misguided by the central bank's rate of interest), that breathes subjectivist life into those otherwise meaningless triangles.[6]

Garrison went on to argue that Kirzner's work does more than just give meaning to the Hayekian analytics; it paves the way for the reconstruction of modern macroeconomics along capital-theoretic grounds. Kirzner builds the bridge between choice-theoretic market process theory and capital-theoretic macroeconomic analysis.

After reading Kirzner's *Essay on Capital* and Donald Dewey's *Modern Capital Theory* in the 1960s, Ludwig Lachmann half-jokingly asked Kirzner whether the economists at New York University and those at Columbia University ever talked to one another. Admittedly there is something of the tone and method of an isolated scholar in *Essay on Capital*. One might think that Kirzner was simply trying to work through the material in capital theory and figure it out for himself without much interest in engaging his contemporary peers in economic debate. But Kirzner's focus on older "debates" in capital theory related to the works of Böhm-Bawerk, Irving Fisher, and Frank Knight, as well as his discussion of "waiting" and "capital measurement," provide the tools necessary to address more contemporary debates such as the "Cambridge Controversy" as well as increasing returns and path dependency. Ralph Pfouts's review of Kirzner's *Essay* for the *American Economic Review* points out a key Kirzner insight: one cannot ignore the subjective "element of decision making which can be encompassed only by the multi-period planning approach to capital theory."[7]

ACKNOWLEDGMENTS

We would first like to thank wholeheartedly Israel Kirzner for his unparalleled contribution to economic science. Kirzner's research program has deeply enriched the discipline and has shed light on some of eco-

---

6. See Roger Garrison (1997), "The Undiscountable Professor Kirzner," *The Freeman* 47 (8), pp. 511–13.

7. See Ralph W. Pfouts (1968), "Review of *An Essay on Capital* by Israel Kirzner," *American Economic Review* 58 (1), p. 196.

nomics' most difficult puzzles. Economists owe him an immense intellectual debt.

The publication of The Collected Works of Israel M. Kirzner would not be a reality without the participation of Liberty Fund, Inc. We are extremely grateful to Liberty Fund, and especially to Emilio Pacheco, for making this project possible. To republish Kirzner's unique œuvre has been on our minds since our time spent at New York University in the 1990s—where one of us was a professor (Peter) and the other was a postdoctoral student (Frédéric). We are thrilled to know that current and future generations of economists and other scholars will have easy access to Kirzner's works.

Finally, we wish to thank Rosemarie Fike for her invaluable help in the publication of this volume.

Peter J. Boettke and Frédéric Sautet

ESSAYS ON CAPITAL
AND INTEREST

ESSAY 1 INTRODUCTION

The republication of the three essays which make up the body of this book offers an opportunity to place these papers in the context of more widely known twentieth-century developments in the area of capital and interest theory. As the sub-title of this book announces, each of these papers was written in the spirit of the Austrian tradition in economics, and specifically in order to clarify and develop what I have understood to be the Misesian position on these issues. The first of the three essays (Essay 2 in this book) was published in 1966, and dealt only with capital theory. Mises was still alive and active at that time, and he reviewed the essay before its publication. The second essay, published in 1976 (Essay 3 in this book), had been written in 1974 as a contribution to a symposium on the economics of Ludwig von Mises, who had died about a year earlier; the essay covered Mises's views on both capital and interest. The third essay (published in 1993) had been written in the late 1980s in an attempt to clarify (as much for myself as for others) what Mises (and of course Fetter) could possibly have meant by a theory of interest which recognized only time preference as the root cause of the phenomenon of interest, with what seems to be no recognition at all for any productivity-of-capital element in causing the interest phenomenon.

At the time the first of these three essays was written the Austrian tradition was widely perceived as having long died out. The subjectivist concerns which inspired that essay were almost invariably brushed aside in the profession generally as, at best, purist worries holding only trivial implications for economic theory, let alone policy. By the time the third essay was published, Austrian subjectivism had, in a resurgence quite remarkable in the history of economic thought, once again captured the attention of many (especially younger) economists. The insights of Ludwig von Mises are today no longer dismissed as old-fashioned economic philosophizing (or worse). It is now recognized that the methodological tenets which have shaped the course of mid-twentieth-century neoclassical economics have diverted the attention of economists from key insights which are essential for understanding the way in which economies in fact work. A number of these insights have, during the past two decades, been rediscovered in the work of Mises and the Austrian tradition (including, particularly, the contributions of Friedrich Hayek).

For the most part, the rediscovery of Misesian subjectivism has tended to illuminate modern Austrian understanding of the market process, without regard to intertemporal considerations. Relatively little modern Austrian attention has been paid to further developing Misesian insights into the role of capital in the full market process, and into the theory of interest.[1] (A good deal of recent attention has of course been paid to refining and restating the Hayekian theory of the business cycle. And certainly this theory is deeply embedded in Böhm-Bawerkian capital-theoretic insights. However, a fairly strong case can be made that when Hayek developed that theory at the end of the 1920s from the sketched outline offered many years earlier by Mises, he was not yet as fully alive to the subjectivism of Mises's general approach as he was later to become. It is this which, for this writer, explains why the recent Austrian work on Hayekian cycle theory seems, on the whole, to fail to draw on the subjectivist, Misesian, tradition which the contemporary Austrian resurgence has done so much to revive.) So the Misesian approach to problems of capital and interest developed in the essays in this book may be able to make a contribution to that broader, subjectivist understanding of economic processes and relationships which is emerging from the contemporary revival of the Austrian tradition in economic thought.

During the second half of the twentieth century (that is, the period since the publication of Mises's *Human Action*) a number of developments in the treatment of capital and interest problems occurred, of course, outside Austrian economics. In particular a celebrated "grand debate" arose (mainly during the 1960s) between the defenders of neoclassical orthodoxy in the theory of capitalist distribution, and the radical critics of that theory (the latter often identified as the Italian-Cambridge School—the Cambridge being, of course, the UK Cambridge).[2] In this debate, with its unmistakably ideological overtones,[3] the neoclassical defenders were largely relying on Irving Fisher's theory of interest with its related framework of capital theory, a framework in which productivity elements were prominently present. The Austrian (that is, the Böhm-

1. For an example of recent attention to subjectivist theory in the area of capital and interest problems, see Garrison (1985).

2. The term "grand debate" was applied by Ludwig Lachmann (1973a). An account of the debate from a protagonist of the Cambridge (UK) side is given in Harcourt (1972). An assessment from the other side is provided by Blaug (1974).

3. For a comment on the ideological overtones of the debate, see Solow (1975).

Bawerkian) roots of this neoclassical framework were to some extent recognized in that debate. What was not recognized at all was that that neoclassical "Austrian" framework was by no means the only intellectual progeny of Böhm-Bawerk's seminal work on capital and interest. Alongside the better known Fisherine development of Böhm-Bawerkian doctrine there emerged an entirely separate filiation of Austrian ideas in regard, especially, to the theory of interest. This tradition emerged particularly in the pure time-preference theory of interest espoused by Fetter and later Mises. While this second Austrian tradition, too, derived in large part from Böhm-Bawerk, its more consistent subjectivism seems attributable also to more sensitive appreciation of the Mengerian legacy. We shall argue below that the failure of the two sides in the above "grand debate" to recognize the existence and relevance of a third option—the more subjective version of Austrian theory—rendered that debate both incomplete and inconclusive.

THE MENGERIAN LEGACY

For the Austrian tradition subjectivism was, of course, the key, revolutionary, insight. The classical economists had attributed the regularities governing economic phenomena to the objective physical and biological conditions under which societies exist. The Austrians, on the other hand, found these regularities to have their roots in the valuations and the decisions of acting human beings. For other marginalist schools of economic thought in the post-1870 era, economic regularities reflected the interplay of both the objective physical conditions governing production and supply and the subjective preferences underlying consumer demand. The Mengerian view, however, relegated the objective conditions governing production to the passive background upon which the actions of purposeful human beings impinged. What *actively* shaped subsequent economic phenomena was seen to be *only* the actions of such purposeful human beings. This way of seeing the economic process was expressed perhaps most clearly in Menger's well-known conception of "orders" of productive factors.

Goods which confer utility directly to the consumer are "goods of lowest order"; resources which produce consumer goods are "goods of higher order" (in an ascending ranking which treats the resources most remote from the finally consumed good as goods of highest order). For Menger the significance, the economic value, attached to productive factors was perceived as being derived not directly from the objective productive potential of those factors, but strictly from the resulting valuations which consumers (or their surrogates, the entrepreneurs) place upon them as being useful in promoting consumption utility.

It is not difficult to see how this Mengerian refusal to accord *intrinsic* importance to the productivity of resources carries implications (not only for the theory of value, in which these implications have been recognized from the beginning, but also) for the theory of capital. In exactly the same way as Austrian value theory had no place for "cost of production" as an independent explanatory element (coordinate with "consumer utility") in the causation of economic value, a Mengerian capital and interest theory could have no place for the productivity of capital as an independent explanatory element in accounting for the structure of prices (including, especially, the phenomenon of interest). All prices, including interest, are brought about strictly by the actions expressing the valuations of purposeful human beings.

This implication of the Mengerian legacy was in large part lost sight of in Böhm-Bawerk's theory. In his monumental exploration into the role of time in production, and in the resulting development of his theory of capital and interest, Böhm-Bawerk seemed unable to avoid permitting the physical productivity of roundaboutness (or of time, or of waiting) to play an independently explanatory role in accounting for the phenomenon of market interest. So that subsequent interest theorists (particularly Irving Fisher) came to develop "Austrian" theories of interest which could hardly be considered Mengerian. Fisher's theory (and thus the mainstream of subsequent theorizing on capital and interest) has been considered Austrian in that it followed Böhm-Bawerk in emphasizing the role of time (both in enhancing the productivity of other resources and—through time-preference considerations—in shaping consumer decisions). But that theory must be considered as inconsistent with the fundamental Mengerian insight in that it treats the productivity of waiting as an independent explanatory element in accounting for the phenomenon of market interest.

It was thus Mises, in his 1940 *Nationalökonomie* rediscovery and further development of Fetter's pure time-preference theory of interest, who was to refine Böhm-Bawerkian theory and redirect it along Mengerian lines. In his slashing review article on Mises's book, Knight (1941) perceptively recognized this—and saw it as grounds for dismissing Mises's entire approach to the theory of capital and interest. In other words, Knight was attacking Mises not only because he was, like Böhm-Bawerk and Fisher, emphasizing the role of time in production (whereas for Knight the foundation of wisdom in this area consists in recognizing that "in a stationary economy, all production and consumption are strictly simultaneous; the waiting period is zero; there is none"; ibid., p. 420). Rather, he was attacking Mises for his "original and naive or absolute 'Austrianism'" (ibid., p. 422)—by which he apparently meant Mises's Mengerianism. (This reading of Knight's attack is reinforced by his own explicit rejection of Mises's frequent and favorable references to Menger's conception of the "order" of goods. On Knight's sweepingly dismissive attitude to this conception of Menger's, see also his highly critical introduction to the 1950 English edition of Menger's 1871 *Grundsätze*, p. 25.) For Knight, Mises's cardinal sin was not so much his emphasis on the role of time *per se*, as his denial of primary explanatory significance to the objective *productivity* of time.

MENGERIAN AUSTRIANISM AND THE CAMBRIDGE CONTROVERSY

As indicated earlier, we wish in this Introduction to draw attention to a certain incompleteness surrounding the Cambridge controversy. In that controversy mainstream neoclassical theory was under relentless attack by economists seeking to reverse the marginalist revolution and to return to the classical perspective. The critics, especially insofar as they were following Sraffa (1960), argued for an economics in which the objective conditions of production determine economic events, with virtually no role assigned to consumer demand. We wish to emphasize that what was overlooked in that debate was the existence of a third theoretical approach (a "Mengerian" approach) to capital and interest issues, in which the *entire* explanatory burden is assigned to consumer valuations. Our task in developing this critical observation regarding the Cambridge controversy is complicated by the fact that the *ideological* component of that controversy seems at first glance to place the mainstream neoclassical position squarely in Mengerian territory. In order to avoid confusion, therefore, it is necessary briefly to review this ideological element in the controversy.

From the Cambridge (UK) perspective, the error of mainstream neoclassical capital and interest theory consists in its explanation of distribution as being determined by the conditions of supply and demand. Given consumer preferences, resource availabilities and technological possibilities, the share of output going to capitalists as interest income is determined through the interplay of consequent supply and demand conditions. A different level of interest income would generate a suboptimal level of capital use: either consumers would be denied current consumption enjoyments without the justification of sufficiently worthwhile later increase in output, or else they would be enjoying current consumption at the cost of available, and preferred, later production (which might have been achieved through the maintenance of a higher level of capital use). The ideological element in the mainstream approach here being attacked is thus the "consumer sovereignty" claim held to be implicit in that approach. The Cambridge (UK) critics, denying the supply-and-demand determination of income distribution under capitalism, were denying that capitalist income shares benignly express (and cater to the satisfaction of) the preferences of the consuming public.

Now, the doctrine of consumer sovereignty appears closely tied to the Mengerian insights mentioned above. It was Menger who emphasized that the entire structure of prices (and thus factor incomes) is to be attributed to consumer preferences and valuations. Certainly, the Austrian development of the theory of the market saw market prices of both consumer goods and factor services as the expression of the relative valuations held by consumers. Yet, as indicated above, we shall maintain that the mainstream neoclassical theory under Cambridge attack can in no way be identified as Mengerian.

For the Cambridge critics the objectionable character of neoclassical theory arises out of its identifying interest as the additional value generated by productive capital. It is this feature of the theory which provides justification for the incomes enjoyed by capitalists: they are merely enjoying the value of what their capital has created for consumers. But what we have called the Mengerian (that is, the Menger-inspired) theory of capital and interest expounded by Mises in his 1940 book, emphatically rejects the interpretation of interest as a value of marginal product. For Mises's pure time-preference theory (as for Fetter's theory), capital productivity is neither a necessary nor a sufficient cause for interest. Interest is seen not as the value of any additional product but as expressing the difference between the valuations of a given prospective receipt by a consumer, made at different earlier dates. So Mises's theory of interest cannot possibly incur Cantabrigian wrath on account of its identifying interest with additionally produced product. In regard to this specific issue the "extreme" Austrianism of the pure time-preference theory seems in fact to coincide substantially with the view of the Cambridge critics. Yet, in regard to the *general* "ideological" bone of contention between the neoclassical and the

Italian-Cambridge school, the Misesian theory must certainly be seen by the latter school as an enemy. Indeed, this Misesian theory depends, far more radically than does the mainstream neoclassical view, upon the key Mengerian insight (that incomes reflect consumer evaluation of the productive contributions of resources).

That this is the case is seen immediately from the basis upon which the pure time-preference theory *rejects* all productivity theories of interest. That basis is in fact precisely the Austrian insight into the relationship between factor-service values and the value of output. All final output, Fetter (following Böhm-Bawerk) had argued, must be swept back by the market process to the original factors of production from which that output proceeded. (That is, the market values of the original factors can be relied upon to tend to reflect the full value to consumers of final output.) If one refuses (as indeed Böhm-Bawerk had himself refused)[4] to recognize time as a productive resource, this reasoning must inevitably lead to denial of independent productivity to any but the original factors of production.

So while the Misesian theory coincides with the Cambridge view at least in denying that interest is a productivity return, it offers to that view an "ideological" profile which must be fully as unattractive to it as that of the mainstream neoclassical view. For the pure time-preference perspective, interest emerges in intertemporal exchanges in which freely interacting market participants express their prospective relative valuations of receipts/sacrifices of different dates. Interest income so received is an entirely defensible reflection of consumer sovereignty (in regard to the intertemporal allocation of utilities).[5]

It is this third alternative (to both the Cambridge-classical approach and the mainstream neoclassical approach) which was, unfortunately, entirely overlooked throughout the course of the Cambridge debate. Confusion in this regard seems to have been compounded due to the circumstance that the mainstream neoclassical view itself was partly derived, as we have seen, from Austrian intellectual roots (in the Böhm-Bawerkian theory).[6] Let us turn to examine some of the radically subjectivist (and thus certainly Austrian) aspects of the Misesian approach, and to observe how this subjectivism renders this approach invulnerable to the powerful

4. On this point, see Böhm-Bawerk (1959b, pp. 97f.; 1959c, p. 196).

5. On this point, see the discussion toward the conclusion of Essay 4 below.

6. For a treatment of the mainstream neoclassical theory of capital and interest which emphasizes its Austrian roots, see Hausman (1981, pp. 37ff.).

criticisms leveled from Cambridge (UK) against the mainstream neoclassical view.

SUBJECTIVISM, RESWITCHING PARADOXES AND ALL THAT

In the course of the Cambridge debate it was the reswitching and capital reversal paradoxes which cast the deepest shadow upon the mainstream neoclassical theory of distribution. Yet, as we shall see, these paradoxes present no problem at all for the explanation of interest contained in the Misesian theory of capital and interest.

The problem posed for the neoclassical theory by the phenomenon of "capital reversal" is well known. Capital reversal occurs when a change in the rate of interest is associated with a seemingly "perverse" change in adopted production technique—for example, when a reduction in the interest rate implies a switch to "the less, not the more, time-consuming, or roundabout or capital-intensive technique" (Yeager, 1976, p. 313). That capital reversal is at least theoretically possible was conceded by major exponents of the neoclassical position in the 1960s (Samuelson, 1966; Ferguson, 1969, pp. xv, 265f., 269f.). That this concession implies serious difficulties for the neoclassical view of interest as the supply-and-demand price of a productive service, has been emphasized by many writers:

> If capital is an input into production whose value measures its quantity and whose marginal product decreases with its quantity, and if the rate of interest is proportional to the marginal product of capital, then the rate of interest and the value of capital must be inversely related. How can one regard capital as a factor of production if . . . firms find it profitable to use *less* capital when its price (the rate of interest) declines? When an input becomes cheaper one should expect firms to find it profitable to use relatively more of it. Something is drastically awry. (Hausman, 1981, p. 76)

Capital reversal erodes the notion of a demand curve for capital and thus the view of interest as a "true scarcity price" (introduction to *Capital and Growth*, ed. G. C. Harcourt and N. F. Laing, Penguin Books, 1971, p. 23).

For our purposes it is worthwhile to underscore the fact that these difficulties in the neoclassical position arise entirely from its view that the demand curve for capital (or time, or waiting, or roundaboutness) expresses the demand for the productive services of capital (or of time, etc.). It is only because the rate of interest is seen, in the neoclassical view, as an index of the scarcity *of these productive services* that the possibility of capital reversal appears to play havoc with the notion of a well-behaved, downward-sloping demand curve playing a conventional role in the market determination of the interest price. From the perspective of a Misesian, pure time-preference approach to interest, therefore, a demonstration that a lower rate of interest might make it more profitable to employ an apparently *less* time-consuming technique of production would seem to present no *direct* challenge. Interest is not offered, in this view, in order to command the productive services of time; the shape attributed to the curve of marginal productivity of time is thus of no relevance to the market causation of interest. What may be a problem for productivity views of interest can create no difficulty for the pure time-preference view. We must point out, however, that while this argument is correct as far as it goes, it is not, by any means, enough for the purposes of such an argument.

It may, after all, properly be objected that while the Misesian theory escapes the *particular* problem posed for productivity theories by the possibility of capital reversal, it must nonetheless confront an altogether parallel difficulty. Surely a reduction in the rate of interest must, for the pure time-preference theory too, be expected to lead to the employment of *more* time-consuming methods of production (even if for reasons that have nothing to do with the productivity of time). For the pure time-preference theory there are likely, at any given rate of interest, to exist possible time-consuming processes of production that are not adopted only because the necessary outlays, including interest, are too large to be justified by the prospective future output. Surely a reduction in the rate of interest must tend to transform some of these (hitherto "too long") processes of production from unprofitable to profitable projects. So a demonstration that a fall in the rate of interest may lead to the adoption of *less* lengthy processes of production must seem to be as much a puzzle and an embarrassment for the Misesian view as it was, for other reasons, for the neoclassical view. To see that this objection is in no sense damaging to the Misesian view, it is necessary to reconsider the very possibility of capital reversal in terms of the *prospective* waiting relevant to the time-preference of the subjectivist economist.

In the literature that applies the capital-reversal notion to the Böhm-Bawerkian temporal context, it is taken for granted that the input-dating requirements for a given production process, together with the associated dates of output availability, unambiguously and objectively define the quantity of time (or waiting, or the degree of roundaboutness) required for that process. It is then shown, for example, that with given prices of inputs, the relative profitability of one technique as compared with a second depends upon the rate of interest—with, say, the first technique being more profitable than the second at the very low rates of interest (say, less than r_1) and at very high rates of interest (greater than r_2), but less profitable at a range of intermediate rates of interest. With such a "reswitching" situation it is clear that at one or other of the two switch points (i.e., either at r_1 or r_2) we are confronted with the paradox that a fall in the rate of interest is associated with increased relative profitability of the technique that calls for *less* "waiting."

But reflection should convince us that the basic premise upon which this reasoning depends is by no means to be accepted without question. This premise is that each technique of production involves a simple, unidimensional "quantity" of time, such that different techniques can be unambiguously "objectively" ranked as involving greater or lesser quantities of time (or waiting). In fact, there is no reason at all to accept this premise. The cases that yield the capital-reversing paradoxes all arise from production processes involving more or less complex dating patterns for inputs and outputs. (In a stylized example made famous by Samuelson (1966), a given quantity of output can be obtained in year 4 from one technique that calls for the input of two units of labor in year 1, and six units of labor in year 3; or alternatively by a second technique of production calling only for the input of seven units of labor in year 2.) It appears obviously mistaken (or at least to involve an arbitrary and possibly misleading oversimplification) to wish to collapse the possibly incommensurable quantities of time associated with individually dated input components of a given complex production technique into a single simple unidimensional quantity of time. The fact that economists ever since Böhm-Bawerk have argued about the "correct" formula through which to square this particular circle, should not mislead us into failure to recognize that such a task can hardly be anything but an arbitrary "simplifying" undertaking.

The truth is, surely, that with positive subjective time-preference assumed, we simply cannot entertain the possibility that, *with respect to a given quantity of physical input,* a decision-maker might, merely as a result of a decrease in the rate of interest (that he must pay for the use of borrowed funds with which to advance payment for the input), choose to assign that input to a *shorter* time-consuming process of production. If then we find that, as interest falls from very high levels to below r_2, technique A is replaced by technique B, while when interest continues to fall even lower and reaches below r_1, technique B is replaced, in turn, by technique A (which had been preferred at very high rates of interest), we should not, surely, conclude that at one of these two switch points the reduction in interest has perversely brought a change to a *less* time-consuming technique. Rather, we should understand that comparing the complex, multidimensional waiting requirements for different techniques *simply does not permit us to pronounce* that one technique involves unambiguously less waiting than a second technique. (In the case of the Samuelson example, for instance, the one technique involves a long wait for the marginal output of the two units of labor and a short wait for the output of the six units, while the second technique involves an intermediate wait for the output of seven units of labor. There is no need—and there need not be in fact any way—to rank the two techniques in terms of their overall waiting requirements.) They involve *different* patterns of waiting, such that both very low and very high rates of interest might make technique A seem the more profitable, while at intermediate rates it is technique B that is the more profitable. There is nothing perverse about this, unless one mistakenly insists that one or other of these techniques involves the greater quantity of time, or of waiting.[7]

It is altogether understandable that theorists who attach significance to the *productivity* of roundaboutness (or of time, or of waiting) do feel it necessary to insist on being able, in principle, to rank different techniques in terms of the "objective" quantities of waiting they respectively involve. After all, if time, or waiting, is being treated as a factor of pro-

---

7. Something similar to the reasoning in the text seems to have been the intuitive foundation for Professor Leland Yeager's exhaustive and lucid discussion of the issues (Yeager, 1976, 1979). Yeager sought to dissolve the capital paradoxes by insisting that "waiting" should not be measured in physical clock-hour terms; rather, that "the amount of it required in a physically specified production process does depend partly on its own price" (Yeager, 1976, p. 345). In this way Yeager argues that, *appropriately measured in terms of the relevant rates of interest,* lower interest rates do always stimulate the use of techniques involving "more" waiting. But the point made here in the text does not revolve around the particular measurement technique to be used in measuring waiting. Rather, we argue that there is no need (and may well be no way) to measure waiting, for the relatively complicated production cases in which the reswitching and capital-reversal paradoxes have their habitat. (See also Hausman, 1981, p. 79, for a critique of the particular measurement technique used by Yeager in resolving these paradoxes.)

duction, it seems reasonable to ask which of the two techniques calls for use of the greater quantity of this additional "resource." What should be emphasized is that, from the subjectivist Misesian pure time-preference perspective, there is absolutely no need to assume any possibility for such unambiguous ranking. In this perspective, time is simply not viewed as an "objective" (or any other kind of) input. A technique of production calls for a specific pattern of dating for its inputs, thus confronting the producer with a correspondingly complex pattern of prospective delays before the output is to be forthcoming. Different techniques involve different patterns of prospective delay; that is all.

COMPLETE AND INCOMPLETE SUBJECTIVISM
IN THE THEORY OF CAPITAL AND INTEREST

From the perspective of late twentieth-century Austrianism, therefore, the Misesian vision of a capital-using economy offers a refreshingly consistent subjectivist approach. In this respect it can be seen, certainly, as building on foundations set by Böhm-Bawerk, but also as redirecting the Böhm-Bawerkian project toward more thoroughly subjectivist insights. There can be little doubt that Böhm-Bawerk's original contribution to capital and interest theory injected a most wholesome dose of subjectivism into that area. For Böhm-Bawerk himself, as noticed above, time was *not* treated as an objective input; it was treated primarily as the central element in the subjectivist notion of time-preference. Yet the ambiguities in Böhm-Bawerk's treatment pointed toward a Fisherine neoclassical theory of interest which would be, on the other hand, more elegant, more consistent and more complete than Böhm-Bawerk's, yet at the same time, quite naturally, cast in a mold in which objective productivity elements were fully as independently important as the subjective time-preference elements. Moreover, the Böhm-Bawerkian concept of the capital structure of an economy, which became so important in the Austrian (that is, the Hayekian) theory of the cycle, lent itself to an interpretation which focused more on the objective qualities and durabilities of physical things than on the expectations and goals embodied in individual plans.

Such an incomplete subjectivism carries with it the danger of coming to see the future course of production as inexorably shaped by the present size and shape of the capital stock, as if that stock itself (rather than the possibly faulty set of plans which brought it into being) governed the course of events. The clarity of the Misesian vision made it no longer possible to fall into such error. That vision deepened the Austrian understanding of the market economy by extending Mengerian subjectivism to encompass multiperiod planning for production and intertemporal market exchanges. Each of the essays in this little book was intended as an attempt at exposition and clarification of this consistently subjective approach to the problems of capital and interest. Their republication together here has been undertaken in the hope that they can better achieve this purpose during the years ahead, in the form of this newly reconstructed intellectual capital good.

Preface to the 1966 Edition of *An Essay on Capital*

This little book was written with the purpose of helping to clarify some of the conceptual problems that surround the foundations of capital theory. Much of recent theories of growth, as well as the more traditional microeconomic theories of investment, depend on capital notions. While this essay does not attempt to come to grips substantively with these problems, it is hoped that its discussions will prove of value to workers in these fields.

The author's debt to the literature is, despite the possibly overcritical tone of the essay, very great and very gratefully acknowledged. Despite the author's dissatisfaction with much of the presentation of "Austrian" capital theory, it is from the great writers in this tradition, from Böhm-Bawerk, Fisher, and Wicksell, to Mises, Hayek, and Lachmann, that he has, directly or indirectly, learned most of what is here set forth.

The author is deeply grateful for research support that made this work possible. In particular are to be mentioned the Relm Foundation and the Research Office of the Schools of Business of New York University. To Professor Robert Lindsay the author is deeply indebted for encouragement given in a number of ways. Some of the ideas set forth in this book were presented to a faculty seminar at New York University; the author's thanks for helpful critical comments then expressed go particularly to Professors Solomon Fabricant and Arnold Sametz. Professor Mises kindly read the final manuscript draft and offered valuable criticism. To all these the author is conscious of a debt of gratitude; he holds none of them to blame for inadequacies in the finished product.

Nora Greig performed an efficient and expeditious task of typing the manuscript. The thanks due to the author's wife for her help during the painful months prior to this book's publication are not capable of being set down on paper.

Israel M. Kirzner

Chapter 1. Unfinished Plans

INTRODUCTION

In economics, more than in other sciences, a good theory is a structure of which the foundations consist of clearly defined concepts. Economists have, indeed, long recognized the substantive importance to their discipline, of careful definitions. The ability to define usefully the terms used in theoretical economic discussion turns out almost invariably to call for the very same insight into economic processes that is required for the enunciation of theoretical propositions themselves. Differences in the definitions assigned to key terms usually turn out to reflect differences in the understanding of the nature of the economic processes to which these terms are relevant. In probably no department of economic science is this more obviously the case than in that of the theory of capital. As long ago as 1836 Whately found that eight of the leading writers on political economy presented divergent views on the nature of capital.[1] More recently Solow has remarked that a man from Mars reading the literature on capital theory would be bewildered by the multitude of the connotations of the term "capital," ranging from stocks of consumer goods for the maintainance of workers, to wine and growing trees, to durable buildings and machinery, and so on.[2] And the characteristic difficulties and controversies that have complicated modern theories of capital are closely bound up with these differing concepts of capital.

In the present essay we are not ambitious enough to set out to develop a Theory of Capital. On the other hand, we are not seeking merely a definition of "capital" (in fact, we are only tangentially concerned with definitions). What we seek is an insight into those economic processes in which capital emerges, and which capital theory hopes to illumine. Such an insight is, of course, a prerequisite for capital theory proper—it may be described as a "prologue to capital theory." And it will provide us with a framework within which to examine and criticize some of the more important of the different notions held to be essential to an understanding of the role of capital in the economic system. In the present chapter such

1. Whately (1836, pp. 231–32).
2. Solow (1963, p. 12); see also Böhm-Bawerk (1959b, book 1, ch. 3) for an exhaustive discussion of earlier competing concepts of capital; see also Fisher (1906, ch. 4, para. 2).

a framework is presented. The subsequent chapters then critically examine some of the more important ideas and problems commonly associated with capital.

A DIGRESSION ON METHOD

The understanding of the nature of capital, and of the economic process in a capital-using market economy, that will be developed in this chapter is based on a consistently followed approach. This approach sees economic theory as the extensively worked out *logic of acts of individual choice*.[3] The light which the economic theorist can throw on an economic process, or on the outcome of such a process, is viewed as deriving from his ability to relate back the process to the individual acts of choice of which the process is made up. Through the theorist's understanding of the decisions made by individuals, and of the way in which these decisions have mutual impact upon one another, and become mutually adjusted to one another, he is able to "explain" the course of economic events, and to understand the probable results that will follow from given exogenous changes operating on the system.

While it may be submitted that the theory of the market as traditionally developed does (at least implicitly) follow this approach, it will be argued in this essay that capital theorists have on the whole, and with unfortunate results, abandoned it. We will in this essay insist on relating everything that is to be said about capital back to our fundamental unit of analysis, the individual decision. At every step we will describe the objects that are present in the economy in terms of the past decisions responsible for their presence, or in terms of the opportunities for further decisions that their presence makes possible:

> The generic concept of capital . . . has no measurable counterpart among material objects; it reflects the entrepreneurial appraisal of such objects. Beer barrels and blast-furnaces, harbour installations and hotel-room furniture are capital not by virtue of their physical properties but by virtue of their economic functions.[4]

We will describe the economic processes in which capital plays a part (or in the course of which changes occur in capital), in terms of the individual plans, choices and decisions of which these processes consist. And when

3. For the antecedents of this "praxeological" approach, see Kirzner (1960, ch. 7).
4. Lachmann (1956, p. vii).

in subsequent chapters we turn to examine some of the problems which writers on capital theory have encountered, we will almost invariably find that these have arisen out of a failure to view things from the point of view of individual plans, and out of attempts to see capital as something that could be understood and manipulated on its own, without explicit consideration of the relevant choices made by purposeful human beings.

INDIVIDUAL DECISIONS AND THE MARKET

Our framework of thought will, therefore, be as follows. Each individual in the market economy is at all times seeking to fulfill his purposes (whatever they may be at the time) to the fullest extent permitted by (a) the resources he has at his disposal *and* (b) the opportunities which, to his knowledge, make it possible to turn his resources to account. These latter opportunities are, in turn, determined by the individual's knowledge of relevant technological possibilities *and* by his knowledge of opportunities for exchange (either of resources or of products) that exist in the market. His decisions (and in particular the bids and offers he makes to the market) seek to exploit these technological and market opportunities of which he is aware. At the same time these exchange opportunities that are available in the market are determined by the decisions which the other market participants are making, in *their* pursuit of their own purposes, in the light of the opportunities that they find available to *them*. The market process consists in the systematic chain of events that ensues from the interaction in the market of the decisions of numerous participants. These decision-makers find, at the outset, that the opportunities that are in fact being offered to them in the market (by virtue of the decisions of others) are different (either more or less attractive) than those originally expected. From the lessons learned in the market in this way, there follows a systematic pattern of adjustment and revision in the decisions made by market participants. This pattern of adjustment constitutes the market process.[5]

Now, this analytical framework is applicable in the first place to an economy in which capital is completely absent—the *"kapitallose wirtschaft."* What it is proposed to do in this essay is to extend explicitly this same framework of analysis to the consideration of an economy in which capital plays a role both in individual decisions and in market activity. We will

5. For a more detailed analysis of the market process on these lines, see Kirzner (1963).

first inquire into the capital-relevant decisions of the individual, against the background of assumed given market opportunities. We will then proceed to consider, in barest outline, the manner in which adjustments and revisions will be enforced upon such individual capital-relevant decisions as a result of the interaction in the market place of such decisions made by numerous market participants. The insights obtained from such an approach will, it is hoped, throw light on the nature of "capital," and provide pointers toward the full development of capital theory.

We will find it to our advantage to proceed very slowly. We must contemplate the kinds of plans which individuals make, we must thoroughly "feel" the opportunities envisaged at the outset, and the way in which, as time goes on, the individual perceives these opportunities to be affected by the actions which he has already undertaken. All this may not seem very exciting; after all we are all continually experiencing precisely these processes. But, as elsewhere in economic theory, progress will be found to follow careful and patient analysis of the pattern of everyday decision-making. We turn, then, first to consider the world of the individual, and, as elsewhere, it will prove useful to do this initially in the most individual of all possible worlds, that of Crusoe.

THE DECISIONS OF CRUSOE: MULTIPERIOD DECISIONS

Crusoe finds himself equipped with definite resources. These are of a number of different kinds. He has land and other natural resources at his disposal; he has some tools; he expects to be able to work at some level of intensity for some number of hours per week. His level of technological knowledge will then identify for Crusoe the array of production opportunities that these resources permit him to choose from. Any program of production that he undertakes involves costs. As seen by the economist the cost to Crusoe of the production program that he adopts consists in the opportunities that he has rejected in order to exploit the program that he has adopted. The rejected opportunities include in the first place the possibilities that were available to Crusoe to enjoy his resources in direct consumption (he could, e.g., have employed his land and his time for sunbathing, instead of for production). In addition the rejected opportunities include all the possible programs of production (leading either to the same products as are being produced by the adopted program, or to different products) that might have been embraced instead.

Since both consumption and production take time, the alternative consumption and production opportunities considered by Crusoe *each con-*

sists of a possible course of action over a period of time. What Crusoe has to choose from is not merely whether to produce apples or pears (as if he were standing before a machine that will vend both or either of these products at the press of the appropriate buttons). He must choose between one time-consuming process of production (in which resources must be applied at definite dates, and from which apples will be yielded at some similarly definite date), and another time-consuming process (in which possibly the different resources must be applied at a different set of dates, yielding pears at some possibly different date). Crusoe's planning is, in other words, *multiperiod planning.* The costs that he incurs through a decision are multiperiod costs.

A word of clarification may be in order in this regard. A person may lie back and plan out future courses of activity that do not involve any immediate actions. A man may plan to spend his next summer in Asia, the following one in Africa, and the one after that in Europe. But he may not be called upon or even be able to do anything about these plans, for the time being. The successful accomplishment of these plans depends on actions that need to be or can be taken only in the fairly distant future. For multiperiod plans of this kind, Crusoe may indeed make decisions now, but he is well aware that such decisions can be revoked at will for some time still to come. Multiperiod plans of this kind are, as yet, clearly not very important.

But there is room for a far more important class of multiperiod plans. Crusoe may, for example, plan to grow wheat. This plan involves the decision to plow now, together with the intention of sowing and harvesting at appropriate dates in the future. *Before* Crusoe plows his land, the opportunity to grow wheat is one out of an array of competing production programs each of which, let us say, calls for some immediate initial action. While the respective initial actions may each be only small steps on the way to the final respective goals, the decision to make one such initial act *is* a decision to embark on the long-range production program of which this initial act is the first step. Insofar as a plowed field precludes at least temporarily the carrying out of certain alternative possible production programs, the decision to plow is more than a decision to plow, it is a decision to grow wheat. The decision to plow is part of a genuine multiperiod plan. The essence of a plan is that each of the activities embraced in the plan is coordinated with the other planned activities. Each portion of the plan "fits in" with the other portions: it depends on their fulfilment, and their fulfilment depends on its fulfilment. A multiperiod plan of the kind we are considering is a similar case. The activities which such a plan calls for currently, "fit in" with those which the plan envisages for the future. Plowing now is required if the sowing and harvesting planned for the future are to be able to be carried out. And the current plowing is undertaken only on the assumption that future sowing and harvesting will in fact be undertaken as well.

It is now of importance to examine Crusoe's position and outlook at three different points in time. We must appraise his situation (a) *before* he has taken any steps toward the implementation of a multiperiod plan; (b) *after* a multiperiod plan has been successfully executed in full as originally planned; and (what will be most important for this essay), (c) at some *intermediate* point in time, when the course of actions envisaged by the multiperiod plan have been commenced, but have not yet been completed.

(a) Before the initial steps of the multiperiod plan have been undertaken, Crusoe has nothing to look back on except completed history. Whatever he may have done in the past has been done. He recognizes, of course, that his present stock of resources and his own personal present situation are the end result of all past history. But, on our assumptions, he is no longer concerned with the appraisal of his past performances, and, again, he has not as yet unfinished plans to complete. He is able to plan freshly for the future unencumbered by past commitments.

He has before him, as discussed above, a number of alternative possible plans of multiperiod action. His choice of one of these commits him to the rejection of the others (the term "rejection" includes of course the possible mere postponement of these other plans). He is aware, in other words, that the plan he is adopting calls for a planned pattern of actions over the future, and that the execution of these actions precludes many other possible actions.

On the other hand it may be that the initial steps required for his adopted plan are identical with those required for initiation of several alternative plans. Plowing may be necessary for the cultivation of other crops besides wheat. In this case he is aware that his immediate decision does not commit him irrevocably to his adopted plan. (In fact, he may in this situation deliberately postpone to the last possible moment the final decision as to which multiperiod plan to adopt, making only sure that his immediate actions are those required to advance whatever plan he will ultimately adopt.)

Or again, while the initial steps toward fulfilment of the adopted plan may be able to be turned to subsequent account in the advancement only of this plan, and be of no avail for the fulfilment of any others, these steps may yet not commit him irrevocably to this adopted plan. Crusoe may be aware that his plan can be scrapped before being brought to fruition. The actions required by the adopted plan for its final stages may simply be replaced by other actions that will lead to other results, if so desired. In other words Crusoe is at the outset aware that his adoption of a particular plan, and even his embarkation on possibly irrevocable initial steps toward its fulfilment, do not by any means necessarily preclude the possibility of subsequent decision-making in respect to this plan, and do not free him from the responsibility of making such later decisions.

Aware of all this, then, Crusoe must, at the outset, select the multiperiod plan to be adopted. Since his is a multiperiod decision, it involves employment of more than merely those resources of which he is *currently* in command, and provision for more than merely *current* enjoyments. His plan depends on his being able to command resources of definite qualities and quantities at definite future dates; and it envisages the provision of output to minister to wants and enjoyments that can as yet be felt and desired only by anticipation. Clearly a multiperiod plan involves the *expectations* that Crusoe holds, not only concerning the technological efficacy of the actions which he contemplates, but also concerning the future course of events as he expects them to unfold (in the absence of any actions on his own part). And his multiperiod plan envisages the introduction of specific changes into this otherwise expected course of events, as a result of his planned actions. The degree of uncertainty with which Crusoe is able to forecast the future course of events (as they are expected to unfold in the absence of action on his own part), will vitally affect the particular multiperiod plan that he adopts, and will, especially, decisively affect the degree of flexibility that he will wish his adopted plan to possess (that is, the degree in which he will wish to reserve the final, irrevocable, decisions for only later stages in the fulfilment of the adopted plan).

The "initial steps" that have been mentioned in the foregoing discussion may take on any of numerous forms. They may consist in acquiring dexterity in the performance of particular operations; or in the acquisition of necessary raw materials and other supplies; or in the construction of tools or other equipment required for subsequent operations; or in preliminary operations on raw material that will prepare it for subsequent further productive operations. Finally these initial steps may (as in the celebrated textbook examples of Crusoe fishing-net construction) consist in the provision of consumption services for the satisfaction of needs expected to arise during the further course of the adopted plan's fulfilment (needs which would be able to be provided for at later dates only at the expense of the adopted plan itself).

(b) We turn to examine Crusoe's situation *after* a particular multiperiod plan has been finally executed. Crusoe may wish to *appraise* his completed performance. In the light of the knowledge and experience gained in the meantime, he may wish to reexamine the wisdom of his having made the decisions that he did make (both at the outset of the multiperiod project, and at subsequent opportunities for plan revision). He may, in this way, now consider the results actually achieved by the executed plan to be more or to be less significant than originally anticipated; he may now consider the results that might have been achieved by the alternative, rejected projects, as more, or as less significant than originally imagined. Again his maturer judgment (and his *ex post* knowledge of the course of events during the time of the plan's fulfilment) may have taught him that the range of alternatives from which he *might* have been able to choose at the outset was actually different from what he had originally believed. Some projects originally believed to be out of reach may now perhaps be seen to have been perfectly feasible; other plans originally believed to have been feasible may now be seen to have been out of reach.

Crusoe may, in this way, seek to determine whether he has "gained" or "lost" by the fulfilment of his project. He will judge himself to have gained, if the alternatives which (hindsight shows) he rejected appear less important than the results actually achieved by his adopted project. He will judge himself to have suffered loss if the achieved results rank less important than these rejected alternatives.

Again, by observing Crusoe's situation, from the outside, so to speak, after the completion of his project, one may be able to assess "objectively" the difference which this completed course of action has made to Crusoe's situation. One compares Crusoe's observed situation today with his observed situation at the time the multiperiod course of action was first undertaken. One may be able to measure certain differences, or one may at least be able to describe these differences. And in this way one may succeed in describing the observable achievements of the multiperiod plan's execution. We notice immediately, of course, that the outsider's appraisal of the impact of the project upon Crusoe's situation need bear no recognizable relationship whatsoever to Crusoe's own assessment of his gain or loss from the project (as discussed in the preceding paragraphs). The outside observer sees only measurable or describable differences between two *actual* situations—"before" and "after." Crusoe himself, while fully aware of, and very interested in these "observable differences," assesses his own gain and loss by comparing an actual situation ("after") with *hypothetical* ones (that *might* have been achieved through alternative courses of action).

Since we are considering Crusoe's position *after* a multiperiod plan has been fully completed, and *before* any other further plans have been considered, any assessment of this position must, it should be observed, be exclusively a "backward-looking" appraisal, not a "forward-looking" one. Since he has as yet considered no further plans for the future, Crusoe is unable to measure what he has already achieved, by measuring what these achievements can enable him to accomplish in the future. All that can be done is to examine Crusoe's current possessions and circumstances, and compare them, as discussed above, either ("objectively") with his situation at the outset of the multiperiod project, or (from a "profit and loss" point of view) with the hypothetical situations that might have been achieved by means of the rejected plans. The implications of this absence of a "forward-looking" view of Crusoe's situation are unusual enough to deserve emphasis. Crusoe's failure to consider further plans means that the things in his possession have significance for him only by their presence at this moment. The stocks of food that he may possess affect his situation now, not at all through their capacity to provide nourishment in the future, but merely by "being there" at this moment (for whatever this is worth). The tools in his workshop, the clothes in his wardrobe, the roof over his head are of significance to Crusoe, at this time, not because of their capacity to render service in the future, but simply by their momentary presence.

This unusually narrow way of looking at things is pointed out here not at all because of its own importance. Quite the contrary, it is being pointed to here only in order to emphasize the exceedingly unrealistic nature of the situation to which it is relevant. The contemplation of this narrow and limited evaluation by Crusoe of his possessions will, surely, confirm that a state in which all past plans have already been completed, and in which no future plans whatever are under consideration, is utterly inconsistent with what we know of living human beings. Long before a multiperiod project has been completed, we may expect Crusoe to have adopted, or at least considered, plans for the future.

In fact, reflection must surely convince us, the very concept of the "final completion" of a multiperiod plan project is probably an unsound one. Such a concept presupposes, as we have done thus far in the discussion, that the original plan called for a series of actions designed to achieve definite goals at specific future dates, *with no other goals but these in mind.* What is far more characteristic, surely, is that the original plan envisages the achievement of the definite future goals with full awareness of the fact that successful achievement of these goals will make possible, and will necessitate, the formulation of further subsequent plans. While in the original formulation of the multiperiod plan these further plans may well have been left completely open for the time being, we may, in a very real sense, consider the original multiperiod plan as extending indefinitely into the future. So we will *never* be able to find Crusoe in the position of having *any* multiperiod fully completed. Crusoe is *always* in the position of having future plans under consideration; or, perhaps more correctly, he is always in the middle of an incomplete long-range project (the final stages of which may not as yet have been definitely selected).

These considerations underscore the importance to be attached to our next task, (c) the consideration of Crusoe's position at some intermediate point in time, when the course of actions envisaged by his multiperiod plan has been commenced, but not yet completed.

THE HALF-FINISHED PROJECT

At intermediate points in time, Crusoe finds himself with what amounts to a half-finished project on his hands. He has already performed some of the actions initially called for by his multiperiod plan, and he now has before him a program of further actions, prescribed by the plan for its subsequent stages. Crusoe appraises his present situation both by looking ahead and by looking back.

Looking back he is aware on the one hand of what has already been achieved through the initial actions. On the other hand, he is in a position to consider again those courses of action that were rejected in order to embark on his own adopted plan. All this is similar to the situation considered in the preceding pages, when we imagined Crusoe to have fully completed his multiperiod plan.

Looking forward to possible revisions in his originally planned program of actions Crusoe may see matters from either of two (equivalent) points of view. First, he may, realistically, look at the future from the point of view of one who is, as he *is,* in the middle of a project, the further stages of which have yet to be finally determined. On this view of things he finds himself faced with the task of choosing the way in which to *complete* the project which has been started; the program of actions called for by the original blueprints presumably make up one of the alternatives from which this choice is to be made. Alternatively Crusoe may look at the future from a completely fresh point of view. He may choose not to view his task as that of completing something already begun. He may see himself faced with the task of selecting anew a multiperiod plan to be *commenced now*, just as he had selected the originally adopted project—a major difference being, however, that *now* he has at his disposal the fruits of the unfinished originally adopted project. Of course, it may be that the new multiperiod plan Crusoe will now select may turn out to consist of the very same program of actions that were required by the originally adopted plan for its final stages, commencing from this point in its development.

Clearly these two ways of viewing the future are for all practical purposes completely equivalent. Both views will, with the knowledge available at any given time, lead to identical plans for the future. The difference between the two views is merely in the way Crusoe looks at things. In particular it is *a difference in the way Crusoe may look at the interim results of the steps taken so far in fulfilment of the originally adopted plan.* From the one point of view these results are seen as a half-finished project. From the second point of view they are seen merely as data, along with other available resources, on the basis of which the new project now to be drawn up can be planned. The former view sees the interim results of the earlier steps taken as the outcome of (a portion of) an earlier *plan*. The second view sees these results "positively"; this view is not concerned with how these data came into being, it is not concerned with the "planned" character of these results. To the first view a plowed field represents the intermediate stage on the way to an originally planned wheat crop. To the second view a plowed field is simply a field ready to be sown, if one so wishes.

Just as Crusoe himself may look at the interim results of the first steps of the original plan from these two different points of view, so too can the outside observer see things from the same two viewpoints. If this outside observer wishes only to understand the *new* plan for subsequent action that Crusoe makes, at the intermediate point in time, then we have seen that, no matter which of the views Crusoe adopts, he will settle on the same plan for further action. On the other hand, if the outside observer wishes to understand how the present intermediate situation came about, then of course he must view the situation as what it really is—the outcome of a plan that has not yet been fully carried out. It is worth noticing, moreover, that the non-positive view is able not only to explain how these results came about, as already mentioned; it is able, in addition, to *interpret* the significance to Crusoe of any tangible *things* that have been yielded by the first steps of the originally adopted project. To the "positive" observer this possibility is not open. To him, for example, a stock of consumption goods is simply a stock of consumption goods. Not only has this observer no interest in explaining how the stock came into existence; he has, for that very reason, no clue as to its purpose. The fact is, of course, that for the "positive" observer, this stock of goods *has* no purpose, until Crusoe starts afresh to consider the possible plans which his resources make feasible.

But to the non-positive observer, things are quite different. To him, a stock of consumer goods may, for example, be seen not merely as a stock of food, but as provisions prepared in anticipation of a long process of production ahead. This insight not only explains how the goods came into being (as part of an earlier plan); it provides, at the same time, immediate recognition of these goods as having (at least up to the present) a very definite function. The positive observer can describe the tangible things that Crusoe now finds at his disposal, *only in physical terms.*[6] He is unable to describe them in terms of *function* because he takes cognizance of no plans in which they play a role. The non-positive observer, on the other hand, is able to describe the tangible things that Crusoe now has at his disposal (as a consequence of the unfinished project), in terms of their function, i.e., in terms of the specific purposes which these things were, in the original scheme, designed to advance.

Imagine that our "outside observer" could observe *two* islands, each with its own isolated Crusoe, who each started out from identical circumstances, and who each undertook the same multiperiod project, commencing on the same date. Suppose that after some time period the observer examines the situations in both islands. Then, if the observer adopts the "positive" view, he must compare the two situations in terms of purely physical description. He may not even say that "tools" exist on one or both islands (since the term "tool" implies function).[7] He certainly

---

6. He may, of course, similarly be able to describe these things in terms of their physical history, by referring to the physical things or services used in their construction.

7. See, e.g., Hayek (1949, p. 59; 1955, p. 27).

cannot say that the stock of goods possessed by the one Crusoe is "better" than that of the second Crusoe, in the way in which the non-positive observer can say this. The latter (non-positive) observer can compare the two islands not merely by physical description of their situations, but also by assessing the degree in which each Crusoe has succeeded in bringing his project closer to fulfilment.

To the non-positive observer a plan that has not yet been fully carried out may present any of numerous possible spectacles. Everything will depend on the particular plan originally selected, and on the initial steps already taken in its fulfilment. It may be that the observer will find difficulty in discovering tangible evidence of any progress at all by Crusoe toward fulfilment of the original plan. This may be the case, for example, if the initial steps of the plan called merely for the acquisition by Crusoe of a particular skill. Or perhaps the observer will find stocks of raw materials and supplies prepared for subsequent use. Or perhaps he will find tools and equipment that Crusoe has constructed for subsequent use. Perhaps he will find that preliminary operations have already been performed upon the raw materials—he may find a real half-baked cake in the oven. Or he may find that Crusoe has (as discussed earlier) merely laid up a stock of consumption goods in preparation for a period of time during which attention to the plan will preclude the provision of such goods.

As we have seen, such an observer will describe the tangible things that are at Crusoe's disposal (as a result of the earlier stages of the multiperiod plan) in terms of their function. That is, he will look *back* to the original plan, to discover what use that plan envisaged for these things, in the *future* that is still yet to come. This seems the most natural logical sequence; the observer is able to describe the tangible resources Crusoe now has at his disposal, by reference to a known earlier plan. But it may be that the observer may employ an inverted logical sequence. It may be, for example, that the observer has no prior knowledge of the multiperiod plan originally adopted by Crusoe. But when this observer sees a hammer and nails, let us say, he is able to infer from this that Crusoe has, in his past planning, envisaged some stage in the fulfilment of his project that will call for the hammering in of nails. This inference, it should be noticed, derives from the relatively *specific* character of hammers and of nails. Hammers are not very useful except for hammering in nails, nails are clearly designed to be hammered. This specificity enables the observer to infer what use the plan intended for the items under observation; it may also enable the observer to infer what other items are planned to be constructed. Many things can be used only in conjunction with complementary goods. Things which are highly specific in production will require very definite complementary goods.[8]

Similarly the observer may be able to infer something of the plan that was originally adopted, by taking note of the durability of the tangible things constructed during the early stages of the plan's fulfilment. Should he find goods that will be able to render service for many years to come, this will tell him something of the length of future time for which the original plan made fairly detailed provision (unless, of course, one knows that the techniques available to Crusoe did not enable him to have control over the durability of the item under observation).

One may, in this way, be able to associate the tangible things available to Crusoe, with rather detailed and fairly definite inferences as to the plans which can be presumed to have been responsible for their existence. So that our non-positive observer may, without prior knowledge of these plans, ascribe definite presumed functions *to these tangible things themselves*. And he may compare two Crusoes without prior knowledge of their several plans, merely by this kind of insightful examination of the tangible things that the two Crusoes respectively possess. He may take significant notice, for example, of the fact that Crusoe A has tractors at his disposal, while Crusoe B has only wooden plows. He may be quick to notice that Crusoe A's equipment reveals many stages of production and considerable time to intervene between the application of "original" resources and the emergence of consumers' goods, while Crusoe B's equipment reveals no such lengthy "period of production."

Valuable and sagacious as these conclusions of the observer be, it is to be emphasized (and for the purposes of this essay, emphasized most strongly) that these descriptions, while they may superficially be thought to apply to the "tangible things" themselves, in full reality apply *only to the plans* (of which these things are, at present, the interim expression).

Nevertheless, the insights obtained in the preceding paragraphs do serve to underscore something that we have already, in a general way, been aware of. This is that, starting from any given starting point, the plans which Crusoe will make depend, in highly sensitive fashion, upon the particular tangible things over which he has control. Should the equipment at his disposal be of durable character, should he have at his disposal

8. See Lachmann (1956, pp. 2–12).

a large reserve stock of consumer goods, he will be able to make *different* plans for the immediate and the more remote future than he would be able to without them. Should he have tractors at his disposal he will make different plans than he would if he had only wooden plows in his sheds.

As mentioned earlier, these reflections on the situation as it appears to Crusoe (or to Crusoe's unseen observer), at some intermediate point during the fulfilment of Crusoe's plans, gain in significance from the fact that, realistically, *any* moment in Crusoe's life is likely to be such an "intermediate point." Crusoe is likely always to be in the middle of some plan that has been commenced but not yet completed. So that if one wishes to assess Crusoe's potential capabilities for the future provision of output, one is likely to start by examining the tangible things he has at his disposal at the present time. One is able to read Crusoe's future consumption capabilities, so to speak, from the state of his present possessions. This opens up new possibilities of significance for the task that we are surveying in these few pages (that of examining Crusoe's situation at some intermediate point during the fulfilment of a multiperiod plan). One may undertake such a task, it now appears, not only for the sake of describing Crusoe's situation at that point in time. One may undertake it to gain prevision of the future. (This is related to, but of course not identical with, the approach to the description and measurement of the tangible things Crusoe has at his disposal that, as discussed earlier, ran not in terms of physical characteristics but in terms of function, or prospective usefulness.)

This way of looking at things may, however, lend itself to illegitimate overextension. We have seen that an insightful observer is able to perceive, in the tangible things Crusoe has at his disposal at an intermediate stage in the development of a project, the adopted plan of which these tangible things are the interim expression. There is now a not entirely desirable possibility, that these tangible things may now be looked at exclusively from a converse point of view. They may be seen as being *nothing more* than the present tangible reflections of streams of future output. One may be tempted to see an oven now as being the "intermediate form" in which countless future loaves of bread are, at the present time, reflected. The error in such a view would be the subtle one of seeing present tangible goods as *being themselves* an intermediate form of future output, without paying attention to the *plans* (either past or future) which have to be constructed with reference to the employment of these tangible goods, before any future output at all can be forthcoming.

The undesirable aspect of this view is thus its tendency to suggest that the future streams of output *automatically* flow out of present resources, and that these resources represent nothing more (and nothing less!) than the entire prospectus of future history telescoped into presently tangible form. There is, it should be apparent, nothing automatic about the way in which Crusoe's future streams of output arise from his currently available body of resources. At almost every step of the way Crusoe has opportunities to modify earlier plans, to fill in details in earlier outlines of plans, to devise entirely fresh plans. What will be yielded by Crusoe's resources simply depends on what Crusoe decides to do with his resources.

It is true, of course, that when a multiperiod plan (or some successive stages of such a plan) of Crusoe has been successfully carried out as originally planned, he is able, in retrospect, to ascribe the goals achieved to the past resources employed. And it is true that one may then say that the course of events during any period of time is merely the consequence of the immediately preceding state of affairs; and thus that the entire skein of subsequent history was merely the unraveling of what was somehow already present (in "bottled-up" form) at the very outset. But this is able to be said only because the plans actually adopted and executed during this history are taken for granted (and are implicitly used in the description of the resources originally available). Moreover, it should be observed that in retrospect significance attaches almost exclusively to states of affairs at points in the past when *new* plans were made, or when *alterations* were made in earlier-laid plans. No particular significance attaches to an earlier decision to permit a half-baked cake to remain in the oven, as originally planned, until fully baked. A statement that a fully baked cake "flowed automatically" out of a half-baked cake (and a hot oven) is not a very important statement at all. The statement gains whatever plausibility it possesses from the circumstance that, in fact, no "new" decisions were made at the time the half-baked cake was permitted to remain in the oven. (Alternative decisions were merely considered and rejected.) But past states of affairs (seen as the basis for the subsequent course of events) are of interest solely because these states of affairs did, in fact, inspire "new" plans. The course of events during a period in Crusoe's history *does* derive from the pre-existing state of affairs—but only because these events depended on the plans which Crusoe adopted, these plans being made at the start of the period, on the basis of the state of affairs prevailing at that date.

We may express these ideas in a slightly different way. We are talking on the one hand of a "state of affairs" at a point in time; and we are talking on the other hand of a "course of events" over a period of time. Whenever one finds Crusoe, one is entitled to inquire as to the "present state of affairs." And this may involve an examination of the tangible things at Crusoe's disposal as a result of the initial stages in the execution of as yet unfinished plans. The description of the present state of affairs may thus be conducted in terms of earlier events leading up to the present, or in terms of the possible courses of events open for choice in the future through the availability of today's resources. Should, however, Crusoe select to complete the final stages of the originally adopted plan as planned, then he will, in retrospect, attach no especial significance to the "state of affairs" at the intermediate point in the plan's fulfilment, *and no especial significance to the array of tangible things that were at his disposal at that time.* When he is at the intermediate point in time, these tangible things are the resources which will determine what further steps he will take. *After* an entire plan has been carried out, Crusoe is aware only of his original goals, and of the final results of his efforts in their pursuit. Looking back at the tangible things that were at his disposal at some past intermediate point, he sees them as nothing more than the means that were necessary to "carry" the actions performed in the earlier stages of the project up to the time when the ultimate outcome of the project has come to fruition. Looking back, those intermediate tangible things merely "stored" the earlier efforts up to the time when their final results could be derived from "them."

CRUSOE AND AN OVERLAPPING SEQUENCE OF PLANS

We have already noticed the artificiality of the assumption that Crusoe chops up his lifetime into separate periods of time, in each of which a new plan is both started from scratch and carried to completion. We have noticed, that is, the artificiality of considering points in time when earlier plans have been fully executed, while new plans have not yet been considered. It is more plausible to think of Crusoe's life as consisting in a series of actions (each one of which is designed to advance *some* plan), such that long before earlier plans (which may, as discussed, each have an infinite horizon) have been "completed," new decisions and plans have already been superimposed on the program that had previously been laid out for subsequent execution.

Complicating as the recognition of this pattern of planning may seem to be, it should be clear that very little of what has been discussed so far in this chapter has thereby lost its relevance. Perhaps the only important respect in which matters have changed consists in the fact that the ideas developed in the earlier discussions are likely to *seem* less obvious in this more complicated case of continual, overlapping decision-making. This is particularly likely to be the case if Crusoe's programs of activity happen to follow a fairly regular and repetitive pattern.

We may imagine Crusoe engaged in various productive activities year after year. At any one time he is employing an array of resources available to him. During any given period of time Crusoe's productive activities are channeled into the provision of goods for consumption, together with the maintenance, periodic replacement, and also the possible expansion of his stock of tangible resources. In this scheme of things, a look at Crusoe's situation at any time will reveal an array of tangible things at his disposal that is not very different in composition from the array of tangible things available to him at other times. Crusoe always seems to be in the middle of a project or projects, and his "state of affairs" is *always* about what it was before.

In these circumstances it is quite easy to overlook the prime importance of Crusoe's *plans,* which are continually being revised and extended and which at all times determine the use to be made of the available array of tangible things. It is easy to overlook the fact that at any one time Crusoe is likely to have a number of projects simultaneously under way, and that these projects will be in various stages of advancement.

But once attention is drawn to these facts, it is impossible to escape the conclusion that the considerations discussed in the preceding sections remain as completely valid and relevant for this more realistic example as they were for the more artificial cases discussed earlier. The "state of affairs" at any point in time may be gauged in part from the composition of the tangible resources then at Crusoe's disposal. And, as before, it will be possible to describe these tangible resources in terms of the relevant plans from which they have sprung, and in terms of the functions designed for them by these plans. It must only be remembered that each bit of tangible resource must be related back to its own (possibly unique) plan. Instead of being in the middle of one project, Crusoe is in the middle of a number of projects, at different stages of incompleteness. That is all. The fact that the overlapping of these different projects leads to a fairly constant periodic volume of output (after replacing worn-out equipment) is quite irrelevant to what has been discussed so far in this chapter. This last point is important enough to require some elaboration.

When Crusoe does in fact engage in activities that repeat themselves year after year, making sure that at all times his stock of tangible things available for productive employment is constant, then the outside observer, and perhaps even Crusoe himself, may lose sight of the role of the *plan* in the system. Crusoe might argue as follows. At each point in time he has control over the (constant) stock of productive tangible things. During each period of time he is able to attain a (constant) level of consumption (after deducting from gross output enough to maintain the constant level of his stock of productive tangible things). Were he not to possess such a stock, then the annual level of consumption that he would be able to produce would be significantly lower. So the steady annual increment in consumption that he is now able to enjoy is clearly associated with the steady presence and employment of his stock of tangible things. It is only the presence at all times of the same stock that makes possible during each period the enjoyment of this increment in consumption output. It is tempting to consider the increment in output obtained in each year, as the result of the *current* presence of the stock of tangible things. After all it would be impossible to keep up the present level of output without currently maintaining the stock of tangible things.

So Crusoe, and the outside observer, might conclude that the significance, for an appraisal of Crusoe's circumstances, of an examination of his stock of tangible things differs from what has been discussed above. Instead of examining this stock for an indication of *future* production potential, for a clue as to the length of future time for which some provision has already been made, it may now be proposed to see Crusoe's stock of tangible things merely as a measure of his *currently* superior productive potential. From this point of view two Crusoes whose present stocks of tangible things are different differ from one another primarily in the sense that one of them has the means to produce more current output than the other. It would be as if the one Crusoe had been endowed by nature with a greater capacity for rendering labor services than the other.

Now, if there were some foreordained law that elevated such a case of constantly maintained output to a role of primacy, then there might be a case for looking at things in this way. For Crusoe himself, in fact, if he attaches especial importance to maintaining a constant pattern of consumption, there can again be no objection to his mentally associating this year's output with the presence of this year's stock of tangible things. Such a mental association might be helpful in achieving the desired constancy in output. But for the outside observer to seize on this mental association as the indicator of which causes bring about which results, is clearly an error. If Crusoe is interested in maintaining a constant level of consumption, then he must *plan* his actions to this end. In these plans, the immediate maintenance intact of the stock of tangible things is required, not for the sake of *current* output, but for the sake of the adopted goal of maintaining the current level of output indefinitely during the future. To do this may call, as discussed earlier, for the simultaneous undertaking of a number of "staggered" projects; Crusoe must commence on new projects while earlier-undertaken projects are still in various stages of partial completion. The age composition of Crusoe's stock of tangible things can be understood, and can serve as a basis for explaining the future, only by steadfastly bearing in mind the particular plans that have brought about the present state of affairs.

MULTIPERIOD PLANNING BY THE INDIVIDUAL IN A MARKET ECONOMY

We turn now to apply the ideas learned from our discussion of Crusoe planning, to planning within the context of a market economy. We consider first the multiperiod plans of individuals. Then we will consider the implications to be drawn from the fact that the data of the market result from the interaction of numerous individual plans.

In a market economy an individual is able to make multiperiod plans with a greater range of freedom than was possible for Crusoe. Crusoe considered the resources at his disposal, made a guess as to the resources likely to be placed at his disposal by the course of future (external) events, and made his plans accordingly, striving to put his resources to use in the most efficient way possible, for the satisfaction of his own anticipated wants. In a market economy, too, an individual considers, just as Crusoe did, the resources at his disposal now and those expected to be made available to him by future (external) events. But the individual in a market economy can make plans which call for the employment of resources that he does not now possess, and that he does not expect to come directly into his possession at all. He is able to do this because he is able to exchange in the market the resources which he does expect to come directly into his possession into the other resources required for the execution of his plans. A special, very important example of this arises from his ability to *borrow* the means to acquire the resources he needs.

An individual will then make multiperiod plans that are limited, not by the particular resources expected to come directly into his possession, but by the arrays of resources expected to be obtainable in the market place through sale of his own resources, or by the terms on which present resources can be borrowed. Moreover, these multiperiod plans may be designed to produce output for which the planner himself anticipates no desire, and which will only later be exchanged in the market for the goods the planner himself expects to consume.

Prominent among the factors that an individual must take into consideration in formulating his plans, will therefore be the *market prices* of (a) the resources that he expects to come directly into his own possession, and (b) the resources that will be required for the execution of the various plans under scrutiny. For the purposes of the analysis of *individual* multiperiod planning, one assumes that these prices are given and externally determined. The existence of these prices (in conjunction with output prices) makes possible the calculation in monetary terms of the *costs* associated with the various projects up for consideration. The relationship between the prices of future output and those of current resources determines the attractiveness of those projects feasible only through the employment of borrowed resources.

But once notice has been taken of these possibilities that are opened up through exchange opportunities on the market, one is able to apply without further significant modification the same ideas that were relevant to the multiperiod plans of Crusoe. Let us take an individual and imagine (as we did with Crusoe) that he undertakes a plan.

At the outset our individual may possess resources and/or may expect to come into possession of resources without action on his part. He may, in addition, consider possibilities of borrowing various resource combinations. He may describe these resources in terms of their physical characteristics, or in terms of the possible functions that these resources can fulfill (in certain combinations). But he may also, in the market economy, describe them in terms of their purchasing power; in particular he can measure their *monetary value*. (Should, indeed, he acquire resources through borrowing, then it may be a sum of money that is borrowed.) Nevertheless, when an individual considers a particular plan of production, he must still at some stage in his calculations deal with it at a technological level. While calculation can now be carried on in monetary terms, the alternative plans being weighed still involve the same real elements that were relevant to Crusoe.

At the technological level it is, therefore, still possible to examine the tangible things that represent the state of an individual's half-finished project. It is still possible to describe these things in terms of past plans, in terms of the functions assigned to these things by these past plans, and in terms of the functions likely to be assigned to these things by the new plans that will be made in the light of changed conditions.

At the same time the facility for calculative purposes that is possessed by money enables the planner to measure the success or failure of his project. In particular it enables the value of the stock of tangible things on the one hand, and that of the flow of finished output on the other hand, to be expressed in homogeneous units of money. The individual concerned is certainly very interested in the relationship between the value of his stock of equipment and that of the annual output that he is able to produce with its assistance.

It is rather important to observe that these possibilities of measurement that exist in a monetary economy carry with them certain fairly subtle temptations to the observer that may avert his attention from the *planned* character of the tangible things that represent the state of an individual's half-finished projects. In our discussion of Crusoe, we came across similar temptations; in a monetary economy these possibilities acquire much greater importance. When the resources with which a project is undertaken and the outputs which are yielded by the project are both measured as sums of money, it becomes easy to forget that the one sum of money represents something which is being striven to be attained, while the other sum represents the means seized upon to further the sought ends. When the state of an individual's affairs is appraised during the course of a project's execution, this becomes even more serious. The tangible things which the individual possesses as a result of the initial stages of fulfilment of his project are valued as a sum of money. To an observer contemplating the magnitude of this sum, there is nothing to indicate that it is the outcome of a planned course of action; and there is nothing to indicate that the original plan envisaged any additional actions to be taken with respect to the things which this sum represents. Nor is there any indication of alternative plans that might be able to turn these things to account.

And yet it is clear that the sum of money is "tied up" in the form of tangible things only for the purpose of gaining still larger sums in the future. It is clear that the larger the sum that is so tied up, the larger will be the future sums that can be so gained. An observer will thus still attempt to gain prevision of an individual's future by an appraisal of his present "state of affairs"; and he will do so by examining the magnitude of the sum of money which the individual has tied up in his projects at any one time. This way of looking at things will do more than merely divert attention from the planning that is embodied in the particular tangible things that this sum of money measures. It will in addition, and as a result, foster the notion (noticed already in our discussion of Crusoe) that the gains that are anticipated for the future will somehow flow automatically from the fund of purchasing power that is at present tied up in the individual's assets.[9] The fact that these future gains are measured in the very same monetary terms as are these assets themselves serves to support this view of things. This makes it all the more easy to consider a fund of money as somehow possessing the capacity *to grow,* almost spontaneously; it makes it easy to think of the assets (which may be expressed in terms of such a monetary sum) as possessing somehow a "productivity" of their own. (This misconceived view certainly seems to fit in only too neatly with the circumstance that on the loan market, sums of money do seem to "grow" automatically with the mere passage of time.)

This misconception depends, it is worth noting, on yet a further consequence of the monetary measurement of assets. This is the misleading impression of *homogeneity* that is imparted by the representation of a set of tangible things by a sum of money. These tangible things may be very different from one another; they may in addition be the interim results of a number of quite separate plans. But this heterogeneity is completely submerged when assets are expressed as a value of money. This leads to an emphasis on the feature common to all tangible things possessed by an individual, viz., the mere fact that they are assets. This facilitates the appraisal of the individual's "state of affairs" in terms of the homogeneous pool of resources over which he has control, and, as seen above, the way is clear to the idea that from this homogeneous pool the future gains will flow more or less spontaneously. In particular, as we shall discover later in this essay, these notions have fostered the idea that, beneath the superficial heterogeneity of the particular stock of tangible goods an individual may possess, there exists a commonly shared characteristic that is responsible for the future surplus that these tangible goods will yield.

The earlier discussions of this chapter will have made clear the mis-

---

9. "Monetary values furnish the common denominator for diverse types of capital goods. . . . Thus it becomes possible to regard capital as a fund of abstract productive power" (Kendrick, 1961, p. 105).

leading nature of such ways of thinking. Of course the tangible things that an individual has in his possession (as a result of earlier stages in the fulfilment of a project) are the source of future gains. This is because the existence of these tangible things places the individual nearer to his goals than he would be without these things. After all, that was why his project called for the provision of these tangible things in the first place. But there is nothing in the mere existence of tangible things themselves that justifies their being looked at as merely the reflection of the future outputs to which they will give rise. This we saw in our discussion of Crusoe. Tangible things will give rise to future outputs only if they are put to use in appropriately planned ways. Even more emphatically must we deny that these tangible things possess some hidden common property that possesses "productivity" of its own, apart from the particular characteristics of the various tangible things, and apart from the various possible plans in which these tangible things might find a role.

INTERACTING PLANS

We must now take up the task of interpreting the significance, for our purposes, of the fact that a market consists of *interacting* individual plans. We do not have numerous Crusoes each formulating his isolated individual plan against the background of market data, but of individuals each of whose plans exercises direct influences on the plans of the others. Let us first recognize the role of division of labor.

Crusoe had first to construct an oven, to grow, harvest and grind grain into flour, and finally to bake bread. In a market economy these various steps in the long process of production leading to bread are broken up into separate self-contained processes. The man who grows wheat does not have to plan its further development into bread; the oven manufacturer's plans need not reach back to iron mining, nor need they extend to wheat-growing or to bread-baking. Each plans his own process. Taken together the plans tend to fit into an integrated pattern. But no single mind has formulated any such overall integrated plan. It is enough for the oven maker to know that there are men willing to sell him iron, that there are men willing to buy ovens from him. And so on.

Of course, each of these stages of production may itself take time, and will involve multiperiod planning on its own account. At any given time each of these individuals will be in possession of intermediate tangible things. From his own individual point of view these things represent half-finished products—where the finished product is simply that which he sells to further participants in the productive process. It is the interaction in the market place of the plans of the various different individuals to undertake different small steps in the overall process of production that may force adjustments in these plans and gradually tends to mold these plans so that altogether they constitute an integrated pattern.

Recognizing the role of the market in bringing about this tendency toward *coordination* among the various stages of production, we are immediately forced to look on the tangible things that are the intermediate products of the individual producers, as having a significance reaching beyond the narrow horizons of these individuals. We look on an unfinished oven not merely as a half-way station toward a finished oven, but as a half-way station toward bread; and we are aware that it is a half-way station along a road that reaches back to the iron mines and to the wheatfields. While the oven manufacturer does not need to know (and certainly not to plan) that his ovens will be used to bake bread, he does know that bakers can be expected to offer him prices for his ovens. And we know that these prices will be offered by the baker as initial steps in the fulfilment of *his* plans to bake and sell bread. So we must indeed see the oven as an intermediate product, the result of the first stages in the fulfilment of a series of (at least partially) interlocking plans whose ultimate end is to produce bread and sell it to the consumer.

This way of looking at things emphasizes the most fundamental of the insights into the market-system that economic analysis has been able to supply—the perception that the plans made in a market interact in a manner that tends to bring about a system of *interlocking* plans.

At the same time economic analysis warns vigorously against the simple assumption that all the plans being made at any one time do in fact interlock perfectly. Such perfection serves as a definition only of the state of equilibrium, a state which can in principle be attained only through the exhaustive operation of the market *process*, carried to its very end against the background of given tastes, factor availability and technological knowledge. Moreover, when, as in this essay, our interest is focused explicitly on the *multiperiod* plans of individuals, the requirements for the perfect interlocking of all relevant plans reach proportions of formidability as to render such a notion of no significance at all except as a theoretical construct.[10] A perfectly interlocking system of individual multiperiod plans would require that plans made now fit in not only with the plans of others

10. See Hayek (1941, ch. 2).

being made now and with relevant plans made by others in the past, but with all other relevant plans to be made in the future.

The existence of a half-finished oven at any time, then, signifies not that plans have in fact been laid to bake bread, but that the oven manufacturer's plans *anticipate*, in effect, the future formulation of such plans. In the case of Crusoe we found that the existence of intermediate tangible things during the course of a project's execution reflected Crusoe's past plans, but represented also currently available resources on the basis of which Crusoe may now wish to formulate new production plans (should he feel his circumstances to have changed). Tangible things might in the end be used for different purposes than those for which they were constructed in the first place. In the market economy this kind of possibility is now seen to acquire additional importance.

In the market economy, too, tangible things may in the end be used for different purposes than those for which they were originally constructed. An oven manufacturer might, in the event of a sudden sharp rise in the price of scrap metal, decide that it is to his advantage to sell his half-finished or even his finished ovens as scrap rather than to continue in his original line of manufacturing. This is quite similar to the possibility we found in the Crusoe economy. Or again, the passage of time may have so adversely affected the market for bread that the oven manufacturer finds himself forced to alter his plans, with respect both to future production and to goods in process. His original multiperiod plans may have been perfectly adjusted with earlier anticipated conditions in the bread market (as exemplified, for example, in the plans for the future made earlier by bakers). Changing conditions have thrown things out of adjustment: new multiperiod plans must be made by the oven manufacturer. Or, at least, he must make revised plans to fit in with different multiperiod plans of others than those originally in mind. This possibility too is rather similar, in principle, to possibilities we have found already in the Crusoe economy.

But a market economy may open up possibilities for altered plans (with respect to the utilization of intermediate tangible things) that have no close parallel in the Crusoe case. An oven manufacturer may have undertaken his line of business under a profound error. He may have entered oven-manufacturing under a badly mistaken impression of the extent of demand for ovens on the part of bakers. The passage of time alters nothing in this case except to provide to the oven manufacturer clearer and clearer evidence of his entrepreneurial error. He may be forced, under such circumstances, to revise his production plans in midstream, and possibly to dispose of his stock of finished and half-finished ovens in ways quite different from those first planned. What has happened here is that the seething agitation that makes up the course of the market process itself has resulted in the alteration of plans. As we have seen, it is precisely this, the enforcement of changes in plans in order to bring different plans into closer mutual adjustment, that is the function of the market process. This is well recognized in the case of single-period plans. What is here being pointed out is that in the context of multiperiod planning, the market process exercises a very special influence. This influence consists in the enforcement of new plans that will, possibly, embrace uses for existing tangible things for which these things had originally not been constructed.

It is of some importance to notice the range of adjustments that may be enforced by the market process in this way. This range is as wide as the range for entrepreneurial error itself. Not only may, for example, machines have been produced to serve industries which have no use for these machines. Machines may have been produced that were designed to be used for a long period of time, and these machines may in fact be used (perhaps more intensively) for only shorter periods. All such errors will lead to disappointments on the part of those who erred in their planning. These disappointments will strike planners primarily in the form of the emergence of market prices for their tangible things that differ from those originally anticipated. As a result they may sell their products to others than the producers for whom they were originally intended.

It should be noticed, however, that disappointingly low prices for tangible things do not *necessarily* mean that these things will be put to uses for which they were not originally planned. It is still entirely possible that the ovens may yet be sold to bakers. The low oven prices may indeed spell severe losses for the oven manufacturer. But these low prices may make it just worthwhile for the baker to continue baking bread. What has happened in this case is that entrepreneurial error on the part of the oven manufacturer has channeled resources into a branch of production (bread-baking) where these resources "ought not" to be employed, as judged from the viewpoint of an omniscient observer. In other words, perfect foreknowledge of market conditions on the part of all entrepreneurs would have inspired multiperiod plans in which bread-baking would now be a smaller industry than is now in fact the case. But the error on the part of the oven manufacturer once having been made, competent entrepreneurship has been able to make the best of a bad situation. The ovens have been put to work, bread-baking has been permitted to exploit the ready-to-hand ovens (even though these ovens would not, on better judgment, have been produced in the first place). In other words the plans originally made for the ovens have been successfully carried through to completion. The only reason for this is that the ovens were produced before the error in their being produced was perceived. The market process has enforced adjustments in current planning in order to exploit, as far as possible, the steps already taken in execution of earlier plans (that ought, nevertheless, not to have been undertaken in the first place). It is not difficult to see how this same pattern might hold true for a Crusoe economy: once he has started on a project, he may decide to continue even though he might now think this project to have been ill-advised in the first place.

THE "STATE OF AFFAIRS" OF AN ECONOMY

Consider the state of an economy at a particular point in time. An examination of the economy reveals the existence of numerous, heterogeneous tangible things. Since we confine our observations to a single instant, this is all that can be observed. How are we to interpret the significance of a particular set of such tangible things? What does the existence of the set tell us about the history of the economy? What basis does it provide for a prevision of the future? Our discussions thus far are sufficient to indicate the way in which these questions may be answered by the economist.

Looking at the economy as a whole, one observes significant similarities to the picture of Crusoe's state of affairs as obtained from the stock of tangible resources available to him at an intermediate point in the fulfilment of his plans. The buildings, the machines, the stocks of raw materials, the tangible things present in an economy at a given time, are all the results of past plans; and they all represent half-way stations along roads intended to lead far beyond themselves. The future output of the economy, as of Crusoe, depends on the present stock of resources.

But whereas we were assuming Crusoe's stock of resources (resulting from earlier steps taken in fulfilment of his multiperiod plans) to be the interim outcome of a *single* integrated plan, the stock of produced things in a market represents the heritage of numberless *separate* past plans. And we have already noticed that these plans can by no means be assumed to have been perfectly interlocking plans. Taken individually each piece of tangible produced good still represents the past plans of its producers and their expectations as to its further employments. But there is not very much more that can be said to preserve the parallelism between a Crusoe economy and the market economy. The state of affairs in a market economy is not the result of a single integrated past plan, nor does it lay the basis for any such future plan. The state of affairs in a market economy represents the status of the numberless individual past plans, and it reveals the extent to which the market process has brought these plans into consonance with one another. At the same time an examination of this state of affairs may reveal the degree to which past plans have *failed* to mesh. This may then indicate the future revisions in these plans that will be necessitated, not by changing underlying conditions (as was the case with Crusoe) but by the mere fact that the conflicts between jarring plans can be expected to result in eventually altered plans.

Nevertheless, despite these very real differences between the market economy and the Crusoe economy, it must be admitted that for some rough-and-ready purposes these differences can be quite usefully ignored. When one observes two Crusoes, one of whom possesses tractors while the second has only a wooden plow, one knows immediately something about the likely respective future outputs of the pair. And when one compares two countries and finds the one well stocked with roads, buildings, machines, and unfinished goods inventories, while the other is relatively poor in these tangible things, one *does* feel that one knows which country will enjoy the greater volume of output. It may be noted that our tendency to make this kind of judgment about a nation's economic future rests, if it is to be at all valid, on an implicit faith in the past and future ability of a market economy to coordinate plans. In the Crusoe case we saw how the future can be surmised from the present array of tangible things only by speculating on the plans Crusoe will make to use these things. In the market economy we can draw conclusions about the future only by assuming not only that individuals will make plans to employ the things they possess, but that they will do so in such a way that these plans will, at least to a large extent, exhibit a meshing and interlocking pattern.

If one is willing to make this kind of assumption then it is entirely in order to assess a nation's future by referring to its current stock of things. This can be done by looking at these things—not, we must insist, as though future output can be expected to flow, automatically and planlessly, from these things, but as though a single integrated plan for the entire economy was in the process of being smoothly carried out, promising the future attainment of some coordinated set of relevant goals.

SOME REMARKS ON THE THEORY OF CAPITAL

Thus far in this chapter little use has been made of the term "capital." During our discussions of multiperiod planning by Crusoe and by individuals in a market economy, use of the term has, in fact, been studiously avoided. We have been exploring the implications of the fact that people make multiperiod plans; we have taken notice of the circumstance that in a market economy multiperiod plans exercise influence over each other just as single-period plans do; in particular we have taken notice of the circumstance that at any given time an economy—whether that of Crusoe or a market economy—will reveal the existence of unfinished projects.

The central theme of this essay is the recognition that significant economic relationships can be revealed by paying attention to the as yet unfinished projects that exist in an economy at each point in time, and to the tangible things that represent the interim status of these projects. We have discovered that many, perhaps all, of the tangible things available at any time represent such "intermediate products"; that the composition of the array of such tangible things present at a given time in the market place, can be explained by reference to the past plans to which these things owe their existence, and to the way in which the market process has enforced a degree of coordination among these plans; and that, insofar as the course of future events depends on the present state of affairs, prevision of this future can be obtained by recognizing the as yet uncompleted plans that were formulated in the past for the further utilization of these tangible things (and of the possible revisions in these plans that may be enforced by the future course of the market process).

The relevance of all this to the concept of capital is not far to seek. The body of analysis generally understood to be embraced by the theory of capital, happens to deal with these same problems. Despite the number of different definitions assigned to the word "capital," the concept is invariably used in theories that attempt to grapple with the relationships between resources at one point in time and outputs of subsequent points in time, and with associated problems. The multiplicity of different formulations of the capital concept attest not only to the elusive nature of the concept itself, but, even more importantly, to the innate complexity of the economic relationships hoped to be elucidated with the aid of this concept, or rather these concepts. The contribution which this essay seeks to make consists in its suggestion of a way of looking at these things that, while not at all novel, has yet, in the area of capital theory, not been followed through with sufficient perseverance or with sufficient consistency.

The remaining chapters of this essay critically appraise in turn some of the more important of the confusing aspects of the capital concept as treated in the literature. These chapters show how confusion frequently seems to have arisen from a failure to exploit the insights that we have obtained during the course of the discussions thus far in this chapter. There has been, it may be assumed, little in these discussions themselves with which issue might be taken. The sole purpose of the discussions has been merely to focus attention on a particular way of looking at things. The point at which we do part ways with other writers on capital theory is with respect to the usefulness for this theory, of this way of looking at things.

Let us consider, for example, the time-honored definition of capital, or of capital goods, that runs in terms of produced means of further production. Factors of production that are not "original," but man-made, are grouped together as capital goods. Now this may be a very useful definition. There is no doubt that many of the tangible things that are capable of being turned to account in production are man-made, and that their having this characteristic may be of considerable significance. But this definition is all too frequently accepted in bald terms, completely ignoring the relevant *plans* that are involved. It is used to focus attention on certain factors of production, and finds a certain uniqueness inhering in this class of objects, viz., their having been obtained by the past productive efforts of men, rather than from direct endowment. The past history of these objects provides a criterion for their definition.[11] Proceeding from this foundation one is then able to discourse further concerning the past inputs, or the "waiting" that are somehow "embodied" in capital goods. And then one is able to formulate propositions that, for example, attempt to relate these past inputs to the contributions that the capital good is able to make to production. If introduced at all, plans play only a subsidiary role in this scheme of things.

The approach that is here being advanced starts out, on the other hand, from the fact that men make multiperiod plans, which, prior to their ultimate completion, result in unfinished projects. Attention is then sought to be trained upon the objects of which these unfinished projects consist, for the purposes outlined above. For these purposes no significance is attached to the physical characteristics or the physical history by which these objects might possibly be grouped apart from other objects. The

11. Hayek (1941, p. 89) has described the definition of capital as the produced means of production as "a remnant of the cost of production theories of value."

fact that these objects have been produced (rather than received as natural endowment) is in itself of little moment. The significance associated with the circumstance that these objects were produced consists in the fact that all production is planned production, so that produced objects are the results of plans. And since these objects are themselves potential factors of production, their production presumably resulted from plans in which their own eventual employment was envisaged.

What we suggest here is that the elusive element in the economic system that economists have been trying to pinpoint by their various definitions of capital and capital goods comes into clear and unmistakable focus as soon as we recognize that at least part of the tangible things present in an economy at any time correspond to the intermediate objects here being discussed.[12] It would seem to us, then, most natural to appropriate the term "capital goods" for the technical identification of such intermediate objects. While no particular importance can be attached to the definitions of particular terms, and another term could very easily be coined for the purpose in question, we offer no apology for saddling the term "capital" with yet one more (different) definition. Confusion would be heightened rather than lessened by the introduction of a new term for the purpose of identifying these intermediate objects. The principal point to be emphasized is that capital goods, thus defined, are distinguished in that they fall neatly into place in a *teleological* framework. They are the interim goals aimed at in earlier plans; they are the means toward the attainment of still further ends envisaged by the earlier plans. It is here maintained that the perception of this aspect of tangible things now available provides the key to the unraveling of the problems generally attempted to be elucidated by capital theory.

The distinguishing characteristic of our capital goods is, then, not a positivist one. Just as a positivist can see in an oven nothing but joined pieces of shaped metal, so will he be unable to distinguish our capital goods from other objects. This is not true of other criteria used to demarcate capital goods from other resources. It remains true, of course, that the identification of a "resource," as distinct from other physical things, cannot be made without reference to human purposes. But for the distinction between capital goods and other resources the criteria employed in the literature would be entirely acceptable to a positivist. Resources that

---

12. Cf. Böhm-Bawerk's definition of capital in terms of intermediate products (1959b, p. 14).

have been produced can be shown to be such by observation; resources that are producible ("augmentable"[13]) can be recognized on purely technological grounds; resources that are non-permanent[14] can be similarly identified. The criterion for the identification of capital goods that is advanced here, on the other hand, cannot be applied on a purely empirical basis. Only *understanding* of the nature of the multiperiod plan enables us to focus attention on the "intermediate objects" under discussion. This is completely consistent with the situation elsewhere in economic analysis. Progress in economics starts with the recognition that goods possess "utility"—in other words that goods provide fulfilment for consumer *plans*. For us the plan is not something that may be invoked (along with other possible explanatory principles) in attempting to explain certain phenomena. Rather, insight into the propensity of human beings to plan imposes the scientific obligation to study the consequences of this propensity. This at once draws our attention to the significant, the relevant features of the real world and provides a theoretical framework into which we may then seek to fit the course of events in this real world.

IS A THEORY OF CAPITAL REALLY NECESSARY?

It will be recalled from our discussion of the Crusoe economy that significance attaches to the "state of affairs" at a point in time primarily when future prospects are being appraised from the point of view of this date itself. The state of affairs that existed at some date already past, when looked at retrospectively, from the vantage point of some later date, is of interest only when one wishes to understand how future prospects must have appeared to those present at the past date; or it may be of interest if this past state of affairs has turned out to have inspired subsequent actions that represented changes in the plan that had previously been mapped out for the future. Where multiperiod plans (or portions thereof) have been successfully carried through to complete execution as originally planned, little interest can attach to past intermediate states of affairs. Nothing that has been accomplished demands explanation in terms of past intermediate states of affairs. Everything can be fully accounted for by reference to conditions existing at the times when decisions were made, either at the initiation of entirely new plans or in the revision of earlier plans.

13. On the "augmentability" criterion, see Kaldor (1937, p. 174); also Hayek (1941, pp. 57–58).

14. See Hayek (1941, ch. 5); also Hayek (1936, pp. 369–70).

It turns out, then, that the course of history in a world in which no plans need to be altered does not call for economic explanation having recourse to intermediate states of affairs. For a world in which there prevails perfect knowledge of future external change and in which the multiperiod plans of all individuals interlock faultlessly, it follows that everything that needs to be explained, outputs, prices, interest rates, and the like, can be explained without seeking causes represented by intermediate states of affairs in the past. For such a world the state of affairs at intermediate stages during the execution of a plan represents only a result, a result that one may wish to explain, but which itself adds nothing to the explanation of the subsequent course of events that could not have been explained by direct reference to past *actions* (applications of input, exchanges, and the like).

It might appear then that a theory of capital is not necessary for an understanding of the chains of cause and effect operating in the real world. Events in a multiperiod model of a market economy would appear to be determined entirely by other events. Past states of affairs, too, are themselves the outcomes of earlier events. Analysis might seem capable of bypassing consideration of these states of affairs, and proceeding directly to the prime causal elements. These are clearly events rather than states. It seems that this, in effect, is the basis for a number of suggestions made in recent years that economic theory (explicitly extended to deal with multiperiod models) can do without a theory of capital altogether.[15]

In defense of capital theory several points ought to be made. In the first place there is room for a theory that will explain how "states of affairs" came to be what they were. A theory is required that should account for the particular array of tangible things available at a given date; the particular types of equipment, the particular degrees of durability of the various things available, the particular stages of completion which the various unfinished products have attained, all these need to be explained. This can only be done by an application of multiperiod analysis for an understanding of the tangible things that emerge when a series of multiperiod plans are, so to speak, arrested in midstream.

More important, a theory of capital is indeed necessary in order to account for the course of events subsequent to a given date. We live in a world in which knowledge of the future is characteristically spotty, so

---

15. Cf., e.g., Blyth (1960, p. 136); Solow (1963, pp. 16, 25); Samuelson (1961, p. 308); Usher (1965, p. 183, n. 1). See also Lachmann (1956, p. v).

that at all times earlier plans are being revised. In addition, we live in a world in which equilibrium is characteristically absent, so that the multiperiod plans of different individuals do not form a faultlessly interlocking system. For this reason, too, earlier plans are being continually revised. These revisions of plans cannot be understood without reference to the stocks of equipment, raw materials, half-finished products and finished products that are available at the relevant dates. What is required is a theory that will explain the new multiperiod plans that will be made, the new forces acting to determine prices and interest rates, outputs, industry size and organization, future rates of accumulation of stocks of new tangible things, and so on, that follow from the presence, at a given date, of a particular array and distribution of capital goods. For all this we require an articulated, fully worked out theory of capital.[16]

In this view of the role of capital theory, we join those writers who have deplored the long-standing, almost traditional, tendency to see capital theory as a mere adjunct to the theory of interest. Interest rates represent merely one particular kind of price—the intertemporal price—that is determined, along with all the other market phenomena, by the multiperiod plans that are being made by market participants. Of course capital theory is involved. But capital theory is required in order to understand the current market price for shoes, just as much as it is required in order to understand the ratio between the future price of shoes and the current prices.

16. Cf. Hayek (1941, pp. 3, 15, 296); see also Griliches (1963, pp. 115–16).

Chapter 2. Stocks and Flows

Despite the controversies surrounding the definition of "capital," there seems, Haavelmo found, "to be at least one aspect of capital which is not very controversial: That capital must have the dimensions of a *stock concept, something at a point of time, t,* and not something per unit of time."[1] As Haavelmo points out, here the agreement on definition ends. Nonetheless the concept of capital as a *stock,* as distinct from other economic variables that are flows, has played a more important role in some approaches to the capital notion than it has in others. This chapter is particularly concerned with these approaches, and will appraise them from the vantage point of the capital concept developed in the preceding chapter.

Our concept of capital too, it will have been observed, sees it as a stock, not a flow. However, the stock of capital is, in our view, seen as the planned outcome of a series of past activities ("flows") and, at the same time, is seen as the basis of plans already (at least partly) formulated for a future series of activities ("flows"). One of the characteristics of some of the alternative approaches which stress the "stock" character of capital is that they employ this "stock" character to permit the analysis of the role of capital in *static* economic models. In other words, because capital itself is not something per unit of time, it is seen as being able to be assimilated into models of the economic system in which no time is permitted to elapse, or at least in which time-subscripts do not matter.[2] It is the "timeless" character thus attributed to capital which has enabled these writers to deal with the problem that Hicks has recently described as: "how is capital to be fitted in to a static theory?"[3]

THE "PRESENCE" OF CAPITAL STOCKS

What is characteristic of these latter approaches is that they admit capital goods into the production function by viewing production as depending simultaneously on *two* kinds of inputs, flow inputs and stock inputs. Out-

---

1. Haavelmo (1960, p. 43, and see also p. 91). See also Fraser (1937, p. 250); Kendrick (1961, p. 102: "Most economists have continued to view capital as a stock"). For further background on the stock concept of capital, see also Schumpeter (1954, pp. 627f.). See also Lerner (1953, p. 545).

2. For a survey of the characteristics distinguishing "static" from "dynamic" systems, see Baumol (1959, ch. 1).

3. Hicks (1963, p. 343).

put results, in this view, from the application of service flows, *in the presence* of stocks of capital. Capital contributes to the process of production by its presence. Vernon Smith sees the "distinguishing characteristic of capital goods" to be "simply that their *presence,* in the form of physical stocks, is required if production is to take place."[4] Haavelmo, dwelling on the stock character of capital, draws from it the "fundamental conclusion" that the influence of capital on output is "due to *capital being present* in the process and not to the fact that certain parts of it are used up in the process."[5] This way of looking at things, Haavelmo believes, removes "the mystery of stored-up land and labor from the definition of instruments of production."[6] (Enke, going even further, insists on the possibility of treating production functions as "instantaneous relations" in which *all* inputs are treated as stocks.")[7]

In this approach, it will be observed, it is the durability of capital goods that is being emphasized. Other inputs, it is being pointed out, contribute to production by being "used up." The essence of capital goods, on the other hand, is seen in their remaining extant even after their "presence" has enabled the "flow" inputs to be transformed into output. The capital goods have, through their presence, provided "services" (without themselves losing any of their potential to provide such services in the future). These "services" may be viewed as flowing, as being "used up," but these services are provided by the mere presence of something that is itself *not* used up by their creation.

It is to be noted that this way of looking at the productive role of capital goods represents, not so much an *application* of their "stock" character, as a (rather dubious) *extension* of this feature. It is one thing to notice that capital goods *exist* at a point in time. It is quite another thing to see the productive usefulness of these goods as consisting in their mere existence. The view that sees the role of capital goods as consisting in their mere presence implies not only that capital goods exist, but that their continued existence over time is completely unaffected by the productive contribution which they make. If, as it may be claimed in its defense, this

4. Smith (1961, p. 64, italics in original).

5. Haavelmo (1960, p. 91, italics in original). For a similar opinion, see Kendrick (1961, p. 103).

6. Haavelmo (1960, pp. 70–80).

7. Enke (1962, pp. 372, 375). While Enke (pp. 369, n. l, 375, n. 23) cites Haavelmo's book in support of his conception of the production function as an "instantaneous relation," there appears reason to question the full justice of this claim.

view of the role of capital goods depends on exclusive concentration upon a given instant, then it has been secured at the price of all the important insights that the recognition of multiperiod planning can confer. The crux of the matter seems to depend, we will attempt to show, on the way one looks at the production function.

A production function can be looked at "positively." As such it represents simply a set of technological relationships. On the other hand, a production function can be looked at as representing *opportunities,* from among which a human being is able to make a choice. Clearly an economics in which market events are seen as the results of deliberately planned actions ought to view production possibilities in this second way, as alternatives from among which planned courses of action may be constructed.[8]

Now, on the first view on the production function (i.e., from a purely technological point of view), there is nothing to deter us from considering thinner and thinner slices of time. We can observe the inputs fed into a process of production during any short period of time, and observe the outputs yielded during this interval. By choosing a sufficiently short interval we can certainly arrive at short processes of production in which, as far as can be observed, part of the yield is to be ascribed merely to the "presence" of certain things, which emerge at the end of the interval in apparently the same form in which they entered the process.

But if we look at a production function from a "planning" or "decision-making" point of view, matters are quite different. We are no longer at liberty to select arbitrarily any interval of time we choose, and to consider it entirely on its own. We are forced to recognize that the plans that men make are *multi*period plans. If we select arbitrarily a slice out of the overall span of time envisaged for a multiperiod plan, we must be prepared to concede that this slice represents only a portion of a plan. What has been planned for this slice of time cannot be understood unless taken within the context of the particular overall multiperiod plan that is relevant.

It follows, then, on this "decision-making" view of the production function, that to treat capital goods as if they were permanent goods, when in fact they have been constructed as part of a plan in which they are to be ultimately used up, is a distortion that ought not to win acceptance

---

8. Current practice generally (and, as it seems to us, unfortunately) follows the "technological" view. This is especially the case with respect to aggregate models. The paragraphs following in the text explain why this practice is especially unfortunate in the capital theory context.

merely because a sufficiently short period of time is being considered. What may be acceptable as a *technological* description of what goes on in a selected short period of time is grossly unsatisfactory as an *economic* description—that is, as a description of the course of events in terms of relevant human decisions that have been made.

This difference between what may be acceptable as a technological description and what is required for the economic description, can be perceived perhaps more clearly by considering a succession of thin slices of time taken together. Let us suppose that the aggregate interval of time is long enough for a capital good to have reached the end of its working life and to have been replaced by another. Now from the positive, technological viewpoint, there can be no objection to a description of the process as having merely required at all times the "presence" of the capital good. And, taking in aggregate the above technological descriptions of what takes place in each of the thin time-slices, this is in fact the total picture obtained. And yet, from the point of view of the decision-maker, what has taken place is far more complicated. Originally the capital good was acquired, in full awareness of its prospective working life, as well as the associated maintenance and operating costs on the one hand, and annual output on the other hand. The capital good was acquired with the intention of "using it up" over its lifetime, in the production of output. Clearly the economic descriptions of what takes place during the various thin time-slices must be capable, at least, of being pieced together into an overall story that does not run in flat contradiction to the economic facts. To do otherwise is to force the description of economic events into a mold no longer suited for economic analysis, i.e., a mold in which events are perceived, not as parts of plans, but as arbitrarily cut slices of history "positively" considered.

STOCK DEMAND AND FLOW DEMAND

Nothing that has been written in these pages should, it is hoped, be understood as necessarily implying criticism of the distinction frequently drawn between "stock demand" and "flow demand," in respect to capital goods. This latter distinction is invoked in analyses of the market forces operating upon the prices of capital goods. It is argued that capital goods involve *two* kinds of market situation. On the one hand, the stock of capital goods at a given date is a datum, and can be expected to be altered only gradually. This characterizes the market for existing capital goods as one for a good that is virtually not able to be produced nor destroyed at all, so that its supply curve is perfectly inelastic. On the other hand, given sufficient time, new capital goods *can* be produced, and existing ones depleted through current use. So that alongside the market forces relevant to capital goods treated as a given stock, there are operative market forces relevant to these goods treated as flows. Recognition of these two sets of interacting forces, it is claimed, provides insight into the process of capital goods accumulation and pricing.[9]

Now this Clower approach, like those discussed in the preceding section, depends on the notion of a *given* size of stock of capital goods, at a given time. Moreover, this approach is able to integrate these two sets of market forces pertaining to capital goods only by assuming that the "flows" of capital goods during a single short time period are small enough to permit the analysis of the price of existing capital goods just as if this stock was, in fact, unaltered in size during the period. In other words, this approach, like the approaches criticized in the preceding section, assumes (at least at one level of discussion) that capital goods are not "used up" during small periods of time. Nonetheless the criticisms of the preceding section do not apply to this approach.

One may indeed entertain doubts concerning an analysis in which the simultaneous critical assumptions are that the stock of capital goods is, and that it is not, constant during the passage of a period of time.[10] But we can find little to quarrel with in the assumption of an unchanging capital stock itself, in this context. What the Clower approach is saying is merely that two kinds of (interacting) adjustments are taking place on the capital goods market: (a) adjustments primarily affecting the prices of *given* goods, and (b) adjustments in the flows of these goods into and out of the sphere of production. Clower chooses to polarize these two kinds of adjustment by talking as if the first kind of adjustment was able to be carried on as if there were no second kind of adjustment at all. The assumed constancy of the capital stock is thus a simplifying one, that does not affect the essence of what is being discussed. It does *not* imply that capital goods are not used up during the processes of production to which they contribute (after all, the whole purpose of the analysis was to integrate the theory of capital goods being used up with that of the stock of existing goods). On the other hand, the approaches criticized in the preced-

9. On this, see Clower (1954). See also Witte (1963); Thalberg (1961).

10. As Clower (1954, p. 68) recognizes, his assumptions are strikingly parallel to those basic to the perfectly competitive model.

ing section emphasize the constancy of the capital stock because, in these approaches, it is of the essence of capital goods that their contribution to production leave these goods intact; capital goods are not used up in production.

ARE CAPITAL GOODS "USED UP" IN PRODUCTION?

We have seen that the Smith-Haavelmo approach to short-run analysis is to treat capital as if it were, unlike other inputs, not "used up" during production. For some capital theorists such a treatment would be to rob capital of one of its essential features. For Hayek, for example, a definition of capital must exclude "permanent resources" from the capital category. It is for Hayek of the essence of capital that it is comprised of resources that have limited life.[11] On the other hand for Lachmann the capital category is broad enough to include resources that never become used up,[12] although, even for the short run, this property is certainly not seen as the crucial capital criterion. For the approach outlined in the preceding chapter, again, whether or not resources are "permanent" is not of first importance; but, on the other hand, where a multiperiod plan of production does envisage the using up of resources over time, then, as we have seen, this approach insists that this aspect of the plan not be suppressed. The differences between these various approaches to the question of handling the using up of capital goods during production is brought out very sharply in the various treatments accorded to the notion of *depreciation*.

Haavelmo cites the views that the "input" from a capital good is simply its rate of depreciation. For Haavelmo this idea is "very dangerous and misleading," and, from the point of view of production theory, "hopeless."[13] Elsewhere he describes this idea more mildly as not perhaps "entirely hopeless" in itself, "but as unnecessarily complicated from a technological point of view."[14] It results, Haavelmo thinks, from a natural tendency to ask what it is that "goes in" in order that the additional product made possible by capital goods should "come out." And, as we have seen, this is, for Haavelmo, an inappropriate question with respect to capital goods. Capital goods play a role in production by merely being present and yielding a flow of "services" during each period of time. There

---

11. Hayek (1941, ch. 5).
12. Lachmann (1956, p. 12).
13. Haavelmo (1960, p. 79).
14. Ibid. (p. 93).

are many processes of production in which depreciation is very slight indeed in comparison to output. This suggests, Haavelmo argues, that for something to "come out" of a capital-using process of production it is not really necessary at all for anything of the capital to "go in." Additional output may be technologically attainable merely by adding the presence of a catalyst, in the form of capital goods. So that even if depreciation of these goods does occur during the course of a process of production, it is wrong to consider this depreciation as the relevant "input." Thus for Haavelmo an isoquant map describing a capital-using process may not be assigned an axis measuring the physical deterioration of capital as one of the inputs.

Enke, too, insists on using a production function in which the presence of capital goods (not their physical deterioration) is relevant to the level of output. However, Enke demands that, for the determination of the optimum mix of capital goods and other factors of production, the cost of capital goods include, besides the interest or rental charge involved, also an item for what he labels "time depreciation." "Time depreciation" during a period of time is a function of the stock of real capital employed, in contrast to "use deterioration" which is a function of output quantity. Use deterioration of capital goods does not affect the cost of using larger or smaller stocks of capital, and hence does not effect the marginal choice between capital and other (non-capital) means of production.[15] In fact, for Enke, use deterioration, while a genuine input, has really nothing to do with the "capitalistic" aspect of a production process at all; use deterioration is a flow input, capital is stocked. On the other hand the presence of capital stocks does involve time depreciation, and this does affect the optimum combination of capital goods and other means of production. Enke is thus able to *define* capital in such a way as to distinguish sharply between the employment of capital stocks on the one hand, and the non-capital flow input constituted by the use-deterioration of stocked capital goods on the other. While treating capital goods as means of production by virtue of their presence (as Haavelmo does), Enke yet insists that the *cost* of the presence of these goods include an item to cover their time depreciation.

Enke's argument insisting on the need to allow for time depreciation in the cost calculations involved in the determination of the optimum capital-labor mix affords a further useful opportunity to notice the two

15. Enke (1962, p. 377).

ways of looking at the production function that were mentioned earlier. A production function can be seen as a positive statement of technological relationships, or it can be seen as presenting a set of opportunities relevant to prospective planning. Corresponding to these two views on the production function are two ways of looking at the optimum factor combination obtained by comparing an isoquant map with an isocost line. We have seen that, on the second, "planning" view of the production function, this function must be constructed within an explicit time framework relevant to multiperiod planning. On the other hand, we found, on the "positive" view, a production function can be constructed in principle for arbitrarily cut slices of time, no matter how thin. Now, on the latter "positive" view, the minimization of cost that is required for the optimum factor combination must involve those items of cost that seem *technologically* relevant to that portion of the process of production under consideration during the arbitrarily thin slice of time. Since the time slice may not be relevant to any plan whatsoever, the "cost" (associated with the corresponding portion of the process of production) may not be in the nature of an opportunity cost altogether. If no plan is relevant, there can be no question of forgone alternatives, of genuine *economic* cost. All that is possible is a technological concept of cost, for the determination of which the accountant will seek to assign a value to what has been used up during the time slice. It is for this reason that for Enke the deterioration in capital stocks that has occurred during this time slice (purely as a result of the passage of time) must be charged as part of the cost of commanding the productive "presence" of these stocks during this time.

But on the "planning" view of the production function this treatment is not at all appropriate. The optimum factor combination, on this view, represents one particular course of action (out of the many courses of action that make up the production function) that appears optimal to the producer planning his future activities. For the producer who is contemplating alternative *multi*period courses of action, therefore, an optimum factor combination can exist only in the context of a production function that is itself multiperiod in scope. One can ask what the optimum capital-labor combination is only at times when the producer is able to vary their combination, i.e., when he is forced to decide which combination to adopt in his production plan. If, for example, the producer has already invested in particular specific and immobile capital goods, then the search for the optimum capital-labor mix does *not* have to take account of the cost of these capital goods, insofar as they represent sunk, irretrievable investment. For a producer in this position, therefore, time depreciation is quite irrelevant; in fact, interest charges on the investment will be equally irrelevant. (Insofar as varying intensity of use affects the durability of the capital goods, of course, then "user cost" will certainly be relevant, but this is different from depreciation.) On the other hand, if the capital goods have *not* yet been acquired, then of course time depreciation is a relevant cost; but the entire picture is now one in which the term "depreciation" hardly has a place. If we consider the decision-maker before he has acquired capital goods then his decision involves a comparison between alternative multiperiod projects. A relevant aspect of any such project will of course be the rate at which capital stocks will deteriorate and will require maintenance and/or replacement expenses in order to be maintained intact. (In this "long-run" context, indeed, the sharp distinction drawn by Enke between use deterioration and time depreciation seems quite unimportant.)

Similar considerations apply to Haavelmo's refusal to consider the input of capital goods as consisting of their depreciation. To the economist "input" refers to what the producer must *plan* to apply to a process of production. From the multiperiod planning viewpoint it hardly makes sense to focus attention separately upon one out of a large number of future periods of time. Certainly, if this one period is one for which the process of production will have been already irrevocably fixed by earlier multiperiod decisions, there is little that can be said about it that is relevant to economic (as distinct from technological) considerations. On the other hand, on viewing prospectively a large number of such periods of time in succession, the "input" that is represented by particular capital goods certainly does appear as the investment that will be consumed over the lifetime of the goods, if their life is limited. In other words, for the "short run" Haavelmo would be right to ignore depreciation, but wrong in discussing a capital-using production function involving capital as an input, as if it were relevant to economic decision-making. On the other hand for the longer run, for which decisions with respect to capital goods are feasible, Haavelmo would be wrong to view the production process as one in which these goods are not used up, if in fact they *are* used up (and if this fact is taken into account by the long-run decision-makers). Only if capital goods were completely non-specific and perfectly mobile would decision-making for the immediately following slice of time, however thin, be relevant at all times (during the course of a multiperiod process of production) to the capital goods employed; only then would the Haavelmo-Enke arguments be genuinely relevant.

HICKS AND THE STOCK-FLOW PRODUCTION
FUNCTION: A DIGRESSION

Our discussion of the Smith-Haavelmo use of stock-flow production functions (in which the inputs are flows of labor services in the *presence* of stocks of capital goods) and our criticism of this notion make it of interest to digress briefly to consider a different kind of stock-flow production function that has been employed by Professor Hicks.[16]

Hicks explicitly attempts to construct a production function that should correspond to production processes that take time. To do this he considers a period of time, and notices that at the beginning of the period there exists an initial capital stock, while at the end of the period a closing stock of capital is left over. During the period there are applied flow inputs, and there emerges a flow output. The relevant inputs, argues Hicks, are thus the initial *stock* of capital and the *flow* inputs applied during the period. The outputs are the *flows* emerging during the period, and the *stock* of capital remaining over at the end. Between these four items (flow inputs, stock inputs, flow outputs, stock outputs) there will exist, with given technique, a production relation that can be expressed as the production function.

It is apparent that Hicks' stocks of capital play a quite different role in his stock-flow production functions than do those of Smith or of Haavelmo. For the latter the importance of treating capital as a stock consists in that this enables the process of production to be viewed as one in which capital goods contribute to production without being themselves used up. For Hicks this is not at all the case. On the contrary, he sees the change that occurs in the stock of capital goods between the start and the close of the period as an important aspect of the production process, treating the initial stock as an input and the closing stock as an output. For Hicks the stock character of capital is relevant merely because a "balance sheet" is drawn up at the start and at the close of the period. At given dates there exist particular stocks of capital; during the intervening period flows of inputs and outputs occur. Hicks' time-conscious production function embraces both sets of elements.

In fact Hicks' production function is vastly superior to that of Smith and Haavelmo precisely in its attempt to represent the period of time that a production process requires. It might even at first glance appear that Hicks' production function is identical with that which we have called for in this chapter in order that the function be relevant to multiperiod *plan-*

16. Hicks (1961, pp. 23ff.).

ning. The decision-maker contemplating a particular multiperiod plan is contemplating, just as Hicks describes, the application of an initial stock of resources in conjunction with subsequent additional applications of inputs. It might seem that Hicks has provided us with just the tool that we have been asking for.

This, however, is not the case; Hicks' production function, while not an "instantaneous" function (and thus certainly superior to the Smith-Haavelmo apparatus), is easily seen to be cast on what we have termed "positive" (rather than economic) lines. This is apparent when Hicks discusses the time-shapes of the flow inputs and outputs during the period of the production process. Hicks shows little compunction in principle to slicing up time into thinner and thinner slices; it is apparently of little moment that the resulting production processes, despite their taking up time, are nonetheless merely arbitrary segments of the process as a whole (that is relevant to multiperiod planning).[17]

CAPITAL STOCKS AND INCOME FLOWS

Any discussion of capital in which its "stock" character is emphasized, must sooner or later come to deal with the distinctive concept of capital that is associated with Knight and his followers. Professor Knight's theory of capital will be of particular concern to us in the succeeding chapter; in the present chapter we refer to this theory only insofar as it impinges directly on the stock concept that has been associated with capital.

Knight's view of the economic process is well known. Of prime importance to this view is the sharp distinction that is drawn between agencies that render service and the services so rendered. "What is in fact consumed in economic life is exclusively services, and accordingly, the primary meaning of production is the rendering of service."[18] Unlike the agencies that render service, services themselves do not "exist" apart from their flow in time. Capital goods are simply the sources of streams of service. The latter have existence only as flows in time; capital goods exist at particular points in time. Capital goods are stocks, service streams are flows.

Moreover, by viewing capital goods as sources of flows of services, Knight is able to focus attention on an element common to all such goods

---

17. Ibid. (p. 27).

18. Knight (1956, p. 43). For expository discussions of the Knightian view of capital, see especially Kaldor (1937) and Weston (1951).

(and to Knight both land and labor are to be included along with productive instruments, as capital). The element that is common to all agents of
production is that they constitute "sources" of future service flows. Capitalization of the yield of a source of future service flows provides us with
the value of the source.

By paying especial attention to the case in which a "source" yields a
perpetual steady flow of services (after deducting an amount sufficient to
maintain the source itself at all times), Knight is able to go even further.
Any instrument of production is perceived as a "fund" of capital, a fund
from which there is able to flow such a perpetual steady flow of services.
Productive plant "is measured by the perpetual service income which it
can be counted upon to yield. In other words, plant itself, in its quantitative aspect, is perpetual (regardless of changes in physical form), except
for a possible net disinvestment in society as a whole. . . . Quantitatively
speaking, any two pieces or items of wealth are to be compared as perpetual incomes."[19]

It is important to notice the distinctive features in Knight's conception
of capital as a stock (as opposed to a flow). These features set Knight's approach apart from that of Haavelmo and Smith discussed earlier (despite
some superficial similarities); they set Knight's approach completely apart
from that developed in the first chapter of this essay; in fact the distinction that exists for Knight between stock and flow is quite different from
all the other means by which stocks and flows are kept separate by writers
on capital theory.

For Haavelmo and Smith capital was stocked in the sense that producers required the *presence* of capital goods without necessarily using them
up, in order to raise the output obtainable from the application of flow
inputs. For the approach outlined in the first chapter of this essay, capital
goods are a stock, because they are what is found when the state of an unfinished project is appraised as of a particular date. Similarly for Hicks,
as cited in the preceding section, capital goods are a stock because they
are found when a balance sheet of an economic system (or a segment
thereof) is drawn as of a particular date. For Fisher or for Fraser, discussing the possibility of defining capital, as Knight himself in fact does, so
broadly that *all* items of wealth may be part of capital, capital is yet not
the *same* as wealth: capital is wealth looked at from a particular point of
view; it is the fund of wealth available at a given moment, as opposed to

19. Knight (1956, p. 47).

the flow of wealth produced and consumed during a given period.[20] The distinction between fund and flow that is for Knight of first importance in the theory of capital is quite different from those relevant to these various points of view.

For Knight a special significance attaches to exchange transactions in which a perpetual flow of service is exchanged for an agency which is able (through judicious earmarking, out of the gross yield, of maintenance and replacement reserves) to act as a source of such a perpetual flow. The capital market has the function of ensuring a tendency for such transactions to be carried out on terms in which the rate of discount equates the capitalized values of the future streams of services to the costs of production of the agencies. In a perfect capital market any stream of services of whatever time-shape can be exchanged for a perpetual steady stream at the equilibrium rate of discounting. So that, as already observed, each instrument of production can be viewed as embodying the power to generate a particular perpetual service flow. It is *this* relationship between agencies, or sources, of perpetual steady service flows, on the one hand, and these service flows themselves, on the other hand, that represents for Knight the relevant aspect of the stock-flow dichotomy. The economic world at any given time consists of a stock of "things" each of which is to be viewed as a potential source of a perpetual steady flow of services to be consumed. As of different dates an economy will possess different sizes of capital stocks, as a result of investment or disinvestment. At any one date the potential perpetual flows of future services are represented by the existence of the sources capable of yielding these flows. Capital is the fund from which an endless stream of future income can be drawn.

KNIGHT AND THE PERMANENCE OF CAPITAL

It will be observed that an essential element in the foregoing capital-income scheme is the postulated permanence of capital. Despite the fact that individual instruments of production have only finite productive lives, the capital that is embodied in these instruments is conceived of as permanent: when an instrument "dies" the capital that was embodied in it continues to have existence in the instruments that replace it (these replacements being made possible by the accumulated depreciation allowances set aside from the gross yield of the first instrument). It is only this notion of the permanence of capital that enables a particular instru-

20. Fisher (1906, p. 52); Fraser (1937, p. 250).

ment of production to be viewed as the source of a perpetual steady flow of services.

The permanence of capital as viewed by Knight is, however, not to be confused with the treatment of capital goods at the hands of Smith or of Haavelmo. The latter choose to look upon capital goods as not being used up in production; they are referring to particular instruments of production, and they find it convenient to treat them, when thin time slices are being considered, as if their contribution to processes of production left them in unaltered condition. Knight is not referring at all to particular instruments of production when he asserts the permanence of capital; he is referring to the abstract capital embodied in these particular instruments. Nonetheless, the Smith-Haavelmo approach does possess aspects of similarity to that of Knight. Some of these aspects are of relevance to the matters to be discussed in the succeeding chapter of this essay. Insofar as the present chapter is concerned, the significant similarity is that both approaches look upon capital goods as sources of service flows. For the Smith-Haavelmo view it is convenient to imagine that particular instruments of production are capable (at least for short periods) of rendering services without themselves being used up. For Knight the capital embodied in a particular instrument of production is capable of generating an income flow indefinitely without impairing its capacity to generate further income, because adequate "maintenance" (under which category Knight includes what is generally considered "replacement") can indefinitely "prolong the life" of the agent. (While expositions of Knightian capital theory are sometimes couched in language suggesting that particular agents themselves are permanent in the sense of not being used up in production, this is merely a loose way of referring to the permanence of the abstract capital which, in the Knightian view, is embodied in particular instruments.)

Knight's emphasis on this permanence of capital has been repeatedly attacked as "mystical" or as involving "mythology."[21] In a famous paper[22] Hayek, especially, has attacked the notion of a homogeneous fund of abstract capital represented by the particular heterogeneous non-permanent

21. The terms were used by Böhm-Bawerk (1907, p. 282) and (1895, p. 127) in his criticisms of J. B. Clark and then applied by Hayek (1936) against Knight. See also Kaldor (1937, p. 198); Stigler (1941, p. 309); Mises (1949, p. 512); cf. also Haavelmo (1960, p. 91).

22. Hayek (1936).

resources available at a given date, and the idea that such a "fund" can be transformed from one concrete form into another. Fraser has written of the pure mysticism of Knight's view that the capital invested in particular non-permanent instruments of production is "a kind of substance or vital spark" that lives on after they are used up or disposed of.[23]

Some of the "mysticism" of the Knightian position has been removed by recognizing its assertion of the permanence of capital to be no more than a figure of speech suggested by the economics of the case Knight considers to be typical. In Kaldor's words, "investing in 30 houses, one of which falls due for replacement and is *planned to be replaced* every year *ad infinitum*, is the same thing as investing in a house which lasts forever, while a certain sum has to be paid out each year to keep it in repair."[24] Or, as Dorfman puts it, the Knightian position merely asserts tautologously "that under stationary conditions every capital item entails an obligation for perpetual replacement."[25]

The purpose of employing this figure of speech is clearly that of being able to focus attention on the source-flow dichotomy noticed in the previous pages. So long, the Knightian position would maintain, as economists allow themselves to be preoccupied with the petty problems associated with the limited lives of particular bits of equipment, they cannot hope to be able to stand back and glimpse the underlying long-run economic relationships that transcend the lives of these specific pieces of equipment. For the Knightian position the important feature associated with the holding of a piece of productive equipment is that possession now of this "thing" confers command of a perpetual flow of services; this piece of equipment can be seen as the source of a never-ending stream. This insight is reinforced by the cultivation of a manner of speech in which attention is withdrawn from the concrete, short-lived bit of equipment itself, and turned instead on the abstract "capital" which it may be considered to represent—a capital which, in the above figurative sense, can be viewed as permanent.

The Knightian position thus views the world, and the continuing course of economic events in this world, in a very special way in which the stock-flow dichotomy plays a decisive role. At any given time the world consists of a collection of things. As time proceeds men draw streams

23. Fraser (1937, p. 302).
24. Kaldor (1937, p. 165). See also Stigler (1941, pp. 309f.).
25. Dorfman (1959b, p. 358).

of output by virtue of their possession and judicious maintenance of these things (such maintenance being made possible by the streams of gross output themselves). Nothing is required for the enjoyment of these streams of output except the maintenance of these things. No flows of input have to be applied from outside the system; all possible flows of input, including labor, are seen as emanating from "things" that are possessed and maintained within the system. What an economy may consume over time depends merely on the collection of things that exists and is maintained. It is as if the course of economic events flowed automatically and effortlessly from the stock of things possessed—the only demand made on human decision-making being the requirement that at all times attention be given to allocating a sufficient fraction of the output flow for the maintenance of the capital stock. For an increase to occur in the stream of output, it is necessary to set aside a larger portion of current output for the creation of new resources.

We are not directly concerned in this essay with Knight's productivity theory of interest (nor, for that matter, with any interest theory), but it is of significance to notice how the Knightian view of capital has built into itself the notion of a productivity rate. With all output being considered to flow automatically from the existing collection of resources, we have immediately the notion of a definite rate of flow of output in relation to the existing capital stock. In Knight's view this rate depends on the aggregate stock of capital held at a particular time. The market process is relied upon to guarantee a tendency toward individual producers investing their capital in those ways that will exploit for each of them individually the productivity rate relevant to the economy at a particular time.[26] By these assumptions the Knightian position is thus able to look on *each particular resource* as a source for a future output stream that will flow at the universal productivity rate. The essence of capital theory, in this view, is the analysis of the way these relationships work themselves out through the market, determining interest rates, capital accumulation, the organization of production, and so on.

A CRITIQUE OF THE KNIGHTIAN VIEW

From the point of view of the present essay the fundamental objection to the Knightian way of looking at things is a very simple one. It has already been stated by Hayek in a footnote to his essay on the subject, cited in the

26. See, e.g., Conard (1959, p. 80).

previous section.[27] Hayek points out that an investment (through the sacrifice of a short segment of income flow) yields in the first place only another *limited* segment of income flow (of different time-shape); and that "this limited income stream which is the result of the first investment becomes a permanent income stream only by an infinite series of further decisions when the opportunity of consuming more now and less in the future has to be considered every time. By jumping directly to the desired result, the permanent income stream, Professor Knight slurs over so much that is essential for an understanding of the process that any use of his concept of capital for an analysis of the role of this capital in the course of further changes becomes quite impossible." This presents the objection admirably. The present section will dwell on this objection and attempt to relate it to the conceptual framework advanced in the first chapter of this essay.

It will be recalled that in that chapter the case was presented for a treatment of capital goods that should relate them specifically to a relevant system of production *plans*. Capital goods should be recognized in the first place as the interim result of as yet incompletely fulfilled plans of production formulated in the past. In the second place they should be recognized as playing a decisive role in any new production plans that may be formulated now (including under this heading the possible modification of the later stages of earlier plans not yet completely carried out). It was argued that the theory of the market proceeds by the analysis of individual decision-making and of the way in which individual plans have mutual impact upon one another. The appropriate way to study the role of capital in the economic process, it was therefore maintained, must be found in the similar analysis of the multiperiod plans made in the market. Any concept of capital goods which fails to relate them to multiperiod planning in the manner described is thus of severely limited value for the explicit extension of the theory of the market to the course of economic events over time.

In conjunction with these principles it was also pointed out in the same chapter that the desired recognition of the planned character of capital goods might, nonetheless, lead to error. The assignment of func-

27. Hayek (1936, p. 363, n. 17). See also p. 370: "it has no meaning, in economic analysis, to say that apart from the human decision, which we have yet to explain, the aggregate of all the non-permanent resources becomes some permanent entity." It is to be noted that Hayek does not, however, give this objection central attention. This is especially the case for his *The Pure Theory of Capital* (1941).

tion to particular capital goods (by making reference to the use which had originally been planned for these goods) might lead to overlooking the necessity for additional decision-making in the future. It might thus lead to a view that the presence of a good *automatically* guarantees the flow of services for the sake of which that good was originally produced. It was pointed out that where a steady level of production is maintained continuously for some time there exists a temptation to view the current maintenance of the stock of capital goods as input required for the production of *current* output. In other words there is a temptation to ignore the *planned* character of capital goods maintenance, to overlook the fact that capital goods maintenance is undertaken as part of a series of plans being made for the future—even if only to ensure that future output does not fall below current output. A failure to withstand this kind of temptation involves acceptance of the notion that the *future will take care of itself so long as the present "sources" of future output flows are appropriately maintained.* These kinds of temptations, it was further pointed out, become even more difficult to resist in a system where monetary calculation can be employed. The Knightian approach reflects perfectly the way in which this misleading and unhelpful notion of "automaticity" has been developed into a fully articulated and self-contained theory of capital.

In the Knightian view, indeed, the future course of production is completely determined by the present state of affairs. The instruments of production possessed now are the sources of future flows of output. Because *all* future inputs flows can, in this view, be seen as represented now by something (or some person) that serves as the source of these future flows, and because maintenance of these sources is seen as somehow a matter of mere routine calling for no particular decision-making, we are presented with a picture of the world in which the future is entirely capable of taking care of itself. The future flows automatically from or "grows" out of the present. Professor Knight has himself given us a description of the simplified situation which, it seems, most faithfully mirrors the essential features of the real capital-using world as Knight sees it. Knight draws a picture of an economy, "Crusonia," in which all that is consumed is obtained from "the natural growth of some perennial which grows indefinitely at a constant (geometric) rate, except as new tissue is cut away for consumption."[28] This picture represents a number of abstractions from

---

28. Knight (1944, p. 30). See also Dewey (1963, p. 134) for the opinion that this model contains all that is essential for the theory of capital.

the real world. What is, from the point of view of the present essay, the most arresting and most objectionable of these abstractions is that which portrays the flows of consumption "goods" in the model as forthcoming automatically ("growing") from the capital stock on hand. No room is left for planning, for human decision-making, at the production level. All that is left subject to human decision is how much is to be consumed in each period. Once this has been decided, the future course of events inexorably follows.

What the Knightian view has chosen to do is thus to see the essential elements of the economic process that are relevant to a theory of capital as consisting in those aspects of the problem that do not involve multiperiod planning at the level of production. For the purpose of the analysis which the Knightian theory of capital is designed to contribute we are asked to assume that the appropriate relevant plans will somehow be made. We are told in effect that these plans do not have to be explained; that once we have explained the present state of affairs, we have explained all that de- mands explanation in connection with the entire future course of events. From the point of view of the present essay, it is clear, the Knightian ap- proach has, by this procedure, simply renounced claim to being able to offer an explanation of the course of economic events in a capital-using world. To repeat Hayek's remark once again this concept of capital slurs "over so much that is essential for an undertaking of the process that any use of [it] for an analysis of the role of this capital in the course of further changes becomes quite impossible."

CAPITAL AND INCOME

Our discussion of the Knightian view of capital as sources of perpetual service flows leads us to reflect on the more general capital-income dichot- omy. None of the criticisms leveled at the Knightian approach have any application, of course, to the validity of the capital-income concept as an accounting tool. A distinction between capital and income does not imply that the economic process in fact resembles an everlasting tree that spon- taneously yields fruit every year (as the Knightian view chooses to imag- ine) but merely that someone wishes to distinguish between "the fund of wealth available at a given moment," on the one hand, and "the flow of wealth produced and consumed during a given period" on the other hand.[29] The Knightian view has, in fact, illegitimately transferred these

29. Fraser (1937, p. 250).

(superficially) smooth accounting concepts to a realm of discussion where they do not belong and where their use hides rather than reveals the true chains of cause and effect. Nonetheless critical attention from a capital theory perspective deserves to be paid to the capital-income dichotomy, especially from the point of view presented in this essay. We will discover that this will raise still further problems for the Knightian approach.

Economists have long struggled to formulate acceptable criteria for the distinction between capital and income.[30] Fisher chose to define income as equivalent to consumption. Of the gross output that rolls off the assembly lines during a given period, only that portion which is consumed during the current period should, Fisher argues, be termed current income. All the rest of the gross output consists of goods that will yield consumption services in future periods of time. They should be kept apart from current consumption. Fisher chooses to reserve the term "income" to denote only this latter category.

It is to be noted that both "gross output" and "consumption" are magnitudes that correspond to definite economic entities. It is true that neither the magnitude of gross output nor that of consumption can be known in advance (merely from a knowledge of the initial stock of capital goods) until the appropriate production and consumption decisions have been made. (And, indeed, critics have objected to the use of these magnitudes as measures of current welfare possibilities on the grounds that each of them depends somehow arbitrarily on the pattern of human decisions. Thus Kaldor objects to Fisher's definition of income that it makes income depend on the saving-consumption decision.[31] Similarly Samuelson argues that gross output does not offer a measure of the current welfare possibilities created by production, because gross output is not a definite figure, it depends on the intensity with which one wishes to utilize the existing stock of capital goods.)[32] Nonetheless, at least *ex post,* both gross output and consumption have unambiguous economic meaning.

It is of interest, then, that neither of these two magnitudes has been generally accepted as an income concept. Gross output has been rejected because of the desire for a "net" concept, in the sense to be discussed below.[33] On the other hand, Fisher's insistence on consumption as the ap-

---

30. The classic survey of the attempts has become Kaldor (1955, appendix to ch. 1).
31. Ibid. (pp. 56–57).
32. Samuelson (1961, p. 34).
33. Cf. also Hicks (1963, p. 347).

propriate income magnitude has not found favor because, as noted above, it does not provide a measure of the potential volume of consumption attainable (in the absence of a decision to save). Instead of these two unambiguous economic entities economists have generally searched for a definition of income that should equal "net output." Most of the difficulties surrounding this search have to do with just what is wished to be intended by the "netness" of this latter term. We will discover that net output is a magnitude that corresponds to no well-defined economic category at all, but is imposed artificially upon an account of the actual course of economic events in order to fulfill a specific accounting motive that many people hold to be important.

Matters will be made clearest by referring to the Hicks-Hayek definition of income. This identifies income as the "level of consumption flow permanently attainable."[34] It is the maximum amount one can consume during a period without making it impossible to maintain this level of consumption indefinitely. Gross output is rejected as the income category because if all of it were to be consumed this would mean that the capital goods that contributed to the production of this year's gross output would no longer exist in intact form for next year's process of production; next year's output will be smaller. Consumption is similarly excluded, because a decision to consume very little will mean that one is consuming less than all that could be consumed without diminishing future consumption; such a case constitutes, in some sense which these writers are attempting to make precise, living below the standard set by one's income. What is sought is a criterion by which to separate, out of a period's gross output, that amount which must be plowed back into the production process (if current production possibilities are to be maintained indefinitively) from the portion of gross output that can be consumed (without affecting the continued availability of current production possibilities).

The portion of gross output that is *not* net output in this sense is thus that portion of it necessary to restore (or replace) depreciated equipment to their original quality (so that next year's initial stock of capital goods be not smaller in any way than that of the current year). Intact maintenance of capital requires that this difference between gross and net output not be consumed. Consumption of any portion of this difference must be

34. Cf. Samuelson (1961, p. 45, n. 1); see Hicks (1939, ch. 14); Hayek (1935); Kaldor (1955, pp. 64–67).

considered consumption of capital, not consumption of income. Such consumption of capital constitutes "living beyond one's income"; one is consuming now at the expense of being able to maintain a steady level of consumption over future periods of time.

Useful as such a net output, or income, concept undoubtedly is, it is for the purposes of this essay important to point out that there is no natural economic magnitude that emerges from the description of the economic process which can be identified with the concept. Net output, or income, does not constitute a well-defined economic pie in its own right (such as gross output is, or as consumption is), it is an arbitrarily cut slice of a larger pie.

Economists have long noted the arbitrariness of the capital-income distinction. There is nothing that makes it more natural to seek to maintain a steady income than to seek an income stream of different time-shape. So there is no particular *a priori* importance that is attached to the accounting criterion for the determination of the size of the portion of gross output necessary to maintain capital.[35] But there is still a further difficulty that, from the point of view of this essay, calls for special emphasis.

This difficulty has to do with the notion of "constant income." Hayek alludes to some of the difficulties involved. In order "to give the concept of a constant income stream an objective meaning," he observes, it is necessary "to postulate identity of tastes at successive moments."[36] This is required not only in the sense that relative preferences remain comparable from year to year, but also in the sense that the absolute satisfaction derived from one year's income is the same as that derived from that of any other year. It is not enough to say that an income stream is constant if, looking forward to it *ex ante* from a given date, one feels indifferent as to the sequence of the component elements of the stream. Such a statement has to do with time preference, it does not have relevance to the concept of an income flow that should enable "the level of total satisfaction . . . to be maintained constant throughout."[37] What is looked for is a criterion that should enable one to say that someone is rendered as well-off by this year's income as he was by last year's. We have somehow to compare the actual satisfaction derived this year from this year's income with that derived last year from last year's.

35. See Hayek (1941, pp. 298–99, 335–36); Mises (1949, p. 511).
36. Hayek (1941, p. 159n).
37. Ibid. (p. 158).

This raises what appear to be insuperable difficulties. Economic analysis is never couched in terms that involve the comparison of satisfactions between which an individual is not free to choose. An individual may be free to choose *today* between *prospective* income flows of different time-shapes. He is never in a position to choose, in any but a prospective manner, between a satisfaction on one date and a second satisfaction at a different date. (It is this circumstance that creates the problems associated with welfare comparisons over time, during which relative tastes have undergone alteration.)[38] To compare the satisfaction derived this year from this year's income, with that derived last year from last year's income, is to attempt the same task as to compare A's satisfaction from a steak dinner with B's. Intertemporal utility comparisons, like interpersonal ones, can be made only on an absolute basis; this is outside the province of economic analysis.

It follows that economic analysis can never be invoked in order to describe a particular flow of income over time as being a constant one. Such a description can be made only arbitrarily; we may describe income as constant in money terms or some other arbitrarily selected criterion, but we cannot do so in any absolute sense. All this does not, of course, render the capital-income dichotomy invalid. We may still continue to use the Hicks-Hayek "permanently-attainable-level-of-consumption" definition of income. We are merely forced to recognize that these concepts can be applied only arbitrarily by individuals choosing to do so. For such individuals the application of these concepts may provide criteria for accounting operations in which they may be intensely interested. The capital-income relationship provides such a criterion. Important as this relationship unquestionably is for most of us, it must not be elevated into a tool of economic analysis.[39] It represents an accounting convention, not merely because many people may not be interested in such a distinction at all, but because, in addition, a person can set up the capital-income dichotomy only by making arbitrary judgments of what constitutes for him an unchanged level of satisfaction over time.

The implications of these observations for the Knightian view on capital should be fairly clear. From an accounting point of view there can, as

---

38. See Rothenberg (1961, appendix to ch. 2); Weckstein (1962).

39. The discussion in the text has been carried on at the level of the individual; it applies even more critically at the macro-accounting level.

we have seen, be no objection to making the distinction between capital and income. And from the point of view of the person concerned with maintaining what he (arbitrarily) judges to be a constant income flow, a very special significance does indeed come to be attached to his stock of capital. This stock is an entity which must be maintained intact if the desired constant income level is to be continuously assured. Given this stock of capital the individual is assured of this perpetual income flow; diminish the stock in any way and the individual can no longer look forward to such a flow. The individual may, then, quite justifiably look upon his stock of capital as somehow being the "source" of the prospective perpetual income flow.

But, as we have seen, all this has meaning only from the viewpoint of the individual interested in setting up for himself the capital-income dichotomy. He may reasonably consider his capital stock as merely the source of a prospective perpetual income flow. He may do this by choosing to assume that the capital stock will in fact be appropriately utilized to this end, and by arbitrarily choosing a relevant concept of constant income for his purposes. But all this cannot be done, in a non-arbitrary way, by outsiders. The outsider can observe objectively the size and composition of an individual's stock of capital. He may describe all the possible time-shapes of output and consumption flows that may, under different circumstances, be secured by utilization of this stock of capital. But he is unable to single out one particular time-shape of flow out of the other flows, and pronounce this flow to be a constant income flow of which the original capital stock is to be considered the source. He cannot do this, in the first place, because, as discussed in the previous section, he has no right to assume in advance that the whole series of decisions necessary to secure any one particular output and consumption flow will in fact be made. The discussion in the present section has shown that he cannot do so for yet an additional reason. As an outsider he is unable to determine which of the possible output and consumption flows represents, in the arbitrary judgment of the individual concerned, a level of *constant* income. And, as we have seen, the constant income concept, and with it the capital-as-a-source-of-perpetual-income concept, are meaningless from any other than an arbitrary point of view.

We must conclude, then, that the Knightian capital concept is wholly unhelpful. It represents an extension of the capital-income dichotomy from a realm of discourse in which the essential arbitrariness of the distinction does not matter, to a realm of discourse where it does matter. What was acceptable at the level of accounting turns out to be wholly unacceptable at the level of economic analysis. And with the recognition of the arbitrariness of the capital-income dichotomy must come realization that a capital concept based on this dichotomy cannot be looked to as a tool in economic analysis.

Chapter 3. Capital and Waiting

We turn to take up the aspect of capital that has proved perhaps most fascinating to economists and yet seems to have provided them with their greatest difficulties and with fuel for their fiercest controversies—the relation between capital and waiting. In general economists associate the "Austrian" approach to capital and interest theory with a major emphasis on the time lapse between inputs and outputs—the theory revolving around concepts such as the length of the period of production, or of investment, the amount of waiting thus involved, and the "productivity" of the time concepts so distinguished. On the other hand the Clark-Knight view of the capital and interest problem vigorously disputes the stress on waiting, casting its own theory in terms that not only do not depend on an integration of the waiting concept into the theory of production, but which even challenge the economic meaningfulness of the concept altogether.

The controversy has been alive now for over six decades, with now the one approach, now the other, seeming to hold the allegiance of the bulk of current theorists. In recent years both views have been reflected in the literature; in particular the "Austrian" approach has, as we shall see, been accorded a more respectful hearing than on many occasions in the past. Our task in the present chapter will be to review the principal ideas to be found on the subject of waiting in this modern capital-and-interest literature. We will find much to criticize in this literature: while our greatest dissatisfaction must be with the Clark-Knight tradition, we find ourselves constrained to take sharp exception to many of the ideas used in recent attempts to rehabilitate the Böhm-Bawerkian approach. It will be our position that much of the confusion that has clouded the subject for so long can be avoided without difficulty by adhering resolutely to the *planning* approach—that is, by consistently seeking the explanation of all economic events by referring to the individual human *plans* to which these events can be traced back. What is valid in the "Austrian" approach, in particular, we will maintain, can be vastly improved by explicitly recasting Böhm-Bawerk's seminal ideas within such a "planning"—rather than a technological—framework. It will prove helpful at this stage to preface our discussion with a brief review of our own position on the matter of capital and waiting as developed in the first chapter of this essay. It will be recalled that at the heart of this position there lay the idea of *intertemporal exchanges;* our view of capitalistic production sees it as a particular aspect of such an exchange across time.

CAPITALISTIC PRODUCTION AS EXCHANGE ACROSS TIME

Exchanges across time, it will be recalled, are viewed by the economic theorist as a special case of multiperiod planning by forward-looking decision-makers. The mutual coincidence of the multiperiod plans made by two individuals may make it possible for each of them to gain by exchanging with the other across time: *A* giving up to *B* a quantity of a particular good at one date, and receiving in exchange a specified quantity of a particular good at another date. Even in a Crusoe economy, however, it was noticed, it is convenient to view the plan to engage in a time-consuming process of production as a decision to engage in intertemporal exchange with nature, sacrificing inputs at one date in order to obtain output at a later date.[1]

Viewing production, in this way, as an example of multiperiod planning embracing an exchange across time, we were able to proceed to recognize that the process of production may be so patterned as to afford opportunities for periodic review and possible revision of the original plans. While the original plans envisaged, perhaps, the final completion of a particular time-consuming project, they were laid with the awareness that later events might make it advisable to alter the later stages of the original plan. It became of interest, then, in seeking the explanation of economic events as they unfold through time, to be able to take notice of the states of affairs as they appear at various stages of an as yet *uncompleted* project. Capitalistic production is initiated by plans in which producers find themselves, at the outset, half-way toward their final goals, as a result of the already partly completed projects upon which they are now able to work. What part does "waiting" play in this picture of the process of production over time?

We must at once distinguish between the *prospective* waiting (anticipated at the time when a time-consuming process of production is being planned), on the one hand, and the actual waiting that occurs during the execution of the time-consuming production process, on the other. In our analytical picture of the process of production *only prospective waiting is taken notice of.* Our approach, as always in micro-economic theory, is to

---

1. For a discussion of the insight that Crusoe's activities consist of acts of "exchange," see Mises (1953, pp. 38–39).

trace back economic events to the decisions out of which they sprang. At the time when multiperiod decisions are made, waiting is taken into account *ex ante;* the desirability of the output promised by any prospective production plan (as compared with the inputs whose sacrifice is required) is gauged, in part, by the length of time that must elapse before the output can be forthcoming. When a Crusoe initiates an entirely new project, starting without any partly completed production project to hand, he takes into account the prospective waiting that his plan calls for. When his project is already partly completed, and he is planning its later stages, then he is aware that the waiting time until his final goal is the shorter by virtue of his command over the capital goods produced during the already completed stages of the project. Where the later stages of the project are able to be carried out exactly as envisaged at the very outset of the entire project, then this means that the waiting that was originally undertaken in order to produce these capital goods has fulfilled its ultimate purpose of making it possible to shorten correspondingly the waiting that now has to be undertaken during the later stages of the project as a whole. Where, in a market system based on division of labor, capital goods are purchased by the producers of consumer goods, the price paid for the capital goods will tend to reflect both of these aspects of waiting that are involved. On the one hand the price will tend to be high enough to cover whatever costs of waiting were undertaken by the capital good producer (i.e., the production of a capital good will be undertaken only if it is anticipated that its price will be high enough to cover the anticipated costs of waiting required in its production). On the other hand the price will tend to be bid up to the level that reflects the productive usefulness of the capital good to the prospective producers of consumer goods, reflecting its ability to shorten the prospective waiting needed to be taken into account by these latter producers in making their decisions. The market process will in this way govern the volume and kind of capital goods produced and used in the economy.

It ought to be noticed, moreover, that within the strictly formal context appropriate to micro-economics conceived as the pure logic of choice, it is not really necessary or even helpful to invoke the term "waiting" at all. All that is needed is the recognition that a production plan calls for the sacrifice of inputs at one date in order to obtain output at a later date. The choice made by the prospective producer will depend on the relative positions occupied on his value scale of the inputs and outputs each with its relevant time subscript. That is all.

All this seems obvious enough and elementary enough. And yet we will discover that the dominant schools of capital theory have again and again displayed attitudes toward the role of "waiting" in relation to capital, that in one way or another ignore or deny the simple considerations here outlined. As we will see, this applies both to the current presentations of the Clark-Knight approach, and to recent attempts to present the "Austrian" approach in modern garb (although our objections will of course have different applications to each of the approaches). We take up first that approach to capitalistic production which denies any role at all to "waiting" in the theory of production.

LAGS VS. SIMULTANEITY IN CAPITALISTIC PRODUCTION

In the latter view of things, that of Professor Knight and his followers, no economic significance at all is to be attached to any lag between input and output. Whatever the time pattern that a process of production may follow from a technological point of view, for the economist the picture is one of an instantaneous emergence of product from each step taken in production: "taking production in the value sense, the result is instantaneous, whether in the form of a service (instantly consumed) or in that of a net addition to assets."[2] First of all, it is pointed out, it is not *necessary* to see the result of a productive act only in the final product; "every activity has immediate results."[3] Moreover, in the Knightian view production is appropriately defined as it was for J. B. Clark, only "in relation to economic equilibrium." Production then "consists in using 'productive agents' of all kinds in a relationship of symmetrical cooperation, to provide an unvarying stream of consumable services or satisfactions as the ultimate product." Within the context of this continuous equilibrium-flow of production, the "production of the services consumed in any period of time includes the maintenance of all productive agents and materials used in the economy, including in turn the replacement of any which are worn out or used up." In other words production is defined in such a way that actions taken currently exclusively in order to ensure the continued flow during the *future* of the product service are to be viewed as producing the flow of product service yielded during the *current* period. "Thus under equilibrium conditions production and consumption are simultaneous."[4]

2. Knight (1936, p. 456).
3. Rolph (1939, p. 280).
4. Knight (1946, p. 387); cf. also Stigler (1941, pp. 313–14).

From this "synchronization" perspective the entire Austrian concept of "the gestation period of capital assets" must indeed appear a monumental exercise in futility. As one follower of Knight has recently expressed it, not only is the whole concept itself "fundamentally unimportant"; it has been chewed over to the point of becoming "time-consuming in the classroom and a source of confusion to the young."[5] So long as the "equilibrium" concept of production is adhered to, there is no need to take notice of the ages of the individual components of the capital stock; the "time-structure" of this stock is of no significance. Even in the case of the fifty-tree forest, in which ten five-year-old trees are cut each year and ten seedlings planted, there is no *economic* importance to the age-structure of the forest, so long as equilibrium conditions prevail.[6] In the Clarkian reservoir example "each drop of water coming in at the intake permitted the simultaneous release of a drop at the outlet"; the "average age" of the reservoir being of no economic moment. To point out, as Dorfman has recently done, that "if water improves with age (it sometimes does . . .) then there is an advantage in having a large reservoir," is, technologically, perfectly correct. But, *so long as equilibrium conditions are maintained,* the desired superior quality of water is secured merely through the size of the reservoir, without explicit attention having to be paid to age as such. To go on to argue, as Dorfman has, that Knight is "irrelevant" in stating that in the "stationary" view want-satisfying services are consumed as they are rendered, because Knight ignores "the fact that detention per se can be valuable,"[7] is to fail to understand the *economic* aspect of equilibrium production as Knight wishes it to be understood.

Professor Knight has perhaps best illustrated his view of the economic irrelevance of time lags in production by his picture of Crusonia, an imaginary land where such lags are also technologically irrelevant. In Crusonia, as has been noted earlier in this essay, sustenance is provided by "the natural growth of some perennial which grows indefinitely at a constant (geometric) rate, except as new tissue is cut away for consumption."[8] In such an economy, as Lerner has pointed out, "the period of production is completely arbitrary. The current growth may just as well be considered as due to the stock not being consumed five years ago as to its not being

5. Dewey (1963, p. 134n); see also Dewey (1965, pp. 80 and 201ff.).
6. Cf. Lerner (1953, p. 544).
7. Dorfman (1959b, pp. 354–55). See also Schumpeter (1954, p. 907).
8. Knight (1944, p. 30); see also Dewey (1963; and 1965, pp. 80ff.).

consumed a hundred years ago or to its not being consumed one second ago, so that the period of production concept is quite meaningless."[9] As cited in the previous chapter, the Knightian view of the economic process is one in which the capital of the economy (its stock of productive agents) is permanent, and production consists in drawing forth the steady flow of service which these productive agents are capable of yielding indefinitely. No economic significance can, in this view of things, be attached to technological chains of causation operating over determinate time spans. To the Knightian economist production and consumption are simultaneous.

A CRITICISM OF THE SYNCHRONIZATION VIEW

If the above outline of the Clark-Knight denial of significance to "waiting" in the theory of capitalistic production be accepted as a fair one, then it appears clearly vulnerable to serious objections from the point of view adopted in this essay. The cardinal objection must be that the "waiting," the time lag, that is denied significance by Professor Knight and his followers, is not at all the waiting that is of importance for a theory of capital. Even the acceptance of the relevance of a concept of production based on the stationary state—overcoming one's sympathies for Hayek as he brands Knight's use of this concept "an absurd abuse of words"[10]—does not in any way entail (as the Knightians clearly believe it does entail) the extrusion of waiting from capital theory.

As was pointed out earlier in this chapter, the time lag that a theory of capital must take into account is never anything but a *prospective, ex ante,* notion. The time lags that the synchronization school seeks to persuade us to ignore can only be *ex post* lags. So long as planning for the future does in fact take note of prospective waiting, then a theory of capital based on the decisions made by forward-planning individuals can never avoid coming to grips with "waiting," and with the prospective time lags that make it necessary to anticipate waiting for the output technologically dependent upon contemplated inputs.

Now, there can be no doubt that, whatever Böhm-Bawerk and Wicksell may have *meant,* their expositions of what is usually considered the "productivity" side of their theory fail completely to emphasize the *ex ante* character of waiting periods in production. It is with justification that critics who wished to build a theory of capital without the "period of produc-

9. Lerner (1953, pp. 543–44).
10. Hayek (1936, p. 370, n. 25).

tion," trained their offensive against the *technological* time lag involved in production, the actual time that in fact elapses, during a process of production, between the application of input and the emergence of the desired product. And it is not impossible to understand how an economist might come to consider the specific relationship between the productivity of inputs and the time-length of the production process to be unimportant for the formal, analytical notion of production. But, we must here insist, so long as our theory is to be based on the analysis of decision-making, and so long as we wish our theory to have reference to a world in which *multiperiod* plans are made, we are precluded from doing violence to the time aspect of these decisions. We may, for the purpose of an introductory analysis of the price system, indeed abstract from the multiperiod aspects of the market, treating all decisions in the system as having to do with a single instant. But if we wish to understand the course of economic events over time, including those events that are the outcome of multiperiod plans, we must be prepared to deal with these plans in the way in which they are constructed. Our analytical apparatus must be able to handle decisions in which it is contemplated to sacrifice inputs today *in order* to obtain output tomorrow; and our explanation of states of affairs and of chains of events in the real world must be able to trace them back to such multiperiod plans.[11]

It follows that the arguments employed by the Knightian capital theorist against the concept of the Austrian period of production cannot possibly carry weight in connection with the waiting concept here held to

---

11. It is somewhat surprising that in the literature defending the "Austrian" view from the attacks of Professor Knight, the distinction between "*ex ante* waiting" and "elapsed waiting," made here in the text, was not used with much greater emphasis and with much greater effect. Hayek (1936, p. 364) clearly spells out the distinction; see also Saulnier (1938, p. 273) and Hayek (1941, p. 90). The most vigorous insistence on the *ex ante* character of waiting is to be found in Mises (1949, pp. 477ff.); see also Rothbard (1962, pp. 45, 412–13); Blaug (1962, p. 466). One possibility of defending the "Austrian" view from the criticisms of Professor Knight, that is somewhat parallel to that developed here in the text, has been noticed in the literature. This has to do with Knight's insistence that, no matter how far back one goes into history, one never discovers processes of production in which only pure "original" factors of production are used, so that the distinction between "original" and "produced" factors cannot be made. It has been pointed out that "the services of the resources *accruing at the present moment* might be regarded as 'original factors' as against the services of resources accruing at any subsequent moment" (Kaldor, 1937, p. 158); see especially Schumpeter (1954, p. 908); see also Conard (1959, pp. 21, 112–13).

be of such importance.[12] Even in an equilibrium context, with agents of production ceaselessly yielding a smooth steady flow of net output service, we are not exempt from examining the decisions being continually made to prolong in this way the currently prevailing course of events. The allocation of a portion of current gross productive capacity for the maintenance and replacement of the productive agents is the expression of a *decision* that this allocation be made. While it may be analytically convenient for some of the purposes which the Knightians have in mind to treat the fabrication of such replacements as part of the productive activity yielding the output service forthcoming in the *current* period, such a convention cannot be adopted insofar as concerns the *decision* to allocate current productive capacity for replacement purposes.

It is of service to notice that even in Knight's Crusonia model, which exemplified most powerfully his idea of the arbitrariness of the period of production concept, we may nonetheless still distinguish the anticipated waiting periods here held to be the only ones worthy of economic interest. We saw that in the Crusonia perennial "the current growth may just as well be considered as due to the stock not being consumed five years ago as to its not being consumed a hundred years ago." But, clearly, this is true only with regard to the elapsed waiting to which one seeks to ascribe a specific portion of current growth. In no respect does the Crusonia model exhibit arbitrariness insofar as concerns the *anticipated* waiting that, *at each date of decision-making in the past,* was necessarily taken into account. At each date in the past, five years ago, a hundred years ago, or a second ago, a decision was made as to how much of the existing stock of the perennial should be consumed, and how much of it should be left to grow. Each such decision was a multiperiod one, in which the sacrifice of current enjoyment was weighed against the future enjoyment promised by the conservation and growth of the plant. So long as we do not consider the prospective dates at which enjoyment is anticipated as matters of indifference to the decision-maker, we are forced to recognize that, at each past decision-making date, he took into consideration the anticipated waiting associated with each bit of dated future plant-enjoyment that he

12. The remarks in the text do not deal with one major difficulty associated with the waiting concept, which critics of the "Austrian" approach have emphasized. This has to do with the difficulty of identifying the date of the output that corresponds to a given input, resulting from the "jointness" present in typical processes of production. This difficulty exists for the *ex ante* notion of waiting as it does for the *ex post* concept. See Kaldor (1937, p. 159n); Hayek (1941, pp. 67, 205f.).

was able to contemplate as part of one of the alternative future consumption streams with respect to which he was about to choose the first steps.

THE PERIOD OF PRODUCTION CONCEPT
IN THE CONTEMPORARY LITERATURE

Having reviewed critically the school of thought whose aim is to eliminate the "waiting" concept from the theory of capital, we turn to examine the recent literature in which the "Austrian" approach has, after some refurbishment, been accepted into analytical respectability. In this literature the contributions of Professor Dorfman have commanded the principal interest:[13] one writer has credited Dorfman with "rescuing the concept of the period of production from obscurity and breathing life into it."[14] Much of our discussion will revolve around Dorfman's attempt to provide a modern exposition of the Böhm-Bawerkian theory and a defense of it against the objections raised by Clark, Knight and their followers. As was indicated at the beginning of this chapter, we will discover that our own criticisms of the Dorfman-Austrian approach are at bottom similar to those raised in the preceding section against that of Clark and Knight, viz., that grossly insufficient attention is paid to the *plans* by which capital is accumulated and utilized. Once again, we will find, much of our discussion will have to do with the question of how to view "waiting"—as elapsed waiting or as anticipated waiting.

The aspect of the neo-Austrian position as exemplified by Dorfman[15] to which we wish to draw critical attention can perhaps be brought into sharpest focus by referring to what Dorfman calls the "bathtub theorem." This states that, in a tank *in which a constant volume of water is maintained* (while water flows into and out of the tank), the average period of detention of water equals the given volume of water divided by the rate of flow. If K is the volume of water in the tank, I the rate of flow into (or out of) the tank, and T the average period of detention of water, then $T = K/I$. The bathtub theorem is applied directly to the case of capitalistic production in a stationary economy. The analogue of the given volume of water

13. Dorfman (1959a, 1959b). See also Blaug (1962, pp. 459–78); Uhr (1960, ch. 5). For further signs of the renewed fashionability of Austrian-type capital theory concepts, see Lutz (1961) and Lindahl (1961).

14. Neuberger (1960, p. 150).

15. Besides the contribution by Dorfman (1959a) cited above, presentations of the Austrian position on somewhat similar lines are to be found in Stigler (1941, pp. 278–85); Brems (1959, ch. 18).

is now the stock of capital; corresponding to the rate of flow we have now the level of investment (which in a stationary economy equals the rate of capital consumption); T is the average period of investment.[16] A major purpose of Dorfman's work is to apply the bathtub theorem to a two-sector economy (one in which labor and "machines" are used in one process of production to produce a consumer good, and in a different production process to produce "machines") and to demonstrate the meaningfulness of T in this context. By this demonstration Dorfman is able to refute a major objection to the Böhm-Bawerkian theory that has been raised by Knight and others. This objection rests on the claim that since the existing capital goods were produced with the help of earlier capital goods (which in turn were produced with the help of still earlier capital goods, and so on), the period of production cannot be defined. Dorfman refutes this objection by actually calculating T for a simple two-sector economy.

In addition Dorfman is able to develop, through use of the bathtub theorem, the Böhm-Bawerkian relationships between the stock of capital, the real wage, the size of the labor force and the average period of production, in a stationary (one-sector) economy. Given the first three of these quantities, the average period of production is given by the equation $T = K/Nw$ where N is the size of the labor force, w the real wage, and K is measured in terms of the final product it will ultimately become. (Nw is thus equal to the rate of consumption flow, it being assumed that only workers engage in consumption, doing so without any saving.)[17]

It is in the interpretation of this average period of production T, that Dorfman's emphasis on the bathtub-like character of capital in a stationary economy finds its clearest expression. Alluding to Böhm-Bawerk's interpretation[18] of this period as measuring the length of time for which society can be supported out of its "subsistence fund" (the capital stock) while waiting for the output that will result from currently invested inputs, Dorfman describes this as an "inessential" way of looking at the matter. The bathtub view of things enables us, Dorfman points out, to see T as simply measuring the average length of time for which units of in-

16. For earlier similar treatments of capital in terms of bathtubs or like analogies, see, e.g., Lerner (1944, p. 325); Boulding (1950, p. 193).

17. Cf. Böhm-Bawerk (1959b, p. 365); see also, e.g., Dorfman (1959b, p. 354). On the assumption that labor is expended on each unit of output at an even rate throughout the period, the period of production T is one-half the absolute length of a production process in which a unit of final output emerges.

18. Böhm-Bawerk (1959b, pp. 312ff.).

puts are locked up in the form of unfinished products. Böhm-Bawerk saw the period of production as measuring the delay that the given stock of capital permits to be suffered between the present and the time when the results of current inputs will be available (given N and w). For Dorfman this is an incidental implication of the system. The essence of the matter for Dorfman is that in order for stationary conditions to be fulfilled, the size of the available capital stock determines the detention time of invested inputs (given N and w).

Now, it is by no means our wish to claim that Böhm-Bawerk's understanding of the period of production was primarily an *ex ante* conception. This, regrettably, is not the case.[19] But it is clear that Böhm-Bawerk's view of capital as possessing, as one of its attributes, the character of a subsistence fund (permitting the economy to bridge the time gap between the present and the date when currently invested inputs will finally yield consumption goods) does involve a forward-looking perspective. What the assumption of stationary conditions enables Böhm-Bawerk to do is to show how one particular unchanging attitude with respect to the future (on the part of consumers and capitalists) is able, in equilibrium, to result in the continuous maintenance of the economy's stock of capital, together with its (*ex post*) period of production. For Dorfman this forward-looking perspective on the capitalistic process of production is carefully suppressed. The same seems to hold true of Boulding's "bathtub" presentation of the Austrian concept of the period of production, in which capital is represented as viewed as a "population of 'value.'" "Whenever value is added to [goods] a new value is 'born,' and whenever value is subtracted from them by consumption a value item 'dies.'" It is shown that in equilibrium the average "life" of these "embodied values" is given, as it is for biological populations in general, by the ratio of the size of the "population" to the rate of "births."[20]

Our objection may be phrased in a different way. Böhm-Bawerk's own understanding of capital as a subsistence fund enables his system to incorporate, at least implicitly, the *time preferences* of the individuals in the model. For Dorfman time preferences play no role whatsoever.[21] For

19. See below in this chapter for a critique of the subsistence fund idea.

20. Boulding (1950, p. 193).

21. See Neuberger (1960) for a criticism of Dorfman's excessive emphasis on productivity as an explanation of interest, to the complete exclusion of time preference. Dorfman's refusal to consider the effects of alternative patterns of time preference vitiates also his attempt to prove that present goods are more valuable than future goods

Böhm-Bawerk the subsistence fund notion helps us to recognize that the average period of production—the delay which the system can afford between the date of input and the date of output—depends on how urgently consumption goods are needed for the near future. If w rises, so that T (as given by the formula $T = K/Nw$) falls, this, for Böhm-Bawerk, is a result of the fact that, on average, the consumption needs of the community for the near future have become more urgent. (This is the case because we are assuming, in the Dorfman–Böhm-Bawerk model, that all consumption is out of wages, and that all wages are consumed.) As a result of the increased relative urgency of the need for consumption for the near future (as against the far future), the given subsistence fund now suffices for only a shorter period of delay. For Dorfman, if w rises then T falls simply because the average period of detention of water in a tank of given volume falls when the rate of inflow (and outflow) increases. If the flow of consumption goods provided by the capital stock is drawn down at a greater rate, then, if the size of the stock is being maintained, the average time for which inputs are tied up in the stock must be shorter, the superior productivity technologically possible through longer periods of production cannot be exploited; that is all.

There can be no doubt that the extrusion of time preference considerations from Dorfman's model (and from the similar models of other recent expositors of the Austrian theory) is a concomitant of the refusal to view the period of production as anything but a segment of elapsed clock-time. Time preference enters into economic analysis only when multiperiod decisions are being examined. When constructing a multiperiod plan the individual is comparing *now* the desirability of consuming in the near future with the desirability of consuming in the far future. For the period of production concept to be integrated into a system of multiperiod decisions, it must be envisaged *ex ante*.

For a theory of interest based, on the other hand, exclusively on productivity considerations—and Dorfman recognizes his aim as such[22]—*ex ante* aspects can be dispensed with without strain. Interest emerges in each period simply as the surplus flow of product remaining after wages

---

of like kind and number. The refutation of Dorfman's proof (like that of Böhm-Bawerk's "Third Ground") was provided long ago by Fisher. For a recent careful exposition of the relevant fallacy in the Böhm-Bawerk–Dorfman proof, see Conard (1959, p. 43). See, however, Kuenne (1962a, 1962b).

22. Dorfman (1959b, p. 360).

have been paid; it emerges because the stock of capital has permitted a production period long enough to increase the productivity of current flow inputs so as to yield such a surplus (after paying the flow inputs a return based on their marginal product). No attention at all needs to be paid to the fact that interest payments emerged from the intertemporal exchanges made in the past, as a result of the mutual coincidence of the multiperiod plans made at that time by the market participants. All that is necessary is the technological relationship existing between the length of the production period and the productivity of flow inputs. This technological relationship in no way requires an *ex ante* view of the period of production. If water improves with aging, then the degree of improvement depends on the elapsed detention time of water in the reservoir. The size of the reservoir is important because, with given rate of inflow and outflow, the reservoir size determines the detention period. In this way the improvement in the water yields a return to the owner of the capital stock (reservoir). All else, Dorfman declares, is inessential.

From the point of view of the position taken up in this essay, it ought to be pointed out that the recognition of a technological relationship between the length of the production process and the productivity of flow inputs is, of course, fully taken into account in an *ex ante* approach. In constructing his multiperiod plan an individual takes very carefully into consideration the technological terms of exchange upon which he is choosing between immediate consumption and deferred consumption. The bathtub model of the stationary state can easily be recast into an analysis based on multiperiod decision-making. But in such an analysis it will be impossible to ignore the relative positions taken up, *on the value scale of an individual at a particular date,* by the prospective consumption of given commodities at different specified future dates. It will be impossible to conceive of the flow of interest payments being mechanically yielded as a result of the superior productivity conferred by possession of a stock of capital.

It is worthwhile to observe that it is only the *ex post* conception of the production period that makes it necessary for Dorfman to defend the concept against the Knightian charge, that, in a world in which capital goods have always been produced through the employment of other capital goods, the period of production cannot be defined. We have seen, of course, that Knight's own understanding of the Austrian period of production was (with complete justification) indeed an *ex post* version. So that Dorfman's refutation of the Knightian objection (by, as described earlier in this chapter, actually calculating the production period for a two-sector economy in which machines are used to produce machines) by no means constitutes a case of tilting against windmills. And yet, the task of calculating such a period, as Dorfman had done, or even of demonstrating its meaning, can be avoided by simply denying the relevance of such a period to the theory of capital. As soon as one recognizes that periods of production are of importance only insofar as they are taken into account in the forward-looking multiperiod plans of acting individuals, the entire Knightian objection falls away.[23] If the operator of a Roman iron mine did not introduce into his planning any of the implications of the fact that some of the ore may find its way into the pocket knife of a twentieth-century schoolboy,[24] then no production period extending from Roman times to those of the schoolboy is relevant for the theory of capital, either as applied to Roman industry or to that of the twentieth century. The only periods of production that have relevance to the emergence of interest payments and to the organization of capitalistic production are the periods which prospective decision-makers are able and forced to take into account either directly or indirectly; any periods which cannot be defined are not so taken into account and do not affect decision-making. Such periods of production can, then, hardly be of interest for capital theory.

CAPITAL AND WAITING

Our emphasis on the analysis of the multiperiod *decisions* to which capitalistic production can be traced back can be further exploited to clarify the role of "waiting" in relation to capital goods, and to throw light on the debate concerning the expediency of considering "waiting" to be a factor of production in the capitalistic process of production. Both questions have given rise to considerable confusion.

In the previous section it was pointed out that the time lag separating the date of input application from the date of the emergence of the corresponding output has been variously treated in the theory of capitalistic production. The case was presented in favor of a treatment that would introduce the time lag into analysis exclusively on an *ex ante* basis. In the present section we examine the relationship between "waiting" and *capital* as such; we are directly concerned here not with the period of production as an aspect of the production process, but with the ways in which

---

23. See further above in this chapter note 11.

24. Cf. Böhm-Bawerk (1959b, p. 86); Stigler (1941, p. 205); Schumpeter (1954, p. 908). See also Blaug (1962, p. 470).

capital goods have been considered as themselves "representing" waiting periods variously conceived. The various views that we will notice are all in some way derived from the Böhm-Bawerkian emphasis on the role of time in the theory of production.

(a) Capital as "Congealed Waiting"

Böhm-Bawerk's stress on the fact that the only "original" factors are land and labor, and that capital goods are the intermediate goods produced by the original factors in the course of time-consuming, roundabout, processes of production, has led to the view that capital goods are "stored-up" labor, land and waiting. Capital goods "embody" the past investment of original factors as well as the "waiting" performed in order to obtain these capital goods.[25] In this view of things the productivity of capital goods in the later stages of the production process is to be traced back to the labor, the land and the waiting which these goods represent. This view of capital as a stock of past waiting is (as we will see in a subsequent section of this chapter) closely related to the attempt to treat "waiting" as an original factor of production, and also (as we will see in the following chapter) to the attempt to *measure* capital by the amount of waiting which it represents.

The fundamental objection against using terms such as "congealed waiting" and the like is that this cast of language conduces to a "cost-of-production" way of thinking about capital goods. The truth is that, as Hayek has reminded us, bygones are bygones in the theory of capital no less than elsewhere in economics.[26] A theory of production which commences with a given stock of capital goods need pay no attention whatsoever to the genesis of these goods.[27] This objection applies, of course, no less to descriptions of capital as "stored-up labor and land" (which Böhm-Bawerk himself endorsed)[28] than to the descriptions which see capital as also stored-up "waiting" (which, as we will see in the following section, Böhm-Bawerk rejected because he did not recognize "waiting" as a factor of production).

On the other hand, the very attempt—central to Böhm-Bawerkian thought—to trace back capital to the "original" factors which were invested

25. See Dorfman (1959b, p. 363); Blaug (1962, p. 471). Cf. also Mises (1949, p. 490).

26. Hayek (1941, p. 89).

27. Hayek (ibid.) uses this consideration to reject the "produced means of production" definition of capital goods. See also Hayek (1936, p. 364, n. 19).

28. See, e.g., Böhm-Bawerk (1959b, p. 100).

in the past to produce it, gives a certain value to the "stored-up factors" description of capital. The position which the Austrians were primarily concerned to demote was that which sees capital and capitalistic production in a purely "timeless" context; in this "timeless" view nothing that is of importance for the theory of capital and interest needs to be related to time lags in production. To emphasize the opposite view, which sees the time-dimension of the production process as the cardinal element in the theory of capital and interest, it is of value to be able to stress the fact that capital goods are themselves the results of processes of production begun in the past. This is the rationale of the "stored-up factors" description.

From the point of view adopted in this essay, the issues seem extremely simple. Looking forward to capital goods that have not yet been produced, the multiperiod planner knows what current inputs must be applied, and the length of time which must be waited for the capital goods. Again, looking still further ahead in time, the planner sees the final consumer products able to be produced with the help of the prospective capital goods. If he wishes he may, looking forward in this way, view the prospective capital goods as the concrete vehicles by means of which his current inputs can be "stored-up" in order to yield their final product, consumer goods, far in the future. But clearly there seems little *analytical* convenience in looking at things in this way, from the point of view of the date at which the decision is made to construct the capital goods. When the capital goods have already been constructed, and the economic historian wishes to *explain* analytically how these particular capital goods came to be produced, he must of course do so by referring to the past inputs of "original" factors which the decision-maker long ago decided to invest. From the point of view of the decision-maker himself, with the capital goods at his disposal, the past is of no consequence whatsoever. In his capacity of decision-maker the presently available capital goods are no different, in this respect, than any other factors of production over which he has command. Because to the decision-maker bygones *ought* to be bygones, the *analysis* of the decisions made at this point need likewise pay no attention to the history of the capital goods. To refer to them as stored-up land and labor or waiting adds nothing to the explanation of subsequent events. (Of course, once the capital goods have been used to produce final output, then the economic historian who wishes to explain analytically the course of past events must do so by referring to the original decisions which gave rise to the particular capital goods produced, the availability of which determines, in part, the decisions taken during the final stages of production.)

In an explicitly *ex ante* approach such as this, there seems little to be gained from the use of "stored-up factors" descriptions of capital goods. Where such descriptions *are* used, the appropriateness of including "waiting" as one of the factor services "congealed" in the capital goods depends entirely on one's view of whether to treat "waiting" as a factor of production in the capitalistic production process. This will be taken up later in this chapter.

(b) Capital as a Store of Potential Waiting

We have already seen that Böhm-Bawerk described capital as a "subsistence fund" that enables society to bridge the gap in time that separates the date of input from the date of output. In this sense the length of the production process that society can afford is determined by the size of this subsistence fund. Capital enables society to wait the time required to take advantage of the superior productivity of the more roundabout methods of production. Capital has come, in this way, to be viewed as constituting a fund of "waiting."

Professor Hayek has extensively discussed the errors to which this kind of view can lead.[29] This view sees a given capital stock as making possible a definite waiting period. This notion could be acceptable only if the capital stock consisted of a stock of consumers' goods (or at least consisted of "inchoate" consumers' goods in the sense that the capital stock is able to make possible only one particular future pattern of consumers' goods) *and* if the given pattern of consumption can be assumed. Only in such an oversimplified world can one talk of a capital stock as a definite store of potential waiting. In less unrealistic worlds a "given stock of capital goods does not represent one single stream of potential output of definite size and time shape; it represents a great number of alternatively possible streams of different time shapes and magnitudes."[30] The consequence of the "fund of waiting" way of looking at capital has been to tend to avert attention from the concrete items composing a particular stock of capital, and to treat the stock as if it were homogeneous. And from the notion of capital as a homogeneous fund, it is not far to the idea that this abstract

29. Hayek (1936, pp. 374ff.; 1941, pp. 93, 146ff., 189–90).
30. Hayek (1941, p. 147).

fund somehow has an existence apart from the concrete items of which the stock is composed, an existence which is "permanent" in the sense that the fund "is maintained intact though the things in which it is invested may go and come to any extent."[31]

It may be added that emphasis on the ability of the capital stock to permit a period of waiting, in the above sense, makes it more difficult to accept any distinction that might be made between capital resources and non-capital resources. It would seem that the larger the command possessed over resources of all kinds, the longer would be the processes of production upon which one could enter (because of one's ability to allocate a sufficient portion of one's resources as a whole, toward the satisfaction of one's wants for the nearer future).

Despite these criticisms of the view which sees capital as a store of potential waiting, we ought not refuse to recognize the valuable insights that this view undoubtedly does incorporate.[32] The lengths of the production process upon which one will choose to embark at any time certainly are governed by one's command over the resources capable of yielding products in the relatively near future. And to the extent that one's provision for the future inclines one to invest now in order to be able, in future years, to engage in those longer, more productive production processes which one cannot now afford one is in fact accumulating the resources that will in those future years enable one to "wait" for lengths of time longer than one can now afford to do. These resources will certainly be capital resources. From the point of view of economic history too, there is unquestioned merit in the recognition that one's present ability to undertake lengthy processes of production is to be ascribed to the stock of capital goods built up during earlier years. While the "store of waiting" concept of capital turns out to be of little service for the *theory* of the capitalistic process of production; it does represent an *application* of that theory that is of considerable practical significance.

(c) Capital as a Means of Shortening the Waiting Period

Yet another relationship has been emphasized in the literature as existing between capital and "waiting." In this view capital goods are seen as instruments whose function it is *to shorten* the waiting time necessary be-

---

31. Knight (1935, p. 57).

32. Even Hayek (1936, p. 374) concedes some justification to this view "for didactic purposes."

fore the emergence of the final consumption goods.[33] The possession of capital makes one *nearer in time* to the final attainment of one's goal than one would be without it. Böhm-Bawerk himself did not emphasize this aspect of capitalistic production. (In fact, Böhm-Bawerk actually found it necessary, in discussing the notion of capitalistic production as a *more* time-consuming way to produce, to defend it against the objection that a tailor can produce a coat in a *shorter* time with the help of a sewing machine than without it.)[34]

The emphasis on the shortening of the waiting period made possible by capital goods arises out of a wish to avoid a misunderstanding for which the Böhm-Bawerkian terminology must bear some responsibility. The notion of "roundabout" processes of production has sometimes helped writers to overlook the fact that, wherever undertaken, such processes represent the *shortest* possible route to the finally desired goal. Especially when taken in conjunction with the above discussed views of capital as congealed waiting and as a fund of waiting, the "roundabout" aspect of capitalistic production has been interpreted as implying that the possession of capital *requires* one to wait for the output to emerge.[35] It is the wish to stress the calculated purposefulness and the temporal efficiency of capitalistic production that has given rise to the above description of capital goods as instruments *to shorten* the time for which the final goal must be waited.

Of course a statement that the possession of capital makes one nearer in time to one's goal is open to the objection that this is merely a way of saying that the use of capital goods is able to increase output. Surely, it will be asked, the control over resource services of *any* kind similarly able to increase output can be described as placing the producer within closer reach of his final goal? From the point of view adopted in this essay some light can perhaps be thrown on the matter.

We have seen that capital goods represent the as yet only partly completed projects initiated in the past by multiperiod decision-makers. The time lag originally incorporated in the multiperiod plan was the shortest waiting period necessary to achieve the planned final output and all

33. See Mises (1949, p. 490); Rothbard (1962, p. 45).
34. Böhm-Bawerk (1959b, p. 83).
35. For an apparent expression of this kind of interpretation, notice the following: "Why is a long lived consumption good regarded as a 'capital' good? Because its full enjoyment necessitates an appreciable degree of 'waiting'" (Fraser, 1937, pp. 266–67).

things considered represented the most desirable production plan available. If this project is able to be carried forward to full completion as planned, then, of course, the fact that the waiting time during the closing stages of the project is shorter than the time lag originally incorporated in the entire multiperiod plan is merely the result of the fact that the earlier time-consuming stages of the plan have already been completed. It is this aspect of the matter that is noticed when capital goods—the result of the earlier stages—are described as "shortening the period of waiting." Without these goods the multiperiod project would have to be commenced from the very beginning. Of course, when one considers the final stages of the plan in isolation, this aspect of the matter loses significance. Bygones are bygones; with given capital goods at hand one is, it is true, nearer to the final goal, but the same holds with respect to command over all kinds of productive services. But we have already noticed several times that the significance of capital goods *qua* capital goods emerges only when the entire multiperiod production project is considered as an integrated plan. And from this viewpoint it is indeed useful to recognize that the intermediate tools or other goods that such a plan calls for will represent the *completed* earlier stages of a longer plan. The possession of an acre of farmland renders the owner nearer in time, no doubt, to a bushel of wheat. But insofar as no multiperiod *plan* was involved in making this resource available, there is no particular analytical insight to such a description of the farmland. But the possession of a tractor makes the farmer nearer to the wheat in the sense that earlier periods of waiting were undertaken *in order* to place the farmer in this favored position. Where other views saw the tractor as a store of past waiting, the view here under discussion sees the tractor (because of the past waiting that was deliberately undertaken) as the means whereby the farmer is spared further waiting.

IS "WAITING" A FACTOR OF PRODUCTION?

Our discussion of the various ways in which capital goods have been conceived of as related to "waiting" makes it of interest to take up at this point the question of whether to consider "waiting" as a factor of production. Of course, for a theory of production in which no significance at all is ascribed to time lags between the date of inputs and the date of output, there can be no question of ascribing productivity to time as such,[36] or to waiting. The debate concerning waiting as an independent, "original"

36. For Knight's earlier views on this point, see Knight (1931, p. 198).

factor of production has had relevance only in the context of the Böhm-Bawerkian-type theory of capitalistic production.

Böhm-Bawerk himself vigorously denied the possibility of distinguishing any independent third factor of production to stand side by side with labor and nature. Capital itself is not such a factor, it is merely the intermediate product of nature and labor.[37] All production achieved with the help of capital must be ascribed to the nature and labor which, some time in the past, cooperated in the production of capital. No portion of the value of the final product can be imputed back to any other original factor. This was the basis for the Böhm-Bawerkian rejection of theories of interest based on the productivity of capital itself.

On the other hand it was one of the cardinal features of the Böhm-Bawerkian view of capitalistic production that capital cannot come into existence without prior saving, or abstinence from consumption. "Production and saving constitute equally indispensable conditions of the formation of capital."[38] The question then arises whether saving, or "abstinence," or "waiting" should not be recognized as an independent factor, coordinate with labor and nature, responsible for the productivity later to be displayed by the capital goods thus accumulated. Followers of Böhm-Bawerk who emphasized that aspect of his system which depended on the *productivity* of time-consuming methods of production (as compared with the time-preference aspect), have indeed tended to treat time, or waiting, in this way as a factor of production, measuring the marginal product of waiting and viewing interest as the return to those responsible for the waiting represented by the capital employed.[39]

But Böhm-Bawerk himself refused to treat waiting as a third independent factor. The function of saving, Bawerk insists, "is not in the nature of performing part of the work which is peculiarly its own province. Instead, its function is to see to it that the productive forces nature and labor, which, in any event, must perform the entire work of production themselves, shall not direct their efforts toward any goal but production, that is to say, shall produce capital goods and not consumption goods."[40]

More recent writers have remarked on the "philosophical" aspects of

37. Böhm-Bawerk (1959b, pp. 97–8). Kaldor's rather surprising statement on this point (1937, p. 192) has already been sharply criticized by Schumpeter (1954, p. 901, n. 26).

38. Böhm-Bawerk (1959b, p. 116).

39. Wicksell (1934, vol. 1, p. 177).

40. Böhm-Bawerk (1959b, p. 117).

the debate. Haavelmo refers to the alternatives of regarding time itself as an active productive agent or only as a medium permitting the flows of inputs to cumulate into the product.[41] (On the other hand Haavelmo has elsewhere objected without reservation to treating "waiting" itself as productive: "Certainly it is not the delay in output which itself is 'productive,' but the fact that the more time we spend, the more capital we can construct.")[42] Fraser has discussed at length the appropriateness of treating passive *conditions* of productive processes (among which he includes "waiting") as factors of production side by side with those resources which are more "intimately bound up with the actual technical processes whereby goods are made."[43] Hayek has remarked that time cannot be treated as a factor of production "since no definite 'quantity' of time is given in a way which would enable us to distribute this 'fund' of time in alternative ways between the different lines of production so that the total of time used will always be the same."[44]

Among recent writers it is Professor Dorfman who (taking up a posture of originality that does not appear to be entirely justified) has been most emphatic in treating waiting as an independent, original factor of production. He makes this way of handling the matter—which, as we have seen, Böhm-Bawerk himself rejected—the cornerstone of his rehabilitation of Böhm-Bawerkian capital theory.[45] Clearly we have an unusual kind of divergence of opinion on this question. Some clarification of the issues involved can, we believe, be obtained with the help of the point of view upon capitalistic production that has been developed in this essay. Part of the confusion has to do with the two views concerning the production function (and hence the significance of productive factors) that were discussed in the previous chapter.

It will be recalled that the one view treats the production function in a purely "positive" manner; it is seen as representing simply a set of *technological* relationships. It answers the question: what combinations of ingredients are able to bring into existence the various quantities of the product? The second ("economic") view of the production function, on the other hand, looked upon it as presenting the alternative *opportunities* af-

41. Haavelmo (1960, p. 47).
42. Ibid. (p. 40).
43. Fraser (1937, pp. 208–9).
44. Hayek (1936, p. 377).
45. Dorfman (1959b, pp. 359ff.).

forded by technology from among which the human producer can *choose*. While for most purposes little substantive difference arises as a result of these two different views, we have already noticed in the previous chapter how these views do importantly affect the treatment of capital. We now have before us yet another instance where the two views on the interpretation of the production function do make a difference. Once again we will discover that it is the second of these two views which proves most helpful, and most appropriate for economic analysis.

For, so long as the production function is seen merely as a statement of technological relationships, it is difficult for anyone conscious of the time-dimension of production processes to avoid looking upon time, or waiting, as a productive factor, i.e., as one of the ingredients necessary before the final output is available. Whether as an "active" or a "passive" ingredient, the lapse of time, or waiting, must precede the emergence of the product of a capitalistic process begun with only labor and nature. Labor and nature alone cannot yield output; labor plus nature plus waiting time yield output.

But, when the production function is looked upon from the economic point of view, that is, when the inputs and outputs are viewed as components of alternative production *plans*, the matter looks quite different. Now the production function comprises alternative multiperiod production plans, *each viewed from a point in time before it has been adopted.* Contemplating prospectively one such multiperiod plan, the decision-maker finds, say, that the investment of a certain quantity of land and labor now will yield a definite quantity of grain at a specified future date. Contemplating a second plan, he finds that the investment now of similar quantities of land and labor, in a different process of production, will yield a smaller quantity of grain (at a date so near as to appear for all practical purposes) in the immediate future. It is now clearly possible to maintain that the greater quantity of grain promised by the first plan does not call for any resources above those required by the second plan. The first plan merely requires that the decision-maker decide to adopt the first production process rather than the second, this decision being taken with the awareness that the output is to be available only at the specified future date; once the futurity of the grain has been taken into account as qualifying the utility promised by the investment, no further input "sacrifice" in the form of waiting need be taken into consideration in the production plan. It is as if a boy were to stand with a dime before two vending machines, one of which yields its contents several seconds earlier than the second. For each machine a dime is all that is required. Looking prospectively at both alternatives the boy is merely aware that the contents of the second machine seem further away in time than do those of the first.

Looked at *ex post,* or from a purely technological point of view, such would not seem to be the case. In the technological sense grain is grain. Even if time subscripts be carefully appended, by itself this does not indicate the relative desirabilities of grain at various dates. For a complete technological description of the time-consuming process it is therefore necessary to say that the investment of land and labor at one date, *plus the lapse of a specified time interval,* yields grain at a future date. It is only in the context of the plan, contemplated *ex ante* by the decision-maker, that it is superfluous to say that, in addition to the investment of the labor and land, he must also invest in waiting in order to obtain grain at the future date. But in the planning context such a statement *would* indeed be superfluous; once the planner is aware of the date of the future output, once he takes into account the relative position on his present scale of values of grain-in-the-specified-future, he merely has to recognize that in order to obtain this grain (rather than the smaller quantity of immediate grain) he must invest the labor and land in process one (rather than process two). No further sacrifices need be taken into account. In this sense Böhm-Bawerk was on very firm ground indeed when he pointed out that the decision to save is not a decision to apply additional input of some kind to the production process, but merely a decision to guide the process toward future goals rather than immediate goals.[46]

It turns out, then, not entirely to one's surprise, that (a) when the time-

---

46. A few additional words of clarification may be helpful. It may be objected that even in the "planning" context, it *is* of course possible for the decision-maker to view the first plan as calling for additional input in the form of waiting, in order to obtain the greater quantity of grain. This is perfectly true. Analogously if one pays fifty cents for the privilege of sitting on a hard chair (with the hardness viewed as a necessary evil), one *may* indeed alternatively say that one is sacrificing fifty cents plus the discomfort of sitting on a hard chair for the privilege of sitting on a chair at all. Clearly it may not always be possible to declare without arbitrariness that a certain disutility associated with a particular enjoyment is to be viewed as lowering the relative position of this enjoyment on one's value scale, rather than as an independent sacrifice required as an "input" for the purchase of the enjoyment. The point made in the text is simply that in the planning context it is *possible* (and sometimes even natural) to view the futurity of output as qualifying its desirability (from the point of view of the present)—in which case no separate sacrifice of waiting need be taken into account. This is in contrast to the "positive," technological, description of a process, in which, even when the

consuming process of production is viewed prospectively, it is perfectly feasible to ignore "waiting" altogether when discussing inputs, and to take notice of all the implications of "waiting" that need to be considered, by having due regard to the effect of time preference upon the present desirability of the prospective future outputs; and that (b) when the time-consuming process of production is viewed "positively," on the other hand, there is every justification to notice "waiting" as one of the inputs, and to proceed to discuss the superior productivity of the more time-consuming processes of production selected, as attributable to the productivity of time. Given the strictly *ex ante* point of view adopted in this essay, it should be clear that it is the former of these alternatives that is to be endorsed. Böhm-Bawerk's refusal to recognize waiting as an input—a matter that has frequently occasioned mild surprise—follows consistently from his fundamental insight that interest is a phenomenon that emerges from intertemporal exchange, in which the time preferences of the exchanging individuals are of the essence. It is only in that line of thought (exemplified, say, by Wicksell and by Dorfman) in which Böhm-Bawerkian doctrine has been developed almost exclusively along productivity lines, with almost no attention to time preferences at all,[47] in which the *ex ante* concept of waiting periods is unnecessary, and in which, as a consequence, waiting came to appear naturally as a productive factor with its own marginal productivity and earning its own productivity return.

One further observation on the question of the productivity of waiting is in order. The Böhm-Bawerkian thesis that more roundabout methods of production are more productive was the cause of a great amount of confusion in the subsequent literature. So long as the "productivity" side of the Austrian theory is treated as in a vacuum, it is indeed not an easy matter to establish the universal validity of the thesis. But as soon as Böhm-Bawerk's own rejection of waiting as a factor of production is recalled, and when it is borne in mind that the basis for this rejection exists in the appropriateness of the "plan" approach to multiperiod decision-making in production, the matter becomes much clearer. It is by no means necessary to postulate that more waiting means more product (as must at least be postulated by the purely "productivity" versions of the Austrian theory, in which waiting is a factor of production). All that is needed is the recog-

---

date of output has been specified, it is not necessarily superfluous to notice that a time interval elapses between the investment of inputs and the final yield.

47. Cf. Hayek (1941, p. 420).

nition that "unless waiting is assumed to be pleasant" the only situations which are economically interesting are those marginal ones in which "the utility of extra products has to be balanced against the disutility of extra waiting."[48] At the "margin of roundaboutness" the decision-maker is always careful to make sure that his multiperiod plan does not call for sacrifices of satisfactions in the near future which, in his estimation are not warranted by the yield promised for the more distant future. With more and more resources at his disposal, so that the former sacrifices no longer have to be made, he will be able to exploit the desirable, high-productivity processes which had earlier to be rejected only because of the length of waiting time involved. That such processes can nearly always be assumed to exist has been explained by Hayek.[49]

48. Fraser (1937, p. 387). This formulation of the "law of roundaboutness" has become quite common in recent literature; see, e.g., Hayek (1941, p. 60); Mises (1949, p. 492); Hazlitt (1959, pp. 212, 230); Haavelmo (1960, p. 92).

49. Hayek (1941, p. 60).

Chapter 4. Measuring Capital

The discussions of the preceding chapters have paved the way for a consideration of that knotty problem, the measurement of capital. There exists a sizable literature attempting to grapple with this problem, some writers denying that capital measurement is possible even in principle, some claiming to have discovered the "right" method to achieve such measurement, some arguing that more than one measure is required, others arguing again that no measurement problems whatsoever exist with respect to capital other than those common to all resources. Here we will attempt to clarify the major issues involved, by a consistent application of the positive approach to the analysis of capitalistic production that has been endorsed in this essay. We commence with our own discussion of the capital measurement difficulties, to be followed in the second half of the chapter by a critical survey of the relevant literature.

A DISCUSSION OF THE PROBLEM OF CAPITAL MEASUREMENT

What Should a Measure of Capital Measure?

We consider a market economy at a given date. Each of the individual members of the economy owns some stock of capital goods. Each of these capital goods was produced during some past period of time with some definite process of production, its production having been undertaken in anticipation of and for the sake of its ability to advance subsequent stages of production. Each of these capital goods is now capable of making various contributions to alternative future processes of production including possibly (but not necessarily) the contributions envisaged at the time when these goods were produced. The stock of capital goods available today is the result of the production and consumption decisions made during past history. The future course of history depends on the decisions that will be made with respect to the utilization of resource services that can be expected to be available during the future, including the services of the existing stocks of capital goods.

Now, were the present stock of capital goods to be in some sense "smaller" than what it is, then the streams of output that can be expected from the future would seem smaller, in some anticipated sense, than they actually do seem. One aspect of the capital measurement discussion has to do with attempts to render precise the "quantity" of capital involved in such a statement; this is the search for a "forward-looking" measure of capital.

On the other hand, we have observed that the existing stock of capital goods is the result of choices made in the past. In order to achieve the existing stock of capital goods, sacrifices were made, alternative uses of past resource services were forgone. Clearly if lesser sacrifices would have been made in the past, in some sense, the stock of capital goods existing today would in some sense be smaller than what it in fact is. Another aspect of the capital measurement discussion has to do with attempts to render precise the "quantity" of capital in this kind of statement; this is the search for a "backward-looking" measure of capital.[1]

Or again, the existing stock of capital goods may be considered apart from their past history, and from the future course of production to which they may make contribution. Attempts have been made to pin down some sense in which a quantity notion can be attached to the collection of sheer physical items that make up the capital stock. Sometimes "forward-looking" or "backward-looking" measures of capital have been used, not as being of prime interest in themselves, as for their ability to serve more or less appropriately as substitute measures for the stock of capital conceived of simply as a collection of physical items.

We will take these alternative interpretations of the notion of a capital quantity (which by no means exhaust the full list of such interpretations) as the starting point in our discussion. We consider first the notion of a quantity of capital goods as it relates to the individual decision-maker; then we will take up the notion of the quantity of capital goods in the economy as a whole.

The Quantity of Capital Available to an Individual

Let us first dispose of the necessity to devise a measure of capital goods seen merely as a collection of physical items and nothing more. If one is indeed unconcerned with the economic history leading up to the present existence of the stock, and also not directly concerned with the contribution to future output that these items can make, then there can clearly be little immediate economic interest in any such measure. And even if one's announced interest in the quantity of physical goods is for the purpose of eventually using this physical measure in decision-making with respect to future production, or in the analysis of future production, it is diffi-

---

1. The terms "forward-looking" and "backward-looking" measures of capital were introduced by Hicks (1961). It will be seen that they are used here in a sense somewhat different from that used by Hicks.

cult to perceive its usefulness. The truth is that the heterogeneity of the various physical items in the stock not only constitutes a well-recognized barrier to the construction of such a measure, but represents at the same time the reason why such a measure can play no significant role at all in the analysis of decision-making in the course of capitalistic production. The producer simply cannot afford to ignore the heterogeneity of the various items in the capital stock. The particular alternative combinations of resource services from among which he chooses all depend crucially on the special features possessed by each piece of capital equipment. To treat a given stock of heterogeneous capital goods as a homogeneous quantity must involve either the suppression of the differences that exist between the various items (in which case the resulting measure has no relevance for decision-making in production) or else the assimilation of these differences into the measure, based on weights derived from the importance which decision-makers attach to these differences (in which case the measure is either "forward looking" or "backward looking" and is no longer a bald physical measure at all).[2]

Turning to backward-looking and forward-looking measures of capital we notice first of all the special case in which the most desirable prospective production processes are precisely those which were envisaged at the various dates at which construction of the currently existing capital goods was undertaken. As was observed in the first chapter, this is the situation in which the earlier stages of the multiperiod plans adopted in the past have been carried through successfully without the discovery of anything calling for a revision in the later stages of these plans. A measure of the sacrifices made in the past in order to arrive at the present state of affairs measures at the same time the sacrifices that are rendered *un*necessary by the availability of the capital stock—sacrifices which had in the past been considered justified by the anticipated usefulness of the capital goods. Or, to put it the other way around, a measure of the flow of productive ser-

---

2. As we will discover in the second half of this chapter, an examination of the literature turns up many attempts to measure capital goods in purely physical terms. A widely employed justification for such attempts has been the wish to be able to measure changes in the "productivity of capital," or to examine the production functions in which capital goods appear as inputs (and are thus measured in physical terms). Insofar as interest in these aspects of capital pertains to decisions made by potential producers, the discussion in the text denies validity to such attempts at physical (as distinct from economic) homogenization. On the relevance of "productivity" measurement to the decision-making approach to economic analysis, see Stigler (1961).

vices that the most efficient exploitation of the present stock of capital goods now promises to yield measures at the same time the anticipated productive contribution for the sake of which the goods were constructed in the first place. In this special case the "present state of affairs" appears now merely as a cross-section of the even course of economic history. The sacrifices measured by a backward-looking view of the present state of affairs dovetail faultlessly with the prospective productive contributions made possible by the present state of affairs, as measured by a forward-looking view of this state of affairs. As was noticed in the first chapter, this situation is one in which only fleeting interest attaches to the "present state of affairs." From the vantage point of later dates nothing that needs to be explained about the course of economic history will be seen to have depended importantly upon the state of affairs in such a situation. The case that is of interest for the theory of capital is the realistic one in which the forward-looking measures of the capital stock do not dovetail with the backward-looking measures (e.g., in which the forward-looking measure of capital shows a quantity of it too small to have justified the past sacrifices indicated by the backward-looking measure of the same stock).

It follows, then, that for the cases that are of interest for a theory of capital, the notion of a quantity of capital goods must be spelled out *either* in terms of the past sacrifices that gave us the capital goods in question *or* in terms of the future productive contribution these goods can be expected to make for the efficient producer. In general these two notices will *not* dovetail; the quantity of capital as measured by its prospective contribution to production will not be that quantity for the sake of which the past sacrifices were incurred. It will in general be illegitimate to use a backward-looking measure of capital as an index of its productive capacity, or a forward-looking measure as an index of the past sacrifices incurred.

Backward-Looking Measures of Capital: The Individual

Let us consider the requirements for a backward-looking measure of the capital goods owned by an individual. It will be simplest to consider this problem first in a Crusoe setting. The sacrifices made by Crusoe in the past in order to attain his present state consist of the best alternative uses to which each bit of past input could have been applied at the time when one of the decisions was made that contributed to the production of the capital goods now possessed. At each past date when input was applied toward capital goods production, some "next best" employment of the input was forgone. The aggregate of these sacrifices is what is sought to measure for the purpose of the backward-looking measure of the now existing stock of capital goods. This seems clear-cut enough; but it raises the obvious problem of heterogeneity in ways that are apparently not always obvious.

It is important to realize carefully wherein this heterogeneity problem exists and where it does *not* exist. Heterogeneity is a problem here *not* because of the heterogeneity of the existing capital goods themselves, since we are measuring the stock of these goods in terms not of the physical items making up the stock, but of the past sacrifices responsible for the stock. If past sacrifices were homogeneous in nature, then we would have no heterogeneity problem at all. But past sacrifices are in general not homogeneous, and this for two reasons.

First, the sacrifices involved in past inputs are in general of different kinds. While there is no objection in principle to a search for the "amount of past sacrifice" involved in a stock of heterogeneous capital goods, understanding "sacrifice" as a simple homogeneous quantity, the likelihood is that the alternative outputs forgone in the past were themselves of different kinds. Suppression of these differences (by collapsing all the different sacrifices into a single homogeneous sacrifice notion) may do no particular harm, as far as concerns our purposes in wishing to measure capital in this way, but it does require the solution of an index-number problem.

Second, the sacrifices involved in the production of the capital goods were, in general, made at *different dates*. This involves a heterogeneity problem, almost completely ignored in the literature, that is thrown into focus by an approach which emphasizes the *decisions* associated with the capital stock. A distinction is made in the literature[3] between "point-input" cases (where all the inputs responsible for capital goods were invested at one single date) and "continuous-input" cases (where the inputs responsible for the capital goods were invested continuously over a period of time). Now, in the case of continuous input, we can assume that capital goods must in general be ascribed to a series of decisions made at various dates. It follows, then, that even if the alternative outputs forgone at each of these past dates were to be identical in all observable respects, any attempt to add them together would involve a problem of heterogenity. This

---

3. The distinction is ascribed by Hayek (1941, p. 66) to R. Frisch. See also Lutz and Lutz (1951, p. 5).

is so (a) because the date at which an act of consumption takes place (or is forgone) is an important respect in which it differs economically from other acts of consumption, even when all the acts of consumption are appraised as of *one* particular date; and (b) because in the continuous input case each of the forgone possibilities of consumption *was being valued* at a different date.[4]

For Crusoe these difficulties must certainly appear insuperable. Even if a system of weights is able to be devised that could bring together all the different kinds of enjoyments (rejected during the process of producing the capital goods) into a single quantity of sacrifice, this could be done only with respect to Crusoe's value scale as of one particular date. In a world in which tastes and expectations are in principle free to change there seems no theoretically valid way in which the sacrifices undertaken at various dates can be aggregated.[5] Of course it would still be possible in principle for Crusoe to appraise the aggregate of past sacrifices as they *now* appear to him in retrospect, but it is not clear in what sense this would be able to provide a useful measure of the capital stock. The rationale of the backward-looking measure of capital as we have thus far described it rests on the assumption that where greater sacrifices have been undergone, they were accepted only in order to achieve "more capital" (as viewed in anticipation). This would require a measurement of the relevant sacrifices at the times at which they were undertaken. If one could assume that a plan to construct the entire existing stock of capital goods had been adopted at one date (in advance of the times at which the actual sacrifices necessary would have to be undertaken) there would perhaps be some merit in measuring these sacrifices as of the date at which they were originally envisaged. But barring this special case, even this limited value must be denied to the Crusoe backward-looking measure of capital.

Let us see whether these difficulties arise entirely out of the peculiarities of the Crusoe setting, and can be avoided by transferring the problem to a market economy. Can an individual in a market economy devise a backward-looking measure of his stock of capital goods that should not founder on the heterogeneity problems we have discovered?

---

4. Even in point-input–point-output cases the difficulty will still exist with respect to the different capital goods produced at different dates.

5. See Little (1950, pp. 84–85); Rothenberg (1961, appendix to ch. 2); and Weckstein (1962).

The advantage, for the purposes of measuring "economic quantities," that is conferred by the existence of a market arises out of the possibility of using market prices to overcome the heterogeneity problem by translating quantities of one physical commodity into value terms for comparison with quantities of other physical commodities. The immediate justification for this is that the market in fact permits easy conversion through commerce of a quantity of physical goods into other goods of equal market value.[6] Can we use market prices to measure the sacrifices undertaken during the past in order that the present stock of capital goods be brought into existence? Clearly the current market prices of the items making up the stock will not serve for this purpose. Current market prices reflect the *present* anticipations of the productive usefulness of the capital goods, and thus, we have already noticed, may be quite different from the corresponding expectations held at the time when the capital goods were produced.[7] Our first thought is to add up the market values of the inputs used in the past in the production of today's stock of capital goods, making sure to allow compound interest to accrue at the respectively appropriate rates and for the respectively appropriate lengths of time.[8] (The "appropriate" rate of interest would here be that rate which could, *at the time when input was applied in the past,* have been obtained for a loan of funds for the relevant length of time, i.e., till the present date. It would be incorrect to use the rate or rates of interest that have in fact been ruling *during* this length of time, since we are concerned with the extent of the sacrifice *undertaken* at the time of input application.)

This way of calculating the "cost" of the capital stock would certainly overcome the heterogeneity problem that arose due to the different kinds of alternatives involved in the various applications of input. These would now be expressed in homogeneous terms of monetary value. A particular alternative enjoyment forgone at one date can be added to a particular alternative enjoyment forgone at a second date, because both enjoyments are expressed in monetary terms. Inclusion of accrued interest (as outlined in the preceding paragraph) enables one to compare sacrifices made in the distant past with those made in the immediately preceding past, since they are being measured by the amounts of money *at the present*

6. See Mises (1953, p. 48).

7. "Any measure based on market prices was bound to be forward-looking" (Malinvaud, 1961b, p. 306).

8. Cf. Lindahl (1939, pp. 313f.).

date which these sacrifices could respectively have bought at the dates at which they were undertaken.

But reflection will convince us that we have not yet succeeded at all in obtaining the backward-looking measure of capital which we have been seeking. Our purpose in seeking such a measure was to exploit our understanding of the past decisions which led to our existing capital stock. Knowing that larger sacrifices would have been undertaken only for the sake of a more desirable stock of capital, we sought to use a homogeneous measure of these sacrifices as an index of the size of our capital stock. But all we have succeeded in obtaining is the sum yielded by adding together all the quantities of present money that could have been owned today if, instead of applying inputs at various past dates, their market values in money had been loaned out at the going rates of interest up to the present date. This sum of money is indeed the present money equivalent of the production costs of the goods in our capital stock. But since this sum is composed of money values of costs incurred at *different* past dates, the sum itself is unable to serve as a measure of the "total sacrifice" incurred in the past for the sake of the present stock. The money equivalent of the input applied at one past date may serve as a measure of the sacrifice involved in its application, because the money was an alternative, available at the time, which was rejected for the sake of the capital stock. But since an individual is at no time able to choose between two alternatives the adoption of which require decisions to be made at *different* dates, it follows that sacrifices undertaken at different dates cannot be compared. (A person may pay x dollars in the summer to enjoy a cold shower, this shows he prefers the latter to the former; he may pay y dollars in the winter to enjoy a warm bath, this shows he prefers the bath to the y dollars. But even if $y > x$ this does not prove that the winter bath is preferred to the summer shower. Even though we know that in the winter he prefers y dollars to x dollars, and so also in the summer, we have no decision possibility permitting him to choose simultaneously between summer and winter enjoyments. He may use the loan market to express his *present* preferences between x dollars in the winter and y dollars in the summer, but this, of course, is something different.)

In brief, our individual seeking to measure the quantity of sacrifice involved in his present capital stock by using market values still finds himself confronted with one of the heterogeneity problems that Crusoe found insuperable. The inputs applied at different dates correspond to sacrifices that can in principle not be compared or aggregated. To add the money values of these inputs is to add essentially heterogeneous items together and to delude oneself into believing that, because all the values are money values, the heterogeneity does not exist. The fact is that a dollar sacrificed at one date can no more be added to a dollar sacrificed at a different date than a carrot can be added to a potato. The fact that the carrot and the potato are each called "vegetable" does nothing to alter the matter. Only in the very special case when *all* the past inputs that produced the current stock of capital were committed in one single irrevocable decision (so that all that was sacrificed was valued as of a *single date*) can one hope to use the market value of inputs (as anticipated at the moment of decision) as a measure of the sacrifices undertaken. Only in this case can a backward-looking measure of capital be conceivable.

We conclude that the attempt to measure the "quantity of capital" in an individual's stock of capital goods, by measuring the past sacrifices involved, must be pronounced a failure. In a later section we will discover what additional difficulties stand in the way of constructing, even in principle, a backward-looking measure of the entire capital stock that exists in an economy as a whole. We turn first to consider the possibilities for a "forward-looking" measure of the capital stock of an individual.

Forward-Looking Measures of Capital: The Individual
The rationale of the forward-looking measure of capital is provided by the notion that a larger stock of capital goods ought to make a larger contribution to future output than a smaller stock. The purpose is then to measure the capital stock by the contribution to future production that it is able to make. Capital goods are in this context treated exactly like other resources, and involve no problems of measurement that are not shared in principle by other resources. Several problems present themselves in connection with the construction of such a resource measure. First, there is the problem of reducing to a single quantity all the contributions to output that the stock of capital is able to make during many different future periods of time. Second, there is the problem created by the many alternative ways in which the stock of capital can be used in future production—what precisely do we wish to mean by the "prospective productive contribution" that a capital good is able to make?

As far as the first of these problems is concerned there seems to be no great difficulty, at least for an individual in a market economy. Once the second problem has been solved, that is, once we have identified the particular future output flow which we consider as the prospective contribution to output of the capital goods, then we can simply find the present market value of this contribution by adding together the prospective market values of each bit of the future output flow, appropriately discounted down to the present date (at the relevant rates of interest now prevailing). This will give the individual an "objective" value of the productive capacity of his stock of capital. (Of course, the individual might be more interested in his own subjective valuation of this flow of output. This will permit him to gauge the desirability of the flow by reference to his own private tastes, including time preferences. In general this could lead only to an ordinal measure.)

The real difficulty, it is clear, has to do with the second problem, that of identifying the contribution to future production that we wish to associate with a particular capital good or collection of capital goods. The difficulty is a result of two circumstances, (a) the versatility of capital goods, and (b) the possibilities of substitution between capital goods and other inputs. First, since capital goods may be used in the production of more than one kind of output, we are required to specify the particular product toward the output of which the stock of capital is, for our purposes, considered able to make contribution. Second, since in the production of many products there exists the possibility of using either relatively more capital with other inputs, or relatively less capital, and since future output depends sensitively on the particular ratio between inputs that is employed, it is necessary to specify the degree of capital intensity that we have in mind when we talk of "the productive contribution" of our capital goods.

The fact is, of course, that these difficulties arise from *the necessity to make decisions* with respect to the productive utilization of capital goods, as of other available resources. It is in many respects a misleading simplification to talk as if a given resource were unambiguously associated with a definite flow of output, in the sense that such an output flow is forthcoming automatically from the resource. Until a definite plan has been formulated that shall clearly mark out the part in the production process that a piece of capital equipment is to fill, it is not really meaningful to talk of its "potential contribution to production." This is so not only because, as was stressed in earlier chapters, output does not emerge without decisions being made,[9] but also because as we have now seen, there is more than one use to which a resource can be put, and more than one

9. Cf. the discussion above, pp. 30, 66.

technique by which it can be applied to a given use. We have already observed that it would be inappropriate to use, for this purpose, the original production plan envisaged at the time the capital was constructed; the essence of our attempt to measure capital in a forward-looking manner is to be able, where necessary, to ignore bygones. It appears, then, that the attempt to measure a stock of capital goods in terms of their potential contribution to future output must assume that all the decisions with respect to the utilization of the capital goods have already been made in the light of current conditions. This means, in addition, that the forward-looking measure of the capital stock is able to provide a measure of capital only against the background of given anticipated prices for other inputs and for products (since it is only with the knowledge of these prices that a production plan can be formulated). To measure the potential productive contribution that a stock of capital goods can render, in isolation from the consideration of other factors of production, appears to be an impossible task.

But, once the difficulties and qualifications surrounding a forward-looking measure of capital have been comprehended, it becomes likewise clear that such a measure is in fact obtainable, in principle, without the problems that frustrated the search for a backward-looking measure. The truth is that a capital good *is* measured—no matter what difficulties this task entails, and no matter how inaccurately it is performed—whenever an individual buys or sells the capital good, and whenever, possessing a capital good, he refrains from selling it at the going market price. And the measurement so made is certainly a forward-looking one. The highest price a person will pay for a capital good is set by his estimate of the present value to him of the addition to the future flow of output that the capital good can make possible, taking into account the particular production process in which he envisages the capital good to be applied, and the particular manner in which he envisages it to be used in this process. The fact that capital goods are bought and sold is evidence that individuals are indeed able to compare its productive usefulness with that of other resources, and with quantities of immediately consumable commodities.

Does this mean that an individual can measure the size of his stock of capital by simply finding out its current market value? Not quite. We have seen that a forward-looking measure of capital implies that one has in mind a definite plan for the productive utilization of the capital goods. Such a plan depends on one's expectations concerning the future prices of the different possible products and of the different possible complementary inputs. An individual's forward-looking measure of a given stock of capital goods is thus highly individualistic, depending crucially on his own subjective expectations concerning the future. The market price of a capital good expresses the quantity of capital that it represents to other individuals in the market (the marginal buyers and marginal sellers), based on their expectations. In the absence of an equilibrium situation there is not even a guarantee that the market price fully expresses the expectations of all potential market participants. And even if the market were to be in equilibrium, our individual cannot be sure that he shares the set of expectations upon which the market price is based. So that for an individual who has his own ideas as to the future, the market price does not provide the subjective measure in which he is interested. On the other hand, for an outside observer wishing to see how much capital the market ascribes to a particular capital good, the market price certainly gives him the information he wants provided he remembers that those who do not trade at the going price clearly disagree with the rest of the market as to the size of the capital good's prospective productive contribution.[10]

The Quantity of Capital Available to an Economy as a Whole
We turn now to consider the additional complications that attend the search for a measure of capital, when the capital sought to be measured is that of an entire economy (or is the "average" capital available per head, a concept that implies the aggregation of all the capital available to the group). We will discover that our dissatisfaction with other treatments of this aspect of the capital measurement problem stems more than ever from the prevalent disregard of the *plan* relevance of the capital concept.

Now, if our interest were in the stock of capital conceived as a collection of physical objects, then there would in principle be no especial difficulty with the construction of an aggregate measure of all the capital goods that exist in an economy. All that would be involved would be the addition of the machines that belong to A, to the machines that belong to B, and so on. But we have already shown that we are not very interested in the "size" of the stock of capital goods in physical terms, where this involves the suppression of the economic differences between heterogeneous goods. There seems no reason for our interest to be reawakened in such a concept merely as a result of the widening of the focus of attention

10. On this point, see Smith (1962, p. 487).

to embrace an entire economy.[11] Our interest, then, must still be in the economic aspects of the nation's stock of capital goods, and this raises serious questions concerning the meaningfulness of aggregation in this context altogether.

Supposing, for the sake of argument, that each of the individuals in the economy had succeeded in devising a valid "backward-looking" measure of the capital stock that he possesses. In other words, each individual has a clear quantitative notion of the sacrifice undertaken in the past for the sake of the capital goods he now possesses. Is there any meaningful way of adding these measures of capital together in order to measure the aggregate stock of capital? Clearly there loom formidable theoretical obstacles in the way of adding together the "sacrifices" undertaken by different individuals. The sacrifices we are concerned with are not quantities of objective physical inputs applied; we are concerned with the *subjective* notion of sacrifice undertaken by each individual in his past decisions. There is no way of comparing the subjective sacrifices undertaken by different individuals. Even if each individual had somehow succeeded in expressing his "quantity of sacrifice" in terms of money, the addition together of these sums of money representing the sacrifices of different individuals cannot succeed in representing a meaningful adding together of the different subjective sacrifices expressed by these sums.

But let us disregard this difficulty, let us imagine that somehow the sacrifices of different individuals can be added together into a single aggregate quantity. Can the resulting quantity serve as a measure of aggregate capital? In what sense does the size of this aggregate sacrifice attest to the size of the capital stock? For an individual, the size of the sacrifice that he undertook in the past measures the quantity of capital produced through this sacrifice *as anticipated* at the time the sacrifice was undertaken. Even if the anticipations have been proved incorrect, there may still be interest in measuring the size of the present capital stock as it was anticipated at the time its construction was undertaken. But when we aggregate the sacrifices made by a large number of individuals, whose past anticipations are likely, at least to some degree, to have been mutually contradictory, we obtain a quantity which hardly seems to have any meaning at all. If A anticipated warm weather and produced an air-conditioner at great sacrifice,

11. Even if one were concerned with a centrally planned economy the objections raised above (pp. 95f.) in connection with the individual would apply with equal force to the state.

while B anticipated cold weather and produced an oil burner with similar sacrifice, then it is clear that in no sense did the "society as a whole" made up of A *and* B anticipate conditions in which *both* capital goods are as valuable as indicated by the respective costs of production incurred.

Nor is the situation greatly different when we consider the possibilities of aggregating forward-looking measures of capital. We have seen that the rationale of such measurements is that the "quantity of a resource" is nothing but another way of describing the additional quantity of input flow which the availability of the resource can make possible. Measuring capital in a forward-looking manner expresses the anticipated usefulness of the capital stock to its owner. We have seen that this presumes a definite plan on the part of the prospective capitalistic producer. This plan in turn depends on the anticipations which he holds concerning the plans of others, in particular as these will express themselves as prices of products and of complementary inputs. If we add together the measures of the capital stocks possessed by different individuals, as measured in a forward-looking way, we are likely to be combining, in effect, mutually inconsistent plans. The point of this whole discussion is that a measure of capital differs from a measure of output in that the former, unlike the latter, depends crucially on some definite plan of production in which the capital is to play a role. Whether backward-looking or forward-looking, a measure of capital necessarily involves the consideration of some plan (either past or prospective) in which the capital appears (as end or as means). A measure of output can, at least in principle, be considered apart from the plans to which the output is to be ascribed (although this does not necessarily provide the most theoretically satisfying measure). Because output can be considered apart from individual plans, the attempt to measure aggregate output (whatever other theoretical difficulties it encounters) does not necessarily have to grapple with the problem of mutually inconsistent plans.

Simon Kuznets seems to have something of this in mind when he criticizes the aggregate measure of capital formation as viewed only as "mechanical sums of bookkeeping entries by business firms and individuals." "Even if the purpose were to study capital purchases and consumption as items that influence the decisions of businessmen. . . . This purpose would call for 'motivational' entries which, by and large, are neither additive nor capable of manipulation mathematically, except within a framework of distinct motivational structures."[12]

12. Kuznets (1957, pp. 271–72).

All this may seem quite discouraging insofar as concerns the attainment of a meaningful aggregate measure of a nation's stock of capital. Certainly the definite collections of physical things that are possessed by individuals permit of being conceptually added together to be considered as a single such collection (but without any analytical purpose being served by representing this collection as a unidimensional quantity). But insofar as each individual is able to measure the capital of which his stock of machines consists, in terms of their prospective usefulness to him in production (either as viewed when their construction was originally undertaken, or as viewed currently), it appears clear that the resulting measures are unique to each individual, do not in general permit comparisons between individuals, and yield no meaningful aggregate when added together. To become aware of this is surely a step forward in one's understanding of the nature of capital within the framework of the decisions that make up the productive process.

And yet it cannot be denied that one is left not entirely satisfied with this conclusion. Is it really without meaning to say that the capital per head in country A is greater than in country B? Is it meaningless to attempt to explain the higher productivity of labor in country A by reference to the larger quantity of capital combined with each man-hour of labor? It is indeed difficult to deny that we, in fact, use aggregate concepts of capital in this manner; what is the meaning to be attached to such concepts, and how do they relate to the "individualistic" concept of capital that has been adopted for the purpose of this essay?

Careful reflection on the matter will, it is believed, reveal that the aggregate concept of capital, the "quantity of capital available to an economy as a whole," is, for a market economy, a wholly artificial construct useful for making certain judgments concerning the progress and performance of the economy. When using this construct one is in fact viewing the economy in its entirety *as if* it were *not* a market economy but instead a completely centralized economy over which the observer himself has absolute control and responsibility. When, for example, one is concerned with the size of the stock available to society in a forward-looking sense, what one is really thinking is as follows. Supposing one were to be able to draw up a complete social listing of output priorities and supposing one were in command of all the information necessary to formulate centralized production plans for the future, what is the additional flow of this "social output" during future years, that is to be ascribed to the presence of the nation's stock of capital? One is thus *not* merging the plans of all the individual capital owners who participate in the market economy, one is conceptually *replacing* these plans by a single master plan that one *imagines* to be relevant to the economy as a whole, and against which one gauges the performance of the economy as a whole.[13]

Now, in order to use such a holistic capital concept with consistency, and in a manner parallel to that which we adopt with respect to the individual capital notion, certain assumptions have to be made. If one wishes to talk of the "cost of the economy's stock of capital," in the sacrifice notion of the backward-looking capital measure, it is necessary to imagine that the existing stock of capital has come into being as the result of past integrated centralized decisions over the years. Only then, with the additional assumption of a holistically conceived scale of social values, can one think in terms of the "social sacrifice" involved in the past production of the present stock of capital. Now, so long as this aggregate concept of capital is used with continual awareness of the special assumptions needed to give it meaning, no very great harm can result. But when, as is so frequently done, the aggregate quantity of capital is used in *conjunction with* discussions of the market process, things become very blurred indeed. The truth is that the aggregate concept of capital has meaning only on assumptions according to which all parts of the capital stock are completely integrated with one another. Each piece of capital equipment in the stock is assumed to have been constructed as part of the *same* central plan which led to the rest of the stock. Each capital good has its part to play; no capital good has a function which precludes the full utilization as planned of any other. But these conditions can exist in a market economy (in which planning is centralized) only in the state of equilibrium. The essential function of the market is, after all, to bring individual plans which do *not* mesh, into greater mutual coordination. So it turns out that the aggregate concept of capital presupposes conditions that are not only violated in the real world, but which assume away some of the major problems which it is the task of a market theory of capital to elucidate. It is the realization of all this that seems to have inspired much of the work of Professor Lachmann in the theory of capital, with his wholesome stress

13. Cf. above, p. 43. See also Hayek's (1941, part 2) treatment of capital in which this approach is explicitly adopted (pp. 27, 99) with references to the antecedent literature. The concept of "intact maintenance of capital" for an economy as a whole must be understood in the same way. (See above, p. 67, for the arbitrary judgments required to give meaning to this concept even for the individual.)

on the problems raised by the need for *complementarity* among the different items that compose the aggregate capital stock.[14] And, at the close of his notable review article of Mrs. Robinson's *Accumulation of Capital* (in the course of which he subjects her discussion of the problems of capital measurement to devastating criticism), it is thus that he sums up the future tasks of the capital theorist: "How bold, then, would the next step be, viz. the realization that the notion of a stock of capital which invariably has the 'appropriate' composition required by circumstances, is an obstacle rather than a help to our understanding of the nature of economic progress?"[15]

THE CAPITAL MEASUREMENT PROBLEM IN THE LITERATURE

In the second half of this chapter we turn now to examine critically some of the ways in which the capital measurement problem has been treated in the literature, with special attention to the more recent contributions. Our examination and criticisms will rely heavily on the discussion of these matters that has been presented in the first half of the chapter. Much has been written concerning capital measurement, with the perspective being variously that of economic theorist, statistician, or econometrician. We will discover that many of the points raised in our discussion earlier have been raised somewhere in the literature; we will however also find, unfortunately, that much of the confusion that has surrounded the treatments of these points is to be ascribed to the prevalent failure to place the theory of capital in the context of the relevant *individual plans*. Our criticism of the various treatments of the capital measurement problem will thus repeatedly draw attention to the ways in which awareness of the individual planning context of capital stocks might either have cleared up points that have raised unnecessary difficulty, or might have revealed points of real difficulty that have in fact apparently escaped attention.

Physical Goods or Abstract Fund—What Are We Trying to Measure?
A considerable amount of disagreement has concerned the question of what precisely is being sought in a measure of capital, a measure of physical things or a measure of an abstract capital fund which these physical things supposedly represent. This disagreement has much to do with the familiar controversies concerning the way in which the economist

14. See Lachmann (1956).
15. Lachmann (1958, p. 100).

ought to look on capital in general. J. B. Clark, who argued in favor of the notion of capital as a homogeneous fund of productive capacity, distinguished sharply between the *value* of the capital stock which measures the size of this fund, and the physical description of the heterogeneous capital goods in which the capital fund is embodied at any particular time. Böhm-Bawerk, who rejected the fund concept of capital, saw no reason why the possibility of measuring a stock of capital as a value implies that what is being measured is an abstract quantity apart from the concrete capital goods. To show that capital *has a value*, is by no means sufficient, he argued, to establish that capital *is* a value.[16] The same points were made again in the course of the Hayek-Knight debate during the thirties. Knight contrasted what he considered the discredited notion of capital as "things," with what he considered the appropriate view of it as a "fund," this fund being "thought of as either a value or a 'capacity' to produce a perpetual flow of income."[17] Hayek's objections to this view, cited in earlier chapters, did not deny that the various capital goods possess a "common attribute of being a condition of making investment possible";[18] but in his view this does not at all justify treating "capital" as if it were a quantity of something apart from the particular goods that make up the capital stock. Böhm-Bawerk himself, Hayek charges, was partly responsible for the spurious notion of homogeneity that has given rise to the fund concept, because he stressed the capacity of capital goods to act as a subsistence fund.[19]

It is not to be thought, of course, that the mere search for a single measure of capital, one that should overcome the problems of heterogeneity, necessarily involves the fund notion of capital. While it is true that Samuelson, for example, contrasts the position which refuses to aggregate heterogeneous capital goods into a single capital quantity with what he calls the "Clark-like concept of aggregate capital,"[20] we have already noticed that Böhm-Bawerk was willing to measure capital as a value without conceding anything to Clark. More recent writers, too, have discussed the possibility of two measures, one measuring the physical things in the capital stock, the other measuring the value of the "fund" considered to

16. Böhm-Bawerk (1959b, pp. 60–61).

17. Knight (1935, p. 57).

18. Hayek (1941, p. 93).

19. Ibid. See also Hayek (1936, pp. 372–76). On this point, see also Kendrick (1961, p. 105).

20. Samuelson (1962, p. 193).

be represented by these things. Hicks especially has stressed the need for both capital concepts,[21] both being measurable in principle.

From the point of view adopted in this essay the issues seem quite clear. The only common attribute that different constituent parts of the capital stock possess is that they are intermediate products. This provides no basis whatsoever for their conception as a homogeneous fund of any kind. Nonetheless, as we have seen in the first part of this chapter, there may be, in principle, the possibility of measuring a stock of heterogeneous capital goods in terms of past sacrifice, or of future potential productive contribution associated with them. Clearly what would be sought thus to be measured would be the physical goods themselves, but only by reference to the economic history, past or future, associated analytically with these goods. The stock of physical things that make up capital is not homogeneous. There is no underlying "fluid" (mystic or otherwise) that is represented by these physical things; so that a collection of these things in no sense represents a fund. Nonetheless, since these things are intermediate products—that is, they are (a) the results of earlier production processes and are (b) planned to be used in future production processes— we may wish to *measure* them by the past sacrifices to which they are to be ascribed or by the future yield to which they are planned to give rise. But this does *not* mean that these physical things themselves are to be viewed as a "stock" of past sacrifices, nor as a "fund" of future productive capacity. They are not to be viewed as a stock of past sacrifices, because bygones are bygones; past sacrifices in no sense affect the current economic status of these capital goods. On the other hand they are not to be viewed as a fund of future productive capacity because their ability to contribute to future output calls for a whole series of new decisions to be made; capital goods in themselves are, indeed, potential inputs, but that is all.

The Heterogeneity of Capital as an Obstacle to Its Measurement
Our brief review of the ambivalence with which the literature has treated the capital concept, now as a collection of physical things, now as a homogeneous fund of some kind, leads us naturally to a more general examination of how the physical heterogeneity of capital goods has been handled in the capital measurement literature. Some writers seem to have understood the problem of capital measurement as arising almost entirely out

21. Hicks (1963, pp. 342f.). Cf. also Griliches (1961, p. 118).

of the heterogeneity of the constituents of the capital stock.[22] An attempt to measure a stock of capital must add together entirely different items. At the same time many writers have pointed out that the heterogeneity problem is by no means peculiar to capital.[23] Any attempt to measure the aggregate flow of labor, for example, will very soon run into the same difficulties of adding together fundamentally different entities. Other writers, again, have denied that the heterogeneity of capital is responsible for the characteristic difficulties that surround the measurement of capital. Even if all capital goods were identical, these writers argue, the real problems that plague the measurement of capital would remain.[24]

We have already, in the first half of this chapter, expressed the opinion that no useful analytical purpose is served by a measure that has no other goal than that of deliberately suppressing the heterogeneity that does, in fact, characterize a stock of capital goods. If a measure of capital seeks to discover some factor common to the various different goods, for example, their capacity to yield a product, or their having been produced at a sacrifice, that is one thing. But if the seeker after a capital measure is not concerned with these possible aspects of homogeneity in the stock,[25] if he confines his attention strictly to the present physical aspects of the capital goods, then, we argued, an attempt to construct an index of capital quantity draws away attention from significant aspects of capital, because decision-makers must, in fact, never lose sight of the unique quality of each capital good. And, just as the decision-maker dare not lose sight of capital heterogeneity, so is it unnecessary for the theorist to ignore it. "With our armchair omniscience," Hahn and Matthews remark, "we can take account of each machine separately." Insofar as the capital measurement problem arises from capital heterogeneity it is "no problem at all

22. See, e.g., Dorfman (1959b, pp. 351f.); Boulding (1950, pp. 177–82); Hahn and Matthews (1964, p. 888). See also Green (1964, part 4).

23. Smith (1962, p. 486); Kendrick (1961, p. 107); Domar (1961, pp. 404–5); Andersen (1965, p. 69); Haavelmo (1960, p. 45).

24. Haavelmo (1960, p. 45); Lerner (1953, p. 540); Metzler (1950, p. 292).

25. In the discussion in the first half of this chapter queries were raised as to whether either past sacrifices or future yields do, in fact, present homogeneous aspects of capital. While these questions do not seem to have been raised in the literature on sacrifice, several writers have noticed the problem of heterogeneity in yield. See Kendrick (1961, pp. 108f.); Sen (1960, p. 17); Robinson (1956, p. 119); Lachmann (1958, p. 93).

because we never have to face it if we do not choose to."[26] A number of writers have insisted that the aggregation of capital in the sense of physical things, into a single quantity, is analytically unnecessary.[27] And it has also been pointed out that if an index of physical things *is* constructed, this necessarily injects some kind of value element into the measure, so that the measure is not strictly a physical one anymore.[28]

Heterogeneity has been seen as a problem associated with that of capital measurement in yet an additional sense. Even if all the physical things that make up the capital stock were identical, Lerner has argued, the "measurement of the marginal product of capital still would involve measuring the capital and consumption goods in the same units so as to obtain a pure number for the marginal product of capital that could be compared with the rate of interest." So long as capital goods are physically different from consumer goods, it is argued, homogeneity of the goods making up capital stock would appear not to have solved anything at all.[29] Hicks has somewhat similarly endorsed the measurement of a capital stock as equivalent to a homogeneous fund of consumption goods, partly on the grounds that this makes possible the measurement of a capital increment in the same units as the saving that corresponds to it.[30] For the same kind of reason a number of theorists have chosen to discuss models in which there exists only one physical commodity (such as the perennial in Knight's Crusonia economy discussed in the previous chapters) that can be either consumed or used as capital in the production of more of itself.[31] Dewey has written of the advantage which this model possesses of avoiding the spurious problem of capital measurement.[32] (Compare also Böhm-Bawerk's conception of capital as inchoate consumer goods "so that the whole economy can be thought of as a single consumption-goods sector.")[33]

26. Hahn and Matthews (1964, p. 888).

27. Solow (1956, pp. 101–2); Samuelson (1962, p. 193).

28. Sen (1960, p. 17).

29. See Lerner (1953, p. 540). Note that Lerner's own position is that the marginal product of capital is not the magnitude that should be compared with the rate of interest, so that this problem disappears.

30. Hicks (1963, pp. 344–45).

31. Ramsay (1928); Hahn and Matthews (1964, p. 783); see Lerner (1953, p. 541).

32. Dewey (1963, p. 134n).

33. Dorfman (1959b, p. 355).

On the other hand, however, it has been objected in the literature that the one-product model necessarily slides over interesting aspects of capital theory.[34] From the point of view adopted in this essay one of the principal objections to this one-product simplification is that it obscures the real economic difference between the constituents of stock of capital on the one hand, and both the original inputs and the final output on the other hand. Measurement of capital in terms of an allegedly *equivalent* quantity of consumer goods is one thing (to be discussed briefly later in this chapter); but a model which measures capital as a quantity of consumer goods because the capital consists physically of consumer goods is necessarily viewing the capital stock in entire abstraction from its economic role. It measures the capital stock purely as a collection of bald physical items, misleadingly implying that these items are economically identical with similar physical items that are planned as outputs.

These objections to the artificial homogenization of the capital stock (and especially the achievement of such homogenization by its reduction to consumer goods) are magnified when the capital measure sought is an aggregate one for the entire economy. As already noted earlier in this chapter one of the most fruitful insights into the market process in a capitalistic economy consists in noticing how this process brings about continual adjustments in the decisions of capital goods producers in the direction of more complete *complementarity* between the heterogeneous items that make up the aggregate stock of capital.[35] Models which deliberately treat capital as if it were homogeneous, and measures of capital that not only slur over inconsistent plans on the part of the various owners of capital goods, but treat capital as something with respect to which inconsistent plans are in principle an impossibility, do a disservice to the extent that they facilitate (and have in fact facilitated) the tendency to ignore entirely this aspect of capital theory in the context of the market.

Heterogeneity, Quality Changes, and Forward-Looking Measures of Capital

A special case of heterogeneity exists where a particular capital good, highly specific to a given branch of production, is being produced today in a quality superior to that of the corresponding good produced last year. Both goods are "typewriters," or "locomotives," but the later model is

34. Smith (1962, p. 484).
35. On all this see Lachmann (1956).

"better" than the older one. If an old-model locomotive was considered one unit of capital (when it was new), should a new-model locomotive be considered as more than one unit of capital, and, if so, how much more?—or should we say that one locomotive is still one unit of capital, but that capital has now become more productive? The problem of quality change is one with which statisticians and econometricians have to grapple in a number of contexts; the problem in the present instance is to devise a theoretically valid way of dealing with quality changes in capital goods that should take into account the special nature of capital goods (as against, for example, that of consumer goods). This constitutes a special case of the heterogeneity problem, in that while the two locomotives are different, they are yet both locomotives, so that one's natural reaction is to compare their respective output. This had led to an examination of forward-looking capital measures for possible use in this special case, far more readily than in the general case.

It should be observed that quality change is not the same thing as technological progress. Different qualities of locomotives may, for example, be produced in different years as a result of changing cost conditions. Nonetheless the treatment of quality change has much in common with the treatment of technological progress (and the two seem to have sometimes become confused in the literature). Especially where technological progress is wholly "embodied" in the capital goods being most recently produced—i.e., where the marginal productivities of capital goods produced earlier are not affected by the change[36]—both kinds of change raise virtually identical problems. Should a measure of capital reflect these changes as increasing the quantity of capital (per "locomotive") or as increasing the productivity of capital (per unit of capital)? Clearly this relates to the question of whether to use a forward-looking measure of capital or not. Those who have deliberately avoided forward-looking measures of capital have had to face the same kind of heterogeneity problem that complicates capital measurement in general (except that they have had to repress with some sternness the natural tendency to consider a better locomotive as being "more locomotive," an urge which does not present itself in connection with goods that have no function in common).[37] Among those

36. The distinction between "embodied" and "disembodied" technical change has been elaborated on especially by Solow; see, e.g., (1962) and (1963).

37. See at length Denison (1957).

who have in this context sought alternatives to forward-looking measures of capital have been especially those wishing to be able to talk of increases in the productivity of capital, arguing that forward-looking measures render this impossible by definition (that which produces more simply representing a greater quantity of capital).[38]

On the other hand, those who have considered the use of forward-looking capital measures as a means of homogenizing capital goods of different quality have encountered some of the characteristic problems which such measures necessarily face. Perhaps foremost among these has been the question of defining the output to be imputed to the capital good involved, in the light of the variable proportions in which capital goods may be combined with complementary inputs. One quantity of machines may, with a given quantity of labor, produce the same output that another number of machines (of different quality) is able to produce with the same labor. But it may be that when combined in turn with some other quantity of labor, each of the two sets of machines yields an output different from that of the other. Under these conditions it is not a simple matter to use the forward-looking approach in order to measure the relative quantities of capital in the two sets. This has been a widely recognized difficulty with the forward-looking approach to capital measurement;[39] in the context of the attempt to handle quality changes it has given rise to a good deal of ambiguity and disagreement. Thus Hicks apparently considered a forward-looking measure of capital such that one new machine shall be said to consist of twice the capital represented by an old machine when the new machine produces, together with a given quantity of labor, twice the output produced by the old machine with the same quantity of labor.[40] Green, on the other hand, wishes us to say that the new machine consists of twice the capital represented by the old machine only when the former produces, with a given quantity of labor, as much output as two old machines can produce when combined with the same total quantity

38. See Hicks (1961, p. 30). More recently Hicks (1963, p. 349) has for this reason endorsed the partial use of the "Physical Things" concept of capital. Cf. also Ruggles and Ruggles (1961, p. 389).

39. Ruggles and Ruggles (1961, pp. 388–89); Hicks (1963, p. 345); Solow (1956, p. 102); Green (1964, p. 11); Barzel (1964, p. 142); H. A. Simon cited in Hammer (1964, p. 16, n. 29).

40. Hicks (1961, p. 30).

of labor.[41] One of the forward-looking measures considered (and rejected) by Denison involves yet a third criterion.[42]

Green, in fact, uses his version of the forward-looking measure to deny altogether that such a measure rules out by definition the possibility of increase in the marginal productivity of capital. Disembodied technological progress, he argues, is entirely able to increase the marginal productivity of a unit of capital (as he wishes us to define it).[43] A machine which last year produced, with a given quantity of labor, output in a certain quantity may this year produce a greater quantity of output with the same labor. Green's own measure enables him to read this as an increase in productivity, while Hicks' measure would interpret it as an increase in capital. All this illustrates the treacherous territory that the would-be measurer of capital must traverse in connection with quality change. It must be confessed that Green's argument in this respect, while perfectly consistent as a matter of mere definition, seems nonetheless to be undeservedly seeking the best of both worlds. If one wishes to use a forward-looking measure of capital, one that focuses attention not on past cost, nor on physical specifications, but on output capacity, then it seems strange that a sudden disembodied technological advance which enables each machine to generate double the output it generated previously in each of its possible uses, is to be viewed as leaving the capital stock no larger than it was before.

Moreover, from the point of view of the discussion in the first half of this chapter it should be clear that no great advantage has been won by being able to use a forward-looking capital measure without having to surrender the notion of changes in the productivity of capital. With the focus of our interest centered on the decision-maker, it is clear that the marginal productivities with which he is concerned are never those of inputs in general, or of capital in general, but are always those of individual bits of input (whenever the different bits of input are in fact significantly different from one another). We have seen that the decision-maker's use of the production function concept never homogenizes capital goods of different qualities so that, where the productivity of capital goods is concerned, the notion of homogeneous capital quantity is irrelevant. On the

---

41. Green (1964, p. 94).

42. See his "method (2)," Denison (1957, pp. 219, 227–29). Denison's method (3) is more closely akin to Green's criterion, but is not identical with it.

43. Green (1964, p. 94).

other hand, where an individual wishes to assess his potential future flow of output, and associates the likelihood of this flow concretely with the capital goods at his present command, he is no longer directly concerned with the marginal productivities at all. So that where a legitimate interest in a homogeneous forward-looking capital measure may exist, the specification of the production function (and the possibility of its changing under the impact of technological progress) no longer holds our attention.

And again, pursuing further the views developed in the discussion in the first half of this chapter, the whole search for an "objective" forward-looking measure of capital, involving, as we have seen, all the ambiguities and confusion arising from the treatment of complementary inputs, seems to imply an unfortunate approach to the problem. What is being sought by the writers whom we have cited in the present section is a forward-looking measure of capital that in no way depends on the decisions to be taken with respect to the employment of the capital goods in question. It may almost be described, perhaps, as a technological rather than an economic measure of the output capacity of the capital. What is being sought, in this literature, is a measure of capital that should express its productive potential in the same way as an engineer might express the thermal capacity of a particular fuel. Naturally this capital measure encounters the problems and ambiguities created by the alternative ways in which the capital goods can be combined with the other inputs—the very alternatives which impose the necessity to make decisions. The truth is that when one considers a forward-looking measure of capital one ought to renounce interest in all other aspects of the capital stock in question and inquire only into the output flow which possession of the existing stock promises to generate. From this point of view the forward-looking capital measure measures future prospects; it is of the essence of the theory of capitalistic production that future prospects *cannot* be simply read off from the list of capital goods now possessed. Future prospects represent the output flow expected from a *particular* plan being contemplated with respect to the capital stock now possessed. Only in the context of such a contemplated plan can the owner of a stock of capital measure it in a forward-looking manner.

Market Value as a Measure of Capital

We turn now to review briefly the manner in which the capital measurement literature has dealt with the possibility of using the market prices of capital goods as a measure of the quantity of capital they represent.

As Lerner has observed, this procedure is most tempting; a market value is expressed in terms of homogeneous money, it is a value measure that can be related to income, it corresponds to the way in which the businessman measures his capital, it facilitates calculations involving the rate of interest.[44] Nonetheless, many economists have expressed uneasiness on the matter, both from the point of view of the practical feasibility of the procedure, and from that of its theoretical validity.

As far as concerns the practical feasibility of measuring the quantity of capital represented by a collection of capital goods by reference to their market value, the problem is a simple one. It has been pointed out that the characteristic immobility and specificity of capital goods leads to a high level of transaction costs, with a consequently weak second-hand market. Market prices for most goods in the capital stock are thus difficult to obtain.[45] This difficulty, of course, is of more concern to the statistician than to the theorist.[46]

From the theoretical standpoint the market value measure of capital has been criticized on a variety of grounds. It has been pointed out that market prices reflect individual valuation only as made at the margin, so that the use of market prices to measure the total value of capital is inappropriate. (This criticism is, of course, relevant to the measurement also of other economic quantities, such as that of consumer goods, in terms of market value.)[47] This objection seems a very powerful one with respect to attempts to measure the quantity of capital in the economy as a whole.

It has also been pointed out that, for purposes of comparison over time, not many of the characteristic problems of capital measurement can generally be avoided by the use of market values. As soon as one wishes to make corrections in order to adjust for price changes over time, one is faced with the problem of constructing an index of capital goods prices. But in order to construct such an index one must be able to measure the quantity of capital in units other than money. We are "back to the point where we started."[48] It ought to be observed that this objection has rel-

44. Lerner (1953, p. 539).

45. Hicks (1961, p. 19); Barna (1961, p. 79); Domar (1961, p. 404); Smith (1962, p. 487).

46. However, Mrs. Robinson (1954, p. 120) points out that the narrowness of the market affects the theoretical value of the prices actually prevailing on it.

47. Kennedy (1955, p. 38). See also Knight (1956, p. 47n); Hicks (1963, p. 343).

48. Barzel (1964, p. 142); see also Ruggles and Ruggles (1961, p. 391); Hicks (1963, p. 344).

evance primarily to the use of market values in order to measure capital goods viewed as mere physical goods. When market values are considered (as they were, with limited results, in the first half of this chapter) in order to facilitate a backward- or forward-looking capital measure, the problem of adjusting for price changes is in principle no more difficult than it is in connection with other kinds of economic measurements.[49]

Several writers have objected to the market-value measurement of capital quantity "because we do not identify quantity with money value for any other class of commodities, so how can we justify it for this one?"[50] Lerner, for example, shows how the measurement of labor by its market value might lead to a *reduction* in the quantity of labor (so measured) when the number of man-hours worked is in fact increasing. The confusing consequences for the specification of the marginal product of labor are not difficult to imagine.[51] This objection, too, seems to have relevance only to the measurement of capital in the sense of physical goods; only then can one demand parallelism with the measurement procedures used with the other factors of production. Nonetheless it *is* important to notice the asymmetry between the treatment of other factors of production on the one hand, and of capital (in the forward-looking sense, say) on the other hand. This asymmetry has been noticed by several writers.[52]

A number of writers are dissatisfied with a market value measure of capital because they are interested in a measurement of the quantity of capital partly in order to explain the rate of interest. Since the market values of capital goods necessarily reflect already the rate of interest (at which future yields are discounted), the resulting aggregate quantity can hardly be used as an independent factor in explaining the determination of the market rate of interest.[53] One's appraisal of the seriousness of this objection will depend on the importance one attaches to an explanation of market interest rate determination that rests on the aggregate quantity of capital in the economy. (And it must not be forgotten that, no matter what the market rate of interest, the participants in the capital goods market never lose sight of their own individual *subjective* scales of time

---

49. Cf. Hicks (1963, p. 344).
50. Dorfman (1959b, p. 352).
51. Lerner (1953, p. 539).
52. See, e.g., Hicks (1961, p. 30n). Cf. also Denison (1957, pp. 228f.).
53. Robinson (1954, p. 115); Sen (1960, p. 18); Dorfman (1959b, p. 352).

preference, in their calculations of the present subjective value to them of anticipated output flows of various time-shapes.)

Ultimately, then, the usefulness of market values for capital measurement depends on what precisely it is that one is seeking to measure. If it is physical things that one seeks to measure, without regard to their "capital" character, then clearly market values will not do. Market values reflect the valuations of the market participants. If it is in the past ("cost") history of the capital goods that one is interested, market values can again be of little use; market prices do not in general directly reflect bygone conditions.[54] Only if one is interested in a forward-looking measure of capital do market values hold any promise of being at all useful. The limitations to their usefulness in this regard (especially insofar as concerns the aggregate quantity of capital in an economy) have been discussed in the first half of this chapter.

Cost Measurements of Capital

Among the various proposals toward the measurement of capital that have been put forward in the literature are a group which concern themselves with the *cost* of capital goods. We will now briefly examine these proposals, and discuss their relationship to the "backward-looking" capital measure that was considered (and rejected) in the first half of this chapter.

The attempt to measure the quantity of capital represented by the cost of capital goods has been made in a number of variants. We find (a) real cost measures; (b) cost measures in terms of forgone consumption goods; and (c) a cost measure that differs from either of these two measures which has been proposed by Denison.

(a) Real cost measures seek to measure capital by finding out what inputs the capital goods "embody." If capital good A was produced by 10,000 man-hours of labor, then it is to be described as consisting of twice the capital represented by capital good B, produced by 5,000 man-hours. Good A embodies twice the input embodied by good B. In principle a real cost measure of capital could be devised such that all inputs (including if so considered, "abstinence" or "waiting")[55] should be reflected in

54. On this, see the exchange between Denison and Kuznets, in Kuznets (1957, pp. 275, 283).

55. On the notion of measuring the congealed quantity of waiting "embodied" in capital goods, see Dorfman (1959b) and our discussion above, pp. 88–91.

the measure.[56] Mrs. Robinson, however, has proposed a pure labor-cost measure of capital.[57] The obvious weaknesses of this rather surprising proposal have been thoroughly criticized by a number of writers, among whom we may perhaps include Mrs. Robinson herself.[58] One general objection (over and above these criticisms) thrusts itself forward, from the point of view adopted in this essay, against all real-cost measures. This is that, as explained in the first half of this chapter, they cannot reflect the past sacrifices, subjectively understood, that were undertaken for the sake of today's capital goods. All that real-cost descriptions of capital goods can furnish is the *technical,* not the economic, history of these goods. (Even the inclusion of "waiting" in the real-cost concept that Dorfman has presented does not exempt it from this stricture, because, as discussed in the preceding chapter, the waiting concept used is itself not appropriate to the explication of the economic choices made.)

(b) A second cost measure of capital is that which measures a stock of capital goods by the sacrifice in terms of consumption goods that the capital goods represent. While no thoroughgoing attempt to develop such a measure seems to have been undertaken, a number of writers have discussed the possibility of such a measure, and seem to have assumed its theoretical validity.[59] The basic idea is to reduce the capital stock to "its equivalent" in consumption goods, on the basis of the universal necessity to forgo the latter if capital is to be possessed. If this can be accomplished, if capital can be expressed as its equivalent in consumption goods, we would have a measure that can be compared with income and can be used in conjunction with interest rate comparisons. Such a measure would be a cost measure since it represents the opportunity cost, in terms of immediate consumption, of the capital stock.[60]

While there is a certain initial attractiveness in a proposal to measure

56. See, e.g., Denison (1957, p. 227, n. 13). Cf. also Hicks (1961) for a "backward-looking" measure of capital, the philosophy of which differs considerably, however, from the real cost measures here discussed.

57. Robinson (1954, p. 115; 1956, p. 20).

58. Kendrick (1961, pp. 106–8); Samuelson (1962, pp. 203–4); Lachmann (1958, pp. 94–95); see also Sen (1960, p. 18); Robinson (1954, pp. 115–16).

59. Denison (1957, p. 227, n. 13); Kuznets (1957, p. 276); Robinson (1956, pp. 119–21); Hicks (1963, p. 343).

60. Mrs. Robinson (1954, p. 116), in arguing for a labor cost measure of capital, rejects the consumption sacrifice cost of capital notion, "for the addition to the stock of productive equipment made by adding an increment of capital depends upon how

capital—representing the basis of our anticipations for greater "future" consumption—in terms of the associated sacrifice of "present" consumption, the proposal cannot be pronounced theoretically satisfying. A comparison of the notion of sacrifice involved in such a proposal with that which provided the rationale for the (unsuccessful) search for a backward-looking capital measure in the first half of this chapter at once reveals the inadequacies of the proposal here being discussed. This proposal finds the quantity of consumption goods that has a market value equal to that of the capital stock, and then immediately states the former quantity to be what is forgone in order to maintain possession of the latter. Now insofar as the *individual* capital owner is concerned, it is quite true that the market value of his capital goods expresses the immediate consumption that he rejects in order to ensure for himself the future output flow to be derived from his capital stock. This expresses his subjective assessment of the present value of the future output stream as being greater than the current market price of the capital goods (in terms of its current purchasing power over consumption goods).[61] This, after all, was the reasoning behind the use of the market value of capital as a forward-looking measure. But it is difficult to see how this provides the basis for an aggregate measure of capital (as the writers cited above apparently intend it to be used). It is difficult to read meaning into such a concept as the aggregate present consumption forgone for the sake of the aggregate capital stock. How could a choice be made *now* by the economy as a whole between its entire stock of capital on the one hand, and its "equivalent" in consumption goods on the other? If the sacrifice in consumption goods pertains to that which has been forgone in the *past* during the history of the accumulation of the present capital stock, then, as discussed at length in the first half of this chapter, it is necessary to specify the decisions responsible for these sacrifices, and it is further necessary to gauge these sacrifices in terms of the choices made at the dates of these decisions, and in terms of the value rankings relevant to these dates. Nothing in the brief statements of the proposal here under discussion makes any mention of all this, or of the theoretical difficulties we have already seen all this to entail.

---

much work is done in constructing it, not upon the cost, in terms of final product, of an hour's labor."

61. Green (1964, p. 88), in fact, has used this insight to justify measuring capital in terms of its equivalent in current consumption goods, not as a cost measure, but as a measure of prospective yield.

(c) We refer finally to the rather special cost measure proposed by Denison in his pioneering paper on capital measurement.[62] Denison specifically rejects forward-looking measures of capital, and asks for a measure based on cost. Two machines which, in a given year, would cost equal amounts to produce, are to be described as consisting of equal quantities of capital, in spite of the possibly superior productivity of one of the machines. Denison emphasizes[63] that his is not a real cost measure: two identical machines produced in different years, with different quantities of labor, still represent equal quantities of capital, because in any given year they would be produced at equal cost (since they are identical). In fact, it is clear, Denison's measure is not all a "cost" measure in the sense of measuring the economic sacrifice historically involved. Rather Denison is attempting to measure machines in *physical* terms and reasons that physically equal things can be produced by physically identical inputs in a given year. This provides the rationale for using production cost as an index of physical quantity. One's appraisal of this measure must largely rest on what one conceives it to be that one wishes to measure. Denison's own interest, as developed at length in his paper, is quite a practical one. For those seeking a notion of capital measurement that should help to sharpen one's theoretical concept of the nature of capital and its place in the production process, Denison's measure can be of little assistance.

The Durability of Capital as an Obstacle to Measurement
Our review of the capital measurement literature has revealed a number of aspects of the matter that have given rise to difficulty. In closing this survey we draw attention briefly to one further aspect which, in the opinion of several writers, is responsible for much of the practical difficulty of measuring capital. These writers refer to the durability of capital goods as a source of difficulty.[64] The matter is of some interest in that it reveals what these writers seek to be measured by a capital measure, and also illustrates their view on the economic role of capital in production.

Where two otherwise identical machines are of different durabilities, these writers contend, the market will value the longer lasting machines more highly and will thus distort the measurement of the quantity of cap-

62. Denison (1957, pp. 218, 222–27).

63. Ibid. (pp. 227, 282).

64. Haavelmo (1960, p. 82); Griliches (1963, p. 118); Domar (1961, p. 404); Andersen (1965, p. 69).

ital. What we have here are two identical machines, but the market does not consider them identical. In order to obtain a correct capital measure, it is thus necessary to adjust by reducing the value placed on the more durable machine.

Clearly what is being sought to be measured is "the number of machines," rather than the quantity of capital represented by these machines, in any of the senses usually attached to the term. The focus of attention for these writers is not a period of time long enough for the different durabilities of the machines to make a difference, but rather one so short that each of the "identical" machines be for all practical purposes equal to the other. The search for such a measure of physical things necessarily diverts attention from the future economic history of these things, and also (insofar as different costs may have been incurred for the sake of different durabilities) diverts attention from the past economic history of these things. We are left with the search for a measure of physical things in respect of which varying durability is a distinct nuisance.

More fundamentally, it seems, at least part of the problem raised for these writers by varying durability is to be ascribed to the particular view of the nature of capital that has been discussed in Chapter 2 in connection with the work of Haavelmo and of Smith. It will be recalled that these writers saw the function of capital in production to consist of making its productive contribution by simply being there. In this view the essence of the role of capital is to increase the productivity of the flow inputs while itself not being used up. It follows that, insofar as different machines are capital, their productive contribution is completely independent of their durabilities. Where the market bids the price of the prospectively longer-lived machine higher, this in no way reflects any greater quantity of the *currently stocked* input. With the time aspect of production plans pushed into the background in this way, the first requisite for a measure of capital is to adjust matters so that the varying lives of different machines can be ignored.[65]

---

65. Cf. also Smith (1962, p. 486, n. 3).

ESSAY 3 LUDWIG VON MISES AND THE
THEORY OF CAPITAL AND INTEREST

Students of Misesian economics often agree that the theory of capital and interest occupies a central and characteristically Austrian position in the general Misesian system. That is the reason Frank H. Knight, in his lengthy and critical review article of the first complete exposition of that system,[1] chose to concentrate on "the theory of capital and interest" after deciding to confine his review to "some one main problem which at once is peculiarly central in the structure of theory, and on which [his] disagreement with the author reaches down to basic premises and methods."[2] In that article, Knight identified Mises as the foremost exponent of the Austrian position on capital and interest. In a 1945 article, Friedrich A. Hayek also alluded to Mises as the most thoroughgoing among the Austrians on these problems.[3]

And yet, in his published works, Mises appears to have devoted little attention to the theories of capital and interest until relatively late in his career. His influence on these matters was largely confined to his oral teaching and seminar discussions. As late as 1941, presumably without having seen Mises's *Nationalökonomie,* published in 1940, Hayek remarked in his *Pure Theory of Capital* that, while Mises's "published work deals mainly with the more complex problems that only arise beyond the point at which [this book] ends," Mises had nonetheless "suggested some of the angles from which the more abstract problem is approached [in this book]."[4]

Apart from a 1931 *Festschrift* paper on inconvertible capital,[5] Mises's published work on capital and interest prior to 1940 is confined (apart from casual *obiter dicta*) to a few brief pages in his *Socialism.*[6] On the other hand, there is an intriguing, somewhat cryptic footnote in the sec-

---

Presented at a session of the meetings of the Southern Economic Association, held at Atlanta, Georgia, November 1974.

1. Mises (1940).

2. Knight (1941, p. 410).

3. Hayek (1945, p. 22).

4. Hayek (1941, p. 45).

5. Mises (1931). For bibliographical information on Mises's works I am indebted to Bettina Bien [Greaves] (1969).

6. Mises (1959, pp. 142–43).

ond (1924) edition of his *Theory of Money and Credit*.[7] It makes clear that, since 1912, Mises (a) had given much critical thought to the theory of interest, (b) now considered Eugen von Böhm-Bawerk, while "the first to clear the way that leads to understanding of the problem," nonetheless to have presented a theory that was *not* satisfactory, and (c) hoped to publish "in the not-too-distant future" his own special study of the problem. It is certainly unfortunate that Mises never published such a study and that we are forced to rely on a relatively meager collection of scattered remarks in his larger works in order to understand what he considered unsatisfactory about Böhm-Bawerk's position. Fortunately, while his later works do not include a detailed critical discussion of Böhm-Bawerk's writings, they do provide us with a complete theoretical treatment of the problems of capital and interest, thereby justifying Knight's claim that the theory of capital and interest occupies a central position in the Misesian system. In what follows I shall first summarize Mises's own views on the problems of capital and interest and then discuss the extent to which his views differed from those of Böhm-Bawerk and Knight. In so doing, we shall discover that Mises's later position is, as was noted by both Knight and Hayek, characteristically and consistently Austrian.

MISES ON CAPITAL AND ON INTEREST

Mises's views on capital and interest may be conveniently summarized as follows:

1. Interest is *not* the specific income derived from using capital goods,[8] nor is it "the price paid for the services of capital."[9] Instead, interest expresses the universal ("categorial") phenomenon of time preference and will therefore inevitably emerge also in a pure exchange economy without production.

2. Since production takes time, the market prices of factors of production (which tend to reflect the market prices of the consumer goods they produce) are themselves subject to considerations of time preference. Thus the market in a production economy generates interest as the excess *value* of produced goods over the appropriately discounted values of the relevant factors of production.

7. Mises (1953, p. 339, and esp. p. 24).
8. Mises (1949, p. 521).
9. Ibid. (p. 523).

3. The concept of *capital* (as well as of its correlative *income*) is strictly a tool for economic calculation and hence has meaning only in the context of a market in which monetary calculation is meaningful. Thus, capital is properly defined as the subjectively perceived monetary value of the owner's equity in the assets of a particular business unit. *Capital* is therefore to be sharply distinguished from *capital goods.*

4. Capital goods are produced factors of production; they are "intermediary stations on the way leading from the very beginning of production to its final goal, the turning out of consumers' goods."[10]

5. It is decidedly *not* useful to define capital as the totality of capital goods. Nor does the concept of a *totality* of capital goods provide any insight into the productive process.

6. Capital goods are the results of earlier (i.e., higher) stages of production and therefore are not factors of production in their own right apart from the factors employed in their production. Capital goods have no productive power of their own that cannot be attributed to these earlier productive factors.

In his discussion about capital and interest, Mises did not, to any extent, name the specific authors with whom he took issue. As Knight observed, with respect to the entire volume that he was reviewing, Mises's exposition of capital and interest "is highly controversial in substance, and in tone, though the argument is directed toward positions, with very little debate or *Auseinandersetzung* with named authors."[11]

The hints Mises himself gave, together with a careful comparison of his own stated views with those of other capital theorists, enable us to understand how his views relate to the more widely known theories of capital and interest against which he was rebelling. Such an understanding is of the utmost importance in order to fully appreciate Mises's contribution. In the following analysis I shall indicate the points of disagreement between Mises and the two major contesting approaches of his time on the issue of capital and interest. I shall consider the Böhm-Bawerkian tradition first and then move on to review the (John Bates) Clark–Knight point of view.

10. Ibid. (p. 490).
11. Knight (1941, p. 409).

MISES AND THE BÖHM-BAWERKIAN THEORY

We have already seen that, as early as 1924, Mises had expressed dissatisfaction with Böhm-Bawerk's theory. This may come as a surprise to those who—quite mistakenly—believe the Austrian position on most questions of economic theory, and especially on the theory of capital and interest, is a monolithic one. The truth of the matter is that, while the suggestive brilliance of Böhm-Bawerk's contribution won international recognition as typifying the work of the Austrian School, it was by no means acceptable to other leading representatives of that school. It is by now well known, as reported by Joseph A. Schumpeter, that Carl Menger considered Böhm-Bawerk's theory of capital and interest to have been "one of the greatest errors ever committed."[12] Referring specifically not only to Menger but also to Friedrich von Wieser and to Schumpeter himself, Hayek remarked that those "commonly regarded as the leaders of the 'Austrian School' of economics" did not accept Böhm-Bawerk's views.[13] So we should not be overly surprised at Mises's disagreement with his own mentor's teachings.

Mises's disagreements with the Böhm-Bawerkian theory reflect a consistent theme. Mises was concerned with distilling Böhm-Bawerk's basic ideas from the non-subjective, technical, and empirical garb in which they had been presented. Mises tried to show that Böhm-Bawerk's basic ideas flowed smoothly out of his own praxeological approach, or, in other words, that they could be cast in a strictly subjectivist mold. Knight correctly characterized Mises as taking an extreme Austrian position on interest by refusing to attribute any explanatory role to the objective, or physical, conditions governing production in a capital-using world. As the Austrian theory of value depends on utility considerations, with no recognition accorded to objective costs, so too, Knight explained, the Misesian theory of interest depends entirely on subjective time preference, with no influence attributed to physical productivity.[14] One is reminded of Hayek's penetrating comment concerning the nature of Mises's contribution to economics. Remarking that "it is probably no exaggeration to say

12. See Schumpeter (1954, p. 847). See also Streissler (1973, p. 231).

13. Hayek (1941, p. 46n). For Hayek's criticisms of Böhm-Bawerk's work, see ibid., pp. 414–23. A critique of Böhm-Bawerk by an "Austrian" theorist may be found in Lachmann (1956).

14. Knight (1941, p. 422).

that every important advance in economic theory during the last hundred years was a further step in the consistent application of subjectivism,"[15] Hayek cited Mises as the economist who most consistently carried out this subjectivist development: "Probably all the characteristic features of his theories . . . follow directly . . . from this central position."[16] More specifically, Mises's theory of capital and interest is in disagreement with Böhm-Bawerk's on the following points:

1. *On the role of time*   Mises, while paying tribute to the "imperishable merits" of Böhm-Bawerk's seminal role in the development of the time-preference theory, sharply criticized the epistemological perspective from which Böhm-Bawerk viewed time as entering the analysis. For Böhm-Bawerk time preference is an empirical regularity observed through casual psychological observation. Instead, Mises saw time preference as a "definite categorial element . . . operative in every instance of action."[17] In Mises's view, Böhm-Bawerk's theory failed to do justice to the universality and inevitability of the phenomenon of time preference. In addition, Mises took Böhm-Bawerk to task for not recognizing that time should enter analysis only in the *ex ante* sense. The role time "plays in action consists entirely in the choices acting man makes between periods of production of different length. The length of time expended in the past for the production of capital goods available today does not count at all. . . . The 'average period of production' is an empty concept."[18] It may be remarked that here Mises identified a source of perennial confusion concerning the role of time in the Austrian theory. Many of the criticisms leveled by Knight and others against the Austrian theory are irrelevant when the theory is cast explicitly in terms of the time-conscious, *forward-looking decisions* made by producers and consumers.[19]

2. *On the role of productivity*   As already mentioned, Mises sharply deplored the concessions Böhm-Bawerk made to the productivity theorists. To Mises, it was both unfortunate and inexplicable that

15. Hayek (1955, p. 31).
16. Ibid. (p. 210, n. 24).
17. Mises (1949, p. 485). See also Mises (1960, p. 31).
18. Mises (1949, p. 486).
19. Kirzner (1966, pp. 79, 99; present edition, pp. 80, 97–98).

Böhm-Bawerk, who in his critical history of interest doctrines had "so brilliantly refuted" the productivity approach, himself fell, to some extent, into the same kind of error in his *Positive Theory*. There is some disagreement in the literature on the degree to which Böhm-Bawerk in fact allowed productivity considerations to enter his theory. The issue goes back at least to Frank A. Fetter's remark in 1902 that it "has been a surprise to many students of Böhm-Bawerk to find that he has presented a theory, the most prominent feature of which is the technical productiveness of roundabout processes. His criticism of the productivity theories of interest has been of such a nature as to lead to the belief that he utterly rejected them. . . . [But] it appears from Böhm-Bawerk's later statement that he does not object to the productivity theory as a partial, but as an exclusive, explanation of interest."[20] Much later Schumpeter insisted that productivity plays only a subsidiary role in what is in fact wholly a time-preference theory.[21] It is of some interest to note that when Böhm-Bawerk considered the alternative roles for productivity in a time-conscious theory, he came out squarely for an interpretation that placed productivity and "impatience" on the same level.[22] Böhm-Bawerk made it very clear that he was not willing to identify his position with that of Fetter, who espoused a time-preference theory of interest without any mention of productivity considerations. Böhm-Bawerk remarked that "Fetter himself espouses a [theory which] places him on the outermost wing of the purely 'psychological' interest theorists— 'psychological' as opposed to 'technical.' He moves into a position far more extreme than the one I occupy."[23]

Certainly Mises offered a theory of interest fully as extreme as the one developed by Fetter. Later we shall consider Mises's denial that capital productivity has any role in interest theory.

3. *On the definition of capital*   Böhm-Bawerk defined capital as the aggregate of intermediate products (i.e., of produced means of production)[24] and in so doing was criticized by Menger.[25] Menger

20. Fetter (1902, p. 177).
21. Schumpeter (1954, pp. 931–32).
22. Böhm-Bawerk (1959a, p. 482, n. 112).
23. Ibid. (p. 476, n. 14).
24. Ibid. (pp. 14, 32).
25. Menger (1888, p. 17).

sought "to rehabilitate the abstract concept of capital as the money value of the property devoted to acquisitive purposes against the Smithian concept of the 'produced means of production.'"[26] As early as his work on *Socialism* (1923), Mises emphatically endorsed the Mengerian definition.[27] In *Human Action* he pursued the question even more thoroughly, though without making it explicit that he was objecting to Böhm-Bawerk's definition. Economists, Mises maintained, fall into the error of defining capital as *real capital*, as an aggregate of physical things. This is not only an empty concept but one that has been responsible for serious errors in the various uses to which the concept of capital has been applied.

Mises's refusal to accept the notion of capital as an aggregate of produced means of production expressed his consistent Austrian emphasis on forward-looking decision-making. Menger had already argued that "the historical origin of a commodity is irrelevant from an economic point of view."[28] Later Knight and Hayek were to claim that emphasis on the historical origins of produced means of production is a residual of the older cost-of-production perspectives and inconsistent with the valuable insight that bygones are bygones.[29] Thus, Mises's rejection of Böhm-Bawerk's definition reflects a thoroughgoing subjective point of view.

In addition, Mises's unhappiness with the Böhm-Bawerkian notion of capital is due to his characteristically Austrian skepticism toward economic aggregates. As Mises wrote, "[The] totality of the produced factors of production is merely an enumeration of physical quantities of thousands and thousands of various goods. Such an inventory is of no use to acting. It is a description of a part of the universe in terms of technology and topography and has no reference whatever to the problems raised by the endeavors to improve human well-being."[30] Lachmann suggested that a similar objection to the questionable practice of economic aggregation may have been the reason for Menger's own sharp disagreement with Böhm-Bawerk's theory.[31]

26. Hayek (1934, p. xxvi).
27. Mises (1959, pp. 123, 142).
28. Hayek (1934, p. xxvi).
29. Hayek (1941, p. 89).
30. Mises (1949, p. 263).
31. More precisely Lachmann suggested that Menger was objecting to the notion of the homogenization of capital (Lachmann, 1973a, p. 205).

In place of the Böhm-Bawerkian notion of capital, Mises took over Menger's definition of the term. Thus, in *Human Action*, Mises emphasized at great length that the measurement of capital has significance only for the role it plays in economic calculation. The term denotes, therefore, an accounting concept and depends for its measurement upon a system of market prices. Mises explained that "the capital concept is operative as far as men in their actions let themselves be guided by capital accounting."[32] At another place, Mises wrote: "Capital is the sum of the money equivalent of all assets minus the sum of the money equivalent of all liabilities as dedicated at a definite date to the conduct of the operations of a definite business unit."[33] It follows, in Mises's words, that capital "is inescapably linked with capitalism, the market economy. It is a mere shadow in economic systems in which there is no market exchange and no money prices of goods of all orders."[34] We shall return to several implications of Mises's substitution of the Mengerian capital concept for Böhm-Bawerk's definition.

MISES AND THE CLARK-KNIGHT TRADITION

If Mises's writings on capital and interest diverge from Böhm-Bawerk's theory, they certainly imply a total rejection of the principal alternative to that tradition, the approach developed in the writings of both Clark and Knight. The Clark-Knight concept of capital and the productivity theory of interest came under sharp attack in Mises's major (later) works. As we have mentioned, Knight's review article of Mises's *Nationalökonomie* consisted almost entirely of an attack on Mises's theory of capital and interest, coupled with a restatement and clarification of Knight's own position. By enumerating Mises's various objections to the Clark-Knight view, we acquire, at the same time, a more complete understanding of Mises's disagreement with Böhm-Bawerk. The reason is that the Knightian theory of interest is, as Knight proclaimed, completely opposed to the "absolute Austrianism" of Mises's approach. And what Mises found objectionable in Böhm-Bawerk's theory were, again, just those points in it that he saw as incompatible with a consistently Austrian perspective. So it is entirely understandable why Mises's position with regard to Böhm-Bawerk's theory is clarified by his criticisms of Clark's and Knight's

32. Mises (1949, p. 512).
33. Ibid. (p. 262).
34. Mises (1949, p. 512).

views. We may group Mises's objections to the Clark-Knight position as follows.

1. The Clark-Knight Concept of Capital

Mises had little patience with the notion of capital as a self-perpetuating fund, which he (and others) declared to be sheer mysticism.[35] "An existence," Mises wrote, "has been attributed to 'capital,' independent of the capital goods in which it is embodied. Capital, it is said, reproduces itself and thus provides for its own maintenance. . . . All this is nonsense."[36]

It is easy to see how foreign the notion of the "automatic maintenance of capital" must have appeared to Mises. An approach that concentrates analytical attention—as Austrian economics does—on the purposive and deliberate decisions of individual human beings when accounting for all social economic phenomena must treat the notion of capital as a spontaneously growing plant as not merely factually incorrect but simply absurd.[37] Moreover, Mises sensed that such Knightian ideas can lead men to dangerous mistakes in public policy when they ignore the institutional framework and incentive system needed to encourage those deliberate decisions necessary for maintaining the capital stock and enhancing its continued growth.[38]

The Misesian critique of the Clark-Knight view and his endorsement of the Mengerian capital concept suggest what Mises might have said about Hicks's recent classification of the views of economists concerning the aggregate of productive assets as being either "fundist" or "materialist."[39]

---

35. For a listing of writers who have ascribed "mysticism" or "mythology" to the Clark-Knight concept of capital, see Kirzner (1966, p. 59; present edition, p. 63).

36. Mises (1949, p. 512).

37. As Knight did in his well-known "Crusonia Plant" example (Knight, 1944, p. 29).

38. Mises (1949, p. 840).

39. Hicks (1974, pp. 308–10). According to Hicks, "fundists" are those who see capital as something apart from the physical goods of which it happens to consist at a particular time. The "materialists" are those who refuse to see capital in any sense other than the physical goods that make it up. Hicks's terminology here is quite unfortunate and may lead to a misunderstanding of his own thesis. From what has been said in the text, it would seem that Clark and Knight are what Hicks meant when he spoke of "fundists." It turns out, however, that Hicks classified them as "materialists"! The Austrian school (which is vehemently opposed to the Clark-Knight notion of capital as a self-perpetuating fund) turns out, in Hicks's classification, to be "fundist" because it viewed the stock of capital goods in terms of the multiperiod future plans in

Mises would have rejected a fundism that, by submerging the separate physical capital goods, ends up concentrating on some supposed quality apart from the goods themselves. He would have argued that the recognition of the time-conscious plans of producers does not require that we submerge the individualities of these goods into, say, a notion such as the average period of production. And, as we have seen, he rejected out of hand the Clarkian view—in Hicks's opinion a "materialist" view—that, by abstracting from the multiperiod plans needed to generate output with capital goods, sees these goods spontaneously generating perpetual flows of net income. In fact, Mises would argue, the entire fundist-materialist debate is predicated on the quite unfortunate practice of directing attention to the aggregate of physical goods. The only useful purpose for a capital concept consists strictly in its accounting role as a tool for economic calculation, a role enormously important for the efficient operation of a productive economy. It was, Mises would insist, Böhm-Bawerk's failure to see all this, and his willingness to accept the basis for a fundist-materialist debate, that lent credence to a Clark-Knight view of the real-capital concept, which implied the mythology of a kind of fundism ("perpetual capital") that Böhm-Bawerk himself did *not* accept. In rejecting Böhm-Bawerk's definition of capital in favor of the Mengerian definition, Mises rendered the Hicksian classification inapplicable to his own work.

2. Trees and Fruit

Mises's adoption of Menger's concept of capital made it possible for him to avoid the pitfalls in interest theory that stem from the *capital-income* dichotomy. In everyday lay experience the ownership of capital provides assurance of a steady income. As soon as capital is identified as some aggregate of factors of production, it becomes tempting to ascribe the steady income that capital ownership makes possible as somehow expressing the *productivity* of these factors. This has always been the starting point for productivity theories of interest. Knight's permanent-fund-of-capital view of physical capital is simply a variant of those theories that view interest as net income generated perpetually by the productivity of the abstract capital temporarily embodied in particular lumps of physical capital. The

---

which they enter. The Clark-Knight notion of capital as a fund is therefore quite different from the Austrian notion of a fund. Clearly, in the Clark-Knight view, capital goods are not the representatives of *plans* for future production processes but rather permanent sources of automatic income flow. (See Essay 5, below, pp. 169–78.)

capital stock, in this view, is a permanent tree that spontaneously and continuously produces fruit (interest).[40] Mises was explicit in concluding that this erroneous view of interest results from defining capital as an aggregate of produced factors of production. "The worst outgrowth of the use of the mythical notion of real capital was that economists began to speculate about a spurious problem called the productivity of (real) capital." It was such speculation, Mises made clear, that is responsible for the "blunder" of explaining "interest as an income derived from the productivity of capital."[41]

The Mengerian concept of capital as an accounting tool enables us to steer clear of such blunders. The accounting concept comes into play only as reflecting a particular motive that calculating human beings display: "The calculating mind of the actor draws a boundary line between the consumer's goods which he plans to employ for the immediate satisfaction of his wants and the goods . . . which he plans to employ for providing by further acting, for the satisfaction of future wants."[42] There is no implication whatsoever that the flow of income thus achieved for consumption—through the careful deployment of capital—is the automatic fruit of the productivity of capital.

3. The Structure of the Productive Process

Perhaps at the core of Mises's rejection of the Clark-Knight productivity theory of interest lies his wholehearted support of the Mengerian insight that the productive process consists of deploying goods of higher order toward the production of goods of lower order. "It is possible to think of the producers' goods as arranged in orders according to their proximity to the consumers' good for whose production they can be used. Those producers' goods which are the nearest to the production of a consumers' good are ranged in the second order, and accordingly those which are used for the production of goods of the second order, in the third order and so on."[43] The purpose of such a scheme of classification is to demonstrate "how the valuation and the prices of the goods of higher orders are dependent on the valuation and the prices of the goods of lower orders pro-

40. See note 37 above.
41. Mises (1949, pp. 263–64).
42. Ibid. (pp. 260–61).
43. Ibid. (p. 94).

duced by their expenditure."[44] This fundamental approach to the pricing of productive factors is able, Mises explained, to lay aside the reasoning of the productivity theorists. *The prices of capital goods must reflect the services expected from their future employment.*[45] In the absence of time preference the price of a piece of land or of a capital good—that is, the price in terms of consumer goods—would equal the undiscounted sum of the marginal values of the future services attributed to it. The productive capacity of a factor cannot, without time preference, account for a flow of interest income on its market value. The phenomenon of interest arises because, as a result of time preference, factor prices reflect only the *discounted* values of their services. "As production goes on, the factors of production are transformed or ripen into present goods of a higher value."[46] For Mises, the important economic characteristic of capital goods is not merely that they can be employed in future production, but that the relationship they bear to their future products is one of higher-order goods to those of lower order. It is this factor that vitiates the productivity theory.

Knight's refusal to grant merit to this reasoning must be seen as a consequence of his rejecting Menger's position that factors of production are really *higher-order* goods. "Perhaps the most serious defect in Menger's economic system . . . is his view of production as a process of converting goods of higher order into goods of lower order."[47] Because the Knightian view of the productive process emphasizes the repetitive "circular flow" of economic activity while denying the paramount importance of a *structural order* linked to final consumer demand, it is possible to simply ignore the Austrian critique of the productivity theory of interest. In essence, this is what Knight did.

MISES, CAPITALISTS, AND ENTREPRENEURSHIP

One final observation concerning Mises's theory of capital and interest is in order. At all times Mises stressed what he termed the "integration of catallactic functions" that takes place in the real world. Real-world capitalists, Mises constantly reminds us, must of necessity—like landowners, laborers, and consumers—be also *entrepreneurs*. "A capitalist [besides

44. Ibid.
45. Ibid. (pp. 263–64).
46. Ibid. (p. 522).
47. Knight (1950, p. 25).

investing funds] is always also virtually an entrepreneur and speculator. He always runs the chance of losing his funds."[48] It follows that "interest stipulated and paid in loans includes not only originary interest but also entrepreneurial profit."[49]

In other words, entrepreneurship exists in capital-using production processes, not only in the usual sense that an entrepreneur-producer borrows or otherwise assembles capital as part of his entrepreneurial function, but also in the more subtle sense that the capitalists themselves, in lending their capital to entrepreneur-producers, are necessarily acting entrepreneurially. While this does not prevent us from analytically isolating the pure capitalist and pure entrepreneurial functions, it does mean that in the real world originary interest and entrepreneurial profit are never found in isolation from one another.

48. Mises (1949, p. 254).
49. Ibid. (p. 533).

THE PURE TIME-PREFERENCE THEORY OF

INTEREST: AN ATTEMPT AT CLARIFICATION

For almost a century a particular theory of interest has been again and again discussed, refuted, defended, ignored, forgotten, and re-discovered; somehow it has managed to survive. This theory is the pure time-preference theory (often to be referred to in this paper as PTPT). For the most part this theory has, especially during the last half-century, languished as a basically discredited, definitely unfashionable, point of view. Yet the theory was never finally interred—nor did it even wholly expire. The theory is often described as Austrian, but, as we shall see, it is not the only and not the best known Austrian theory of interest. In recent decades a certain revival of discussion has emerged surrounding this pure time-preference theory (partly, no doubt, as a result of the modest revival of interest in Austrian economics generally). Almost invariably contemporary economists have reacted to renewed discussions of the pure time-preference theory with utter disbelief and plain bewilderment. These critics have found the theory simply incredible; the idea that the phenomenon of interest is in *no* way dependent upon physical productivity is one that the critics find patently absurd; that serious thinkers should accept this absurdity, they find quite incomprehensible. The present paper does not seek to argue any superiority of PTPT over its competitors in the field of interest theories. Rather we seek to dispel the bewilderment that moderns display in regard to it. This task of clarification will turn out to involve certain "philosophical," extra-economic, issues that are of significance for economists in their own right, in several respects.

THE INTEREST PROBLEM

Much—perhaps all—will turn out to depend on the way in which the interest problem is formulated. For present purposes we adopt a modern formulation of the problem, but wish to emphasize that this formulation is very similar in spirit and character to classic formulations going back to Schumpeter[1]

This paper owes much to countless discussions with Ingo Pellengahr, over a two-year period. His open-minded but persistent questioning concerning troublesome aspects of PTPT helped (and compelled) the writer toward the present clarification. For Pellengahr's own perspective on the matters dealt with in this paper, see references to Pellengahr.

1. Schumpeter (1934).

and Böhm-Bawerk.[2] The modern formulation we cite is that of Hausman.[3] Hausman points out that an "individual's capital . . . enables that individual to earn interest. If the capital is invested in a machine, the sum of the rentals the machine earns over its lifetime is greater than the machine's cost. Why?" Common observation, that is, tells us that possession of a given stock of capital funds can, by judicious investment (say, in a machine) yield a continuous flow of income (annual rentals net of depreciation) without impairing the ability of the capital funds to serve indefinitely as a source of income. The problem is, how this can occur. *Why is not the price of the machine* (paid by the capitalist at the time he invests in the machine) *bid up* (by the competition of others eagerly seeking to capture the net surplus of rentals over cost)—*to the point where no such surplus remains?* We are seeking, then, an explanation for an observed phenomenon which is, in the absence of a theory of interest, unable to be accounted for. Absent a theory of interest, no interest income ought to be forthcoming, except as a transient phenomenon; competition ought to squeeze it out of existence.

Neoclassical theory has, in a variety of versions, seen interest as obtained and paid in return for special productive services of one kind or another. J. B. Clark and F. H. Knight saw capital as providing a flow of productive services, of which interest is the irrepressible expression. Competition does not erode it; ownership of a stock of capital inevitably confers title to a corresponding income flow. (We do not discuss, in this paper, the extent to which this theory in fact addresses the interest problem as formulated above.) For "Austrian" versions[4] of the neoclassical explanation, again, ownership of capital expresses the provision of a special productive service ("waiting") required in order to enjoy the enhanced fruits of more lengthy ("roundabout") processes of production. Competition cannot erode interest income: it *has* to be offered if potential capitalists (with positive time-preference) are to be persuaded to provide the waiting (needed in order to be able to enjoy the enhanced output available

2. Böhm-Bawerk (1959a, 1959b, 1959c) contains translations of three volumes: vol. 1, originally published in 1884; vol. 2, originally published in 1889; vol. 3, originally published in 1921.

3. Hausman (1981, p. 3).

4. As we shall see, there were two "Austrian" theories of interest, both deriving from Böhm-Bawerk, see Hayek (1941, app. 1). One of these, which (unlike Hayek) we identify with Fisher (and describe as neoclassical), is that discussed here in the text. The second is the PTPT, the subject of this paper.

through capital-using production). And, given the productivity of waiting, it *pays* to offer interest in order to elicit that waiting. In the celebrated "Cambridge Controversy" of some years back, this neoclassical view of interest was the *only* view advanced as an alternative to the neo-Ricardian perspective on interest as a surplus (to be explained, not by appeal to market exchange relations, but by "the relations between workers and capitalists including possibly their relative bargaining power").[5]

It will be useful for us to examine more carefully the above-cited "Austrian" variant of the productivity view (actually most carefully developed by Irving Fisher) in order to point up features of the alternative Austrian theory of interest, the pure time-preference theory. The pure time-preference theory (PTPT) was developed, largely from roots in Böhm-Bawerk, by Frank Fetter[6] in the United States, and later by Mises.[7] As Fetter pointed out, Böhm-Bawerk's own position appears in a number of ways to be an inconsistent one, demonstrating at some points the pure time-preference view, at other points the Fisherian physical productivity view. Let us note certain features of the Fisherian "productivity of waiting" theory.

We should note, first of all, that this theory is *not* necessarily vulnerable to the basic Böhm-Bawerkian criticism of all productivity-of-capital theories of interest. Böhm-Bawerk had criticized such theories of interest because they ignore the essential interest problem (as formulated above). It will not do to say that the machine yields interest (in the form of a flow of rentals that is greater than the cost of the machine) because the machine is physically productive. The interest problem consisted in asking why, given this physical productivity, did not the market value of the machine rise to reflect fully the rentals it is able to generate. Of course a tree produces fruit; the interest problem consists in the dilemma posed by the apparent failure of the market price of the tree to equal the value of the total fruit output. Simple theory tells us, after all, that the value of inputs and the value of outputs tend to equality in competitive markets.

The productivity-of-waiting theory of interest escapes this criticism by arguing that *besides* the machine, *besides* the tree, yet another "input" is required in order to command the flow of rentals (or fruit). This additional input is "waiting"; once the services of waiting are properly included in the list of needed inputs, the interest dilemma evaporates. Competition

---

5. Hausman (1981, p. 167).
6. Fetter (1902; reprinted in Rothbard, ed., 1977). Also, Fetter (1914).
7. Mises (1949).

indeed squeezes out all surplus above marginal productivity returns. Interest *is*, in this view, the marginal productivity return on a scarce factor, viz., waiting.

The Fisherian "productivity-of-waiting" theory emphatically recognizes the significance of time preference. It is the circumstance of positive time-preference that renders waiting a scarce, costly factor (to which interest can be attributed as a productivity return). But the interest income that might be considered the reward received by investors to induce them to provide waiting, is at the same time seen as *made possible only by the productivity of waiting*. (It is in this respect, particularly, that PTPT differs from the Fisher theory. For PTPT it is incorrect to see interest income as the "fruit" of anything. Rather PTPT sees interest income as a receipt that results from the pattern of prices governing intertemporal exchanges, with these prices expressing the prevalently positive time-preferences of the participants.)

As a matter of logic, the Fisher productivity-of-waiting theory deals with the interest problem (as formulated above) in impeccable manner. The only way through which the validity of the productivity-of-waiting view (at least insofar as we have presented it thus far) can be challenged, is by disagreeing with the concept of "waiting" as a productive factor service. The critic may refuse to recognize that waiting (or "time") is productive, or is regarded by prospective producers as a scarce factor. The fact that an inevitable time delay must be accepted before current efforts bear fruit, need not mean that time is a necessary *ingredient* in the production process; it may simply mean that this production process is a slow one, yielding a result less valuable (in terms of anticipated attractiveness) than an otherwise similar, more speedy process.

Clearly this question of whether to treat waiting as a productive ingredient must be recognized as a strictly "philosophical" question. No economic reasoning (and certainly no amount of empirical research) can reveal whether time is (or should be treated as) itself an active productive agent or only a medium permitting the flows of inputs to cumulate into the product.[8] Moreover it is conceivable that a given observer may be prepared to recognize time as an active productive agent in some processes of production (the maturing of wine, perhaps?) while refusing to recognize it as such in other time-consuming processes of production (as, per-

---

8. On this, see Haavelmo (1960, p. 47); Kirzner (1966, p. 97; present edition, p. 96).

haps, in considering the operation of an old-fashioned, slower machine as compared with that of a faster, more modern generation of machines). In any event the relevance of the "productivity-of-waiting" theory depends *entirely* on this "philosophical" question. (Part of the dilemma posed by Böhm-Bawerk's own statement of the theory of interest was that on the one hand he explicitly refused to accept time or waiting as an independent factor to stand with labor and nature,[9] yet seemed on the other hand to attribute interest to the physical circumstance that roundabout processes of production are more productive.) If time and waiting are not themselves to be considered productive agents, no interest could emerge as a result of the productivity of time-consuming processes of production (any more than interest can be ascribed to the fruitfulness of a tree).[10]

The basis on which the PTPT is dissatisfied with the Fisher (productivity-of-waiting) solution to the interest problem is thus strictly a noneconomic "philosophic" one—viz., a view of time (and thus of waiting) that sees it (as Böhm-Bawerk himself apparently saw it) as a neutral background medium, rather than as a positive, active ingredient in productive processes. It is this philosophic perspective that underlies the pure time-preference theory to be discussed in this paper. Given this philosophic perspective, then, we note that the interest problem has, therefore, thus far not been touched in the slightest by any productivity-of-roundaboutness considerations.

THE PURE TIME-PREFERENCE THEORY OF INTEREST

The alternative "Austrian" theory of interest that we wish to clarify in this paper, the PTPT, is that pursued consistently by the American Frank Fetter and by Ludwig von Mises. This theory solves the interest problem by appeal to widespread (possibly universal) positive time preference. If, in fact, people do prefer (other aspects of the situation aside) to achieve their goals sooner rather than later, then the dilemma posed by the machine and its rentals, or by the tree and its fruit, dissolves. The price paid for a tree tends systematically to fall short of the sum of its annual fruit yields, because when the tree is bought, the yields are only prospective yields. One is simply not prepared to pay $100 today in order to command $100 worth of fruit in five or ten years' time, no matter how ironclad the contract for the fruit delivery may be. The prospect of $100 available in the

9. Böhm-Bawerk (1959b, pp. 97–98).
10. Fetter (1902).

future has less attractive power than does the prospect of $100 available immediately. The PTPT argues that this solution of the interest problem is entirely sufficient to account for the interest phenomena we observe, in *all* their manifestations, in the simplest consumption loan context (in the pure-exchange economy), or in the most complex of financial-industrial situations. After all, production processes do take time, hence the present price of input services must, given positive time preference, systematically and repeatedly, fall short of the nominal value yielded in the future by their marginal productivity. A portion of currently emerging output must then regularly be retained each year by the capitalist who has, some time in the past, advanced the sums needed to pay for the input services whose output is now emerging. This retained interest income is not caused by, or made possible by the physical productivity of anything.

Such time preference considerations are able, then, to account completely for the phenomenon of interest. They are able, entirely without any appeal to productivity of roundaboutness, to answer the question formulated in the interest problem. On the other hand, as we have seen, the productivity of roundaboutness offered no solution at all to that problem (for those not recognizing waiting or time as a productive agent). Hence, in the view of its protagonists, this "pure" time-preference theory[11] is entirely adequate for its objective; *no productivity considerations can possibly enter at all into the explanation offered for interest.*

It is the latter contention that many theorists, from Böhm-Bawerk's time down to our own, have found simply incredible. These critics of PTPT find it unbelievable that the claim can be made that the market phenomenon of interest is never, in any way, under any circumstances, to be attributed to the productivity of capital or of roundaboutness, waiting, or time. It will be instructive to examine a recurring theme pursued by these critics in expressing their incredulity.

SHEEP, RICE, AND AUSTRIAN HOCUS-POCUS

These critics argue that simple hypothetical examples demonstrate that, at least under certain conditions, a positive rate of interest necessarily emerges, being strictly determined by physical productivity. These examples, the critics maintain, demonstrate that the old argument with which Böhm-Bawerk had demolished the simple productivity theories (viz., the

---

11. See Pellengahr (1986a, pp. 10–11) for several senses in which the adjective "pure" may be understood in the present context. Also, Pellengahr (1986b).

argument that competition ought to drive the market price of the productive agent to the point where it no longer yields a value surplus) cannot entirely drive productivity considerations out of the interest-theoretic picture. Whether or not we can find a logical flaw in the Böhm-Bawerkian argument, the stylized "facts" of these examples prove the argument to be specious. Productivity considerations are clearly sufficient to account for interest. It cannot, therefore, be the case that the explanation of interest must run in *purely* time-preference terms. The examples used by these critics vary in their details. H. G. Brown talked of fruit trees,[12] Irving Fisher talked of sheep,[13] Knight talked of his Crusonia plant (an edible plant that grew at a fixed rate continuously);[14] quite recently Samuelson constructed a rice example to drive home an essentially similar point. What these examples have in common is (a) that they postulate a given rate of physical productivity to the capital stock, a rate invariant to scale of production, or level of wealth; (b) that these examples *appear,* at least at first glance, to escape the impact of the traditional Böhm-Bawerkian argument (against productivity theories of interest) by confining the example to the context of a single-good world (in which the critics believe value productivity measures must coincide with physical productivity rates).[15] Let us examine the most recent of these examples, Samuelson's rice case (which he raised in a discussion of a different doctrinal issue).

Samuelson's case was introduced in the course of a recent critical reconsideration of Schumpeter's zero-interest doctrine.[16] Schumpeter had argued (on the basis of reasoning reflecting Böhm-Bawerk's arguments against the productivity theories of interest) that in a world in circular-flow equilibrium, the rate of interest must be zero, with all output value decomposed into land, rent, and labor wages, with nothing left for any interest share. Samuelson objects that a *possible* technological case refutes the Schumpeterian argument. The case Samuelson identifies is that of 100 units of rice ripening into 110 units of rice during the period of one year, without the input of any labor or any scarce land. This case shows, Samuelson claims, that final value need *not* necessarily be wholly swept

12. Brown (1914).

13. Fisher (1930, p. 193).

14. Knight (1944, p. 52).

15. Brown was dismayed at having been thought by Fetter to have failed to recognize the problem of value-productivity. He believed himself to have successfully avoided this pitfall by his example. See Brown (1926, p. 125, n. 13).

16. Samuelson (1981).

back through the market as factor payments to labor and land; apparently we have 10 units of rice ("real interest income") that can be attributed to no factor service—only to the productivity through time of the initial rice stock. Mere ownership of rice capital confers title to a possible perpetual flow of annual rice consumption income. This annual income is clearly interest earned by the rice capitalist. This income is accounted for entirely by the physical productivity of rice. Samuelson hastens to anticipate the obvious Schumpeterian response. Schumpeter had emphasized that, with interest zero, "the greater magnitude of the forest is *already* imputed back in value to the saplings." So that today's 100 units of rice already have the value of next year's 110 units: "these foreseen changes . . . only conserve the already calculated value of the process," without involving any creation of new value. But Samuelson hotly denounces this response as "pure deception. Real rice *is* being produced net. Kuznets can measure it. You can eat 10 [units of] rice every year and still not impair your circular flow income. . . . No hocus-pocus of backward imputation—of forest to sapling, or rice grain to rice grain—evades the naive fact of productive interest."[17]

It may be instructive to note how this kind of example *appears* to escape the Böhm-Bawerkian critique. Naive productivity theories explain the interest on the capital sum invested in a tree, by virtue of the tree's physical fecundity. Böhm-Bawerk's criticism pointed out that physical productivity does not necessarily mean value productivity. In value terms it is surely still possible, in principle, for the value of the tree to be equal to the sum of the values of all future fruit crops. The presently considered fruit tree, sheep, and rice examples *seem* to escape this problem. One writer has in fact claimed[18] that this is the outstanding virtue of the single-good economy (he is thinking specifically of Knight's Crusonia-plant economy). Rates of productivity can be arrived at directly, since "capital stock" and "income" consist of the same physical entities. No resort need be had to calculation in "value terms," with all its attendant pitfalls. So these productivity examples, from sheep to Crusonia to rice, do indeed demonstrate that, even with zero rate of time preference, present rice exchanges for future rice at a rate that expresses the physical productivity of rice. If *this* demonstration were enough to settle the problem posed by the phenomenon of interest, the issue would indeed be closed. Time preference

17. Ibid. (p. 23).
18. Dewey (1965, p. 80).

need have nothing to do with the emergence of interest; interest as a phenomenon, and the particular *rate* of interest established in the market *can,* it is clear, be entirely explained by physical productivity (at least in certain contexts). Yet the matter is far less simple than this.

INTEREST, OWN-RATES OF INTEREST, AND INTERTEMPORAL EXCHANGE

What these examples demonstrate is that physical productivity affects (or even "determines") the intertemporal exchange rate (the own-rate of interest) on sheep, on rice, and on Crusonia, respectively. One hundred units of 1987 rice exchange, in 1987, for 110 promised units of 1988 rice. With this trade repeated each year, the rice owner can consume 10 units of rice each year ("real interest income") without eroding the ("capital") base that yields this annual income. We shall attempt to show, however, that from the Fetter-Mises PTPT view, these demonstrations do nothing to advance understanding of the general phenomenon of interest; nor do they, as we shall see, demonstrate the impotence or irrelevancy of Böhm-Bawerk's refutation of simple productivity theories.

It may be useful to review the impasse we have apparently reached. On the one hand these sheep and rice stories show that an annual consumption income drawn from the physical fecundity of a source, can in principle be indefinitely enjoyed without eroding the continued existence and productiveness of that source. On the other hand the *logic* of the Böhm-Bawerkian reasoning refuting productivity theories of interest has not itself been addressed—the reasoning has been denounced as hocus-pocus not because of any demonstrated logical fallacy but apparently because these sheep and rice cases are supposed to serve as counter-examples showing precisely that phenomenon which the Böhm-Bawerkian reasoning purported to have proven to be impossible.

Reflection should surely convince us: (a) that the Böhm-Bawerkian reasoning must still be reckoned with—after all, no flaw in its logic has as yet been identified in these examples; (b) that these examples demonstrate the possibility of an income *different* from that for which Böhm-Bawerk sought an explanation; these examples demonstrate the possibility, that is, of an income *which the Böhm-Bawerkian reasoning never questioned;* that (c) since it was the Böhm-Bawerkian reasoning that underlay what we have called the interest problem, *that* interest problem has *not* been touched at all by these sheep and rice stories. Let us try to explain all this. We must return to our original statement of the interest problem.

The interest problem, we recall, asked how it is possible for an individual to invest capital funds in a way that yields a perpetual net income. Why does not the market bid up the price of all the "machines" (in which the individual might plan to invest his capital) so that no net annual yield remains? This question, it should be noted, did not challenge the physical possibility of a tree of infinite life producing an annual crop of fruit (or a tree of finite life producing an annual crop of fruit large enough to permit the planting, out of fruit output, of a replacement tree when the parent tree dies). The question merely asked why, in the absence of any other theory of interest, the market does not bid up the price of the tree to the point where in fact no net annual financial yield is possible from investing in trees. This is what Fetter hammered away at, the distinction between goods and values in this context. "A theory of interest must be *essentially* a value-theory."[19] Samuelson has proven that ownership of rice permits an indefinite stream of annual rice consumption; he has not disproved the contention that the anticipated perpetual flow of rice consumption is already fully recorded in the market valuation of the initial rice source. Samuelson does not, in fact, appear to wish to deny this contention; he appears merely to conclude that this contention constitutes a meaningless incantation which does not affect the undeniable realities of perpetual annual consumption flows—duly measured by Kuznets, or somebody.

One can sympathize with Samuelson's impatience at verbal mysticism that seems out of touch with palpable reality. Moreover we can go a little further; Samuelson was dealing not with any theory of interest, but with Schumpeter's belief that—regardless of productivity—in the state of circular flow no interest at all would emerge. It is easy to sympathize with Samuelson's sense of conviction that his rice example has shown that productivity-interest can indeed emerge in this state of affairs. Yet it must be pointed out that when we turn to a world somewhat richer in assumptions than Samuelson's rice model, it becomes clear that his example (and also the earlier fruit tree, sheep, and Crusonia stories) have in fact failed to identify interest income (in the sense in which we have identified the interest problem) as a productivity return.

One hundred units of 1987 rice are expected to ripen into 110 units of 1988 rice. Suppose that the "value" of the 100 units of 1987 rice has

19. Fetter (1914, p. 257).

indeed risen to anticipate this physical growth. Then in terms of the interest problem (formulated at the outset of this paper) the perpetual annual rice consumption income so made possible *does not present an example of interest*. The annual flow of rice income is indeed adequately explained by productivity—more to the point, there was no "problem" that demanded explanation, at all. There is, after all, no problem constituted by the circumstance that a tree yields fruit annually.

The interest problem would begin, in the context of the rice example, only if in fact the "value" of the 100 units of 1987 rice is somehow lower than that of 110 units of 1988 rice. *Then* we would have the possibility of a sum of abstract capital value serving as a financial source somehow generating a flow of *greater* subsequent value. *That* would indeed appear to fly in the face of economic intuition (since competition ought—absent a theory of interest—to be expected to exclude such a phenomenon). And it is of course *this* interest problem that PTPT solves by reference to the general subjective preference for the achievement of goals sooner rather than later.

What the preceding asserts, then, is that what Brown, Fisher, Knight, and Samuelson have identified as interest income—and which they apparently view as the *only* interest income needed to be discussed—*is in fact not interest income at all* (from the perspective of the interest problem formulated above). On the other hand, that interest income which PTPT deals with—an income which *does* fit the specifications of interest as formulated above—turns out to be something the very existence of which the critics appear to deny. (We recall that Schumpeter, too, was [in this respect only!] on the side of the critics of PTPT: he believed that in the circular flow no pure interest would be present.) Obviously the entire debate appears to have degenerated into a squabble about the meaning of terms.

From the Fisherian perspective the semantic bickering may appear even more deplorable. After all, the Fisherian view is that interest, the income received in return for providing services of "waiting," is *at the same time* the reward received by the capitalists (who provide these services) for their sacrifices (sacrifices which obtain their poignancy from the prevalence of positive time-preferences). A discussion such as the above (in which the issue is made to appear whether the term "interest income" is to refer to the fruits of rice fecundity or to a value differential attributed to time preference) must seem doubly regrettable. Let us go back to basics.

THE INTEREST PROBLEM THAT CALLS FOR
SOLUTION: THE COMPETING VERSIONS

The attention of economists over the centuries has been attracted to the real-world, palpable, phenomenon of interest income largely due to its "surplus" character. Apparently it is possible, in the market economy, to command a steady, regular income merely by possession of a capital stock. As Böhm-Bawerk introduced the phenomenon, "Whoever is the owner of a capital sum is ordinarily able to derive from it a permanent net income. . . . This income . . . arises independently of any personal act of the capitalist. It accrues to him even though he has not moved a finger in creating it. . . . It can be derived from any capital, no matter what be the kind of goods of which the capital consists, from naturally fruitful, as well as from barren goods, from perishable as well as from durable goods, from replaceable as well as from irreplaceable goods, from money as well as from commodities. And, finally, it flows without ever exhausting the capital from which it arises, and therefore without any necessary limit to its continuance. . . . And so the phenomenon of interest presents, on the whole, the remarkable picture of a lifeless thing, capital, producing an everlasting and inexhaustible supply of goods."[20] With this starting point for discussions of the interest phenomenon, it is easy to see how physical fecundity (while it offers a tempting ingredient for interest theorizing) came to be dismissed (in Böhm-Bawerk's chapter refuting the productivity theories). The point is that the entire discussion begins with the assertion that *value*-productivity is a common fact of life; this fact of life was, after all, asserted to hold for barren goods and for money just as it holds for naturally fruitful goods and for commodities. It was this Böhm-Bawerkian identification of the problem as referring to value-productivity that was at the heart of the formulation of the interest problem cited at the start of this paper. Now, the prospective interest theorist can choose one or the other of only two options: he can deny that this interest phenomenon in fact exists (so that there is nothing to be explained), or he must seek an explanation for it within its own framework. Schumpeter chose the first option. Others, implicitly denying the phenomenon that Böhm-Bawerk took as his starting point, focus on physical productivity as a sufficient basis for the (undeniable) *market* phenomenon of interest. But in so doing they have not offered a new explanation for the Böhm-Bawerkian phenomenon: they have simply denied its existence, and cho-

20. Böhm-Bawerk (1959a, p. 1).

sen instead to talk about something else—something easily confused with it (because both might serve plausibly as the underlying basis for the *surface* phenomenon of market interest). PTPT theorists are then entitled to accept the existence of the Böhm-Bawerkian phenomenon and to offer their own explanation for it. From this perspective, then, the situation can be summed up as follows.

First, there is a commonly observed phenomenon of market interest. No one disputes this observation. Second, for Böhm-Bawerk this phenomenon of market interest is simply the expression of the existence of an underlying phenomenon of pure value-productivity. This interpretation of market interest renders the phenomenon insoluble through reference to physical productivity, and leaves it calling out for alternative explanation. Third, PTPT accepts this Böhm-Bawerkian interpretation (and offered time preference insights to account for the phenomenon of value-productivity). Fourth, Schumpeter, while not disputing the Böhm-Bawerkian interpretation of the observed phenomenon of market interest, held that this entire phenomenon is a transient one that would disappear in the state of circular flow. Fifth, other theorists dispute Böhm-Bawerk's interpretation of the observed phenomenon of market interest. In effect these writers deny the existence of the (underlying "value-productivity") phenomenon which Böhm-Bawerk asserted to be reflected in the observed phenomenon of market interest. For these writers the observed phenomenon of market interest reflects nothing more than physical productivity; there *is* no "value-productivity" to be explained. Sixth, finally, for modern theorists following Fisher, the entire discussion in the present section represents an incomprehensible lapse into meaningless mysticism and metaphysics. For these theorists the task of a theory of interest is *not at all that of solving the problem formulated at the start of this paper* (and expressive of the Böhm-Bawerkian formulation at the start of this section). Were the Fisherians to consider *that* (Böhm-Bawerkian) question, they would consider it solved immediately once one has identified "waiting" as a missing factor. Since waiting is a scarce, costly factor, its market value tends to equal *both* its marginal product *and* its marginal cost (in terms of forgone sooner consumption). Interest is *both* the reward for sacrificed earlier consumption *and* the fruits of the enhanced output made possible by waiting. For Fisher and the modern writers the interesting question, and thus the task of interest theory, is (quite apart from possible disputes concerning the existence of the phenomenon to which the Böhm-Bawerkian formulation refers) *nothing more than that of identifying the determinants of intertemporal prices.* In undertaking this latter task, Fisher develops a perfectly adequate framework in which *both* physical productivity *and* time preference considerations have their place.

We may conclude then: (a) most of the modern bewilderment at PTPT stems, we would argue, from the Fisherian unconcern with the interest problem that was posed by Böhm-Bawerk. Most moderns, following Fisher, do not see the task of interest theory to be to account for a phenomenon that somehow (in the absence of a theory of interest) "ought not to exist." As a result, the Fisherian approach finds the PTPT view bizarre (since their own approach finds time preference and physical productivity *both* valuable elements in their theory). We shall return to consider this Fisherian view of PTPT in the subsequent section. (b) Sheep, rice, and other stories introduced to demonstrate the adequacy of a purely productivity theory (and thus to refute PTPT) express a different misunderstanding of PTPT. Without recognizing it, the authors of these examples have in effect denied the very existence of the phenomenon which Böhm-Bawerk identified as that calling for explanation (i.e., the underlying phenomenon of pure value-productivity). From the Böhm-Bawerkian point of view, therefore, these stylized examples deal with a phenomenon which (1) is other than the one Böhm-Bawerk is concerned with, and (2) offers no theoretical challenges ("of course" trees produce fruit!).

We have thus identified *two* distinct sources of modern bewilderment with PTPT. One source stems from an implicit denial of the value-productivity phenomenon seen as calling for explanation in Böhm-Bawerk's view (and in PTPT's view). From this denial it was easy to move to assuming that the phenomenon to be explained by a theory of interest is that which would underlie the market rate of interest *in the absence of* the value-productivity phenomenon—viz., physical productivity. From this latter perspective, PTPT's refusal to accord to physical productivity any role, appears simply incomprehensible. The *second* source of modern bewilderment stems, not from any denial of the phenomenon that Böhm-Bawerk sought to explain, but from an entirely different conception of what constitutes the function of a theory of interest. Whereas for Böhm-Bawerk a theory of interest is called for to account for an otherwise inexplicable phenomenon, for Fisher a theory of interest is called for to identify the determinants of a particular market rate of exchange (viz., the intertemporal rate, which implicitly expresses the rate of interest). From this Fisherian perspective it is easy to understand how bizarre it appears for anyone to deny any role for physical productivity in a theory of interest. We turn to elaborate on this last point. The point turns out to involve an old dispute between Fisher and Böhm-Bawerk, that throws considerable light on the entire issue.

THE EXISTENCE OF INTEREST VS. THE RATE OF INTEREST

"Some writers," Fisher wrote, "have chosen, for purposes of exposition, to postulate two questions involved in the theory of the rate of interest, viz., (1) why any rate of interest exists and (2) how the rate of interest is determined."[21] Fisher dismisses this distinction as being unilluminating, "since to explain how the rate of interest is determined involves the question of whether the rate can or cannot be zero."[22] The purpose of the present section of this paper is (a) to present the case for the distinction criticized by Fisher—a distinction in fact made by Böhm-Bawerk, as we shall see—and (b) to show how failure to understand the rationale for the distinction has generated the widespread modern bewilderment with PTPT referred to earlier.

No better defense for Böhm-Bawerk's distinction need be found than the lucid discussion that he himself provided. Böhm-Bawerk was criticizing Fisher for not distinguishing between "originating forces" and "determining forces." "All interest-originating causes undoubtedly are also determining factors for the actual rate. But not all rate-determining factors are also interest-creating causes. . . . When we inquire into the causes of a flood we certainly cannot cite the dams and reservoirs built to prevent or at least mitigate inundations. But they are a determining factor for the actual water-mark of the flood. . . . Similarly, there are other circumstances besides the actual interest-creating causes that bring about or enhance the value advantage of present goods over future goods."[23] It will be observed that Böhm-Bawerk's distinction faithfully expresses the formulation of the interest problem that he offered (as cited in the preceding section). There is a phenomenon (the existence of interest income) which calls for explanation (just as the occurrence of floods calls for explanation). The required explanation need not necessarily invoke all those "forces" which may be relevant for the determination of the particular rate of interest prevailing in the market. It is true that a complete listing of all aspects

21. Fisher (1930, pp. 13f. and 474) (where Böhm-Bawerk is identified, without specific citation, as having argued for this distinction).

22. Ibid. See also Conard (1959, pp. 13–14).

23. Böhm-Bawerk (1959c, p. 192).

of all the "rate-determining forces" would at the same time explain why the interest rate is other than zero. But to say that all these forces are responsible for the interest phenomenon would be highly misleading. If someone stands amazed at the flow of city traffic along one of its central avenues during morning rush hour, and asks, "Why is traffic so heavy?" the answer to the question should presumably run in terms of the need of people to get to work. It will simply not do to invoke the traffic-light system as an explanation (even partially) for the volume of traffic (even though it is certainly the case that the size of that volume has been, in part, determined by that traffic-light system). For Fisher, it is quite clear, the "problem" of interest is simply to provide a full catalogue of the rate-determining forces. Fisher's analysis leads him, inevitably, to recognize the interaction, among these forces, of physical productivity and time preference. Modern theorists, following Fisher, are understandably bewildered by PTPT statements denying any role for physical productivity. But to endorse the PTPT denial of a role for physical productivity is not necessarily to deny that physical productivity is to be listed among the forces combining to determine intertemporal rates of exchange. The PTPT's denial refers strictly to the problem of accounting for the phenomenon of interest. For the solution of *this* problem, PTPT finds physical productivity to be no more relevant than traffic lights are (for accounting for the phenomenon of morning rush-hour traffic) or than dams are (for Böhm-Bawerk's example of accounting for the occurrence of floods).

PTPT exponents often drive home the irrelevance of physical productivity by pointing out that physical productivity is neither necessary nor sufficient for an explanation for interest (in the sense of value-productivity).[24] They point out how, in the absence of time preference, physical productivity, no matter how great, cannot generate value-productivity. And they point out how, even in a pure exchange world without production processes of any kind, the phenomenon of value-productivity could arise as a result of time preference considerations exclusively. One critic responded to this reasoning by asking whether, based on parallel reasoning, one would conclude that the striking of matches is irrelevant to the causation of fire (since not every match that is struck produces fire, and not all matches that ignite do so as a result of having been struck). The response should surely be that the striking of matches is certainly *highly* relevant to the prevalence of match-ignition, but the striking of matches is indeed far

24. Baird (1982, pp. 303f.).

less relevant for other questions, such as, e.g., why ignition occurs among matches rather than among Q-tips.

Admittedly, some expositions of PTPT have sometimes unfortunately permitted it to be thought that, since only time preference accounts for the *existence* of interest, it follows that a change in the conditions of physical productivity would invariably leave the rate of interest unchanged. But in fact PTPT implies nothing of the kind.[25] It is one thing to maintain that normal daily nutritional needs are in no way responsible for the existence of hospitals; it in no way follows that the extent of such needs is not a factor helping determine the size (and conceivably even the number) of hospitals. *Given* the presence of sickness (upon which the existence of hospitals does depend) a host of unrelated matters may participate in the determination of hospital size. Similarly PTPT theorists do recognize that since the prevalence of positive time preference does generate the phenomenon of interest, it cannot at all be ruled out that other factors (including physical productivity) may affect the determination of its rate. For example, physical productivity may significantly affect the level of wealth, and thus the marginal rate of time preference. All PTPT insists on is that, no matter how significant a role physical productivity may play among the complete list of variables affecting the rate of interest, it is fallacious to refer to interest income (expressing value-productivity) as the fruit of the physical productivity of agents of production. No matter how heavily the costs of the hospital meal service weigh in the determination of hospital size, it remains a fallacy to see a hospital as a sleep-in restaurant.[26]

SOME REMARKS ON METHODOLOGICAL ESSENTIALISM

It will be observed that our defense of PTPT against the bewilderment evinced by its various critics, amounts to a partial affirmation of what has

25. Fetter was quite explicit on this point (1914, p. 247).

26. Economists have frequently argued (e.g., Hayek 1945, pp. 22–25) that whether time preference or physical productivity is to be considered the more important explanatory variable for interest depends on which of them is expressed, in the standard Fisher diagram, by a curve having greater convexity. This makes good sense in regard to the determinants of the interest *rate*. It may be highly relevant to know whether the interest rate is more sensitive to a given marginal change in time preferences, than to a similar marginal change in physical productivity. But for the explanation of the *existence* of interest, these comparisons are hardly relevant. Even if hospital size were somehow more sensitive to changing nutritional standards than to change in the incidence of disease, the *raison d'être* of the hospital remains unaffected.

sometimes been termed "methodological essentialism." Several historians of thought have noticed that for Menger, economic science is a search for *the reality underlying economic phenomena*—for their *essence* (*das Wesen*). In a letter to Walras, Menger asks, "How can we attain to a knowledge of this essence, for example, the essence of value, the essence of land rent, the essence of entrepreneur's profit . . . by mathematics?"[27] This search for essences, reflecting a philosophical approach attributed to Aristotelian influence,[28] would focus, then, not on the land rent paid for a particular parcel of real-estate in a particular year, but upon those essential features of land rent that would be common to all examples of the phenomenon. Similarly an essentialist approach to the interest problem as posed by Böhm-Bawerk would focus not on the list of elements which together determine specific interest rates, but on those elements upon which the interest phenomenon essentially depends, elements without which the phenomenon could in fact not exist. PTPT finds these essential elements for the interest phenomenon in time preference. Physical productivity is *not* such an essential element of interest; but, to repeat, to affirm all this is not to deny that market rates of interest may be related to physical productivity conditions. To assert that, absent time preference, physical productivity is unable to generate *any* interest (in the sense of value-productivity) is not to assert that, *given* time preference, the intertemporal rate of exchange, even in the form of the rate of value-productivity, is unaffected by changes in the physical productivity of machines or of trees. All that is being asserted is that whatever role is played by physical productivity does not permit us to say that interest (value-productivity) *is* the fruit of productive capital. (Rush-hour traffic as a phenomenon may indeed be vitally affected by the timing of traffic lights; nonetheless we understand why it is accurate to describe the phenomenon of rush-hour traffic as "people getting to work," rather than as "the result of traffic-light timing").

From a modernist perspective impatient with metaphysical discussion some of this defense of PTPT against modernist "bewilderment" may appear wholly unhelpful; in fact it may confirm the critics' impression that it is all empty philosophizing unrelated to objective phenomena. If one sees the objective of science as being to account for empirical reality, and one sees the objective of price theory to explain the structure and levels of par-

27. This letter is cited in Hutchison (1953, p. 148).
28. See Kauder (1965, p. 97); Bostaph (1978, p. 11).

ticular prices, then it will seem only natural to seek for an interest theory that explains particular rates of interest. All else must appear metaphysical, irrelevant, and plain confusing. So long as our theory of interest, say, in the form of Fisher's standard diagram (incorporating both intertemporal productive possibilities and time preferences) can show how the market in fact generates its intertemporal rates of exchange (with respect to given physically defined commodities identified at different dates), surely our scientific task has been accomplished—without any essentialist pursuit of some metaphysical reality underlying the explained phenomena. But this modernist impatience can be shown to be unreasonable. Such a demonstration requires that we recognize the nature of the delicate interface between science and ideology. It will prove convenient to present our discussion in the context of brief reference to the celebrated Cambridge Capital Controversy of recent decades.

SCIENCE AND IDEOLOGY: THE CAMBRIDGE CONTROVERSY AND PTPT

For present purposes, we compress our account of the Cambridge Controversy to its barest relevant elements. One side of the debate, representing neoclassical orthodoxy, sees the phenomena of the capitalist economy, especially the assignment of income shares (including interest income) as being phenomena to be understood within the framework of market equilibrium. Market prices (and thus interest) have to be paid if consumers are to receive that which the productive capacity of the market is able to provide, and for which the consumers are prepared to pay. Interest is rendered necessary and thus, in a sense, "justified" by efficiency (i.e., consumer sovereignty) considerations.

On the other hand, the Cambridge (England) critics vigorously deny that interest incomes are "caused by individual exchanges as constrained by technology and the availability of factors of production."[29] These critics see the distribution of income between wage-earners and interest-receivers as being determined by such considerations as the power balance between workers and capitalists, rather than by marginal products, consumer preferences, and factor supplies.

It is not difficult to recognize the ideological implications that can be drawn from each of these two views. As Robert Solow (representing the neoclassical side of the debate) observed, the Cambridge school saw neo-

29. See Hausman (1981, p. 167).

classical theory as "an important part of an apology for private capitalism. It sounds as if capitalists are entitled to their profits."[30] Indeed, Joan Robinson, leading figure in the Cambridge school, asserted very explicitly: "The unconscious preoccupation behind the neoclassical system was chiefly to raise profits to the same level of moral respectability as wages."[31] Clearly the Cambridge critics believe that their own theory of capital provides no such comfort and solace for the capitalist system.

It may be submitted that these asserted ideological implications of alternative capital theories are profoundly important for one's appreciation of what economic science can reveal. While Solow and others[32] believe the Cambridge attack on neoclassicism expresses an anti-capitalist animus, they do not deny the responsibility to deal dispassionately with the Cambridge substantive criticisms and theory. Nor do the Cambridge critics fail to recognize that any ideological dissatisfaction with the implications of neoclassicism must yield to a dispassionate search for logical flaws in that theory. The important point is that such dispassionate scientific debate holds the key to the normative, non-scientific characterization of specific income categories. The neoclassical view of interest permits it to be seen as a productivity return (parallel to the way in which market wages are perceived). This is seen to permit the view that interest is on the "same level of moral respectability as wages." The Cambridge theory is one from which such innate respectability for interest income does *not* emerge. We wish to argue briefly here that the Cambridge Capital Controversy offered an array of alternative theoretical positions that was not exhaustive. A third point of view, not represented in the discussion, but one highly relevant to the underlying ideological concerns, is in fact to be found in the PTPT.

The neoclassical side of the debate saw interest as a productivity return. Any ideological defense of capitalist interest based on this side of the debate will consist in "justifying" interest as the proceeds of enhanced productivity made possible by scarce, costly, waiting. In denying this defense, the Cambridge position will argue that interest *is* not the "justified" proceeds of productivity. (Rather it is a share of "social surplus" somehow acquired by owners of capital.) What needs now to be pointed out is that PTPT offers an understanding of interest income that may be seen as sup-

30. Solow (1975).
31. Robinson (1962, p. 58).
32. Blaug (1974).

porting its moral "respectability," but *without* seeing it as the fruits of productivity. From the PTPT perspective, the neoclassically implied defense of capitalism is flawed. We have again and again pointed out how PTPT does not recognize market interest income as constituting a productivity return; that is not what interest income *is*. On the other hand, PTPT very definitely sees market interest as expressing a market-determined rate of intertemporal exchange. So that PTPT provides a basis, if one chooses to use it for such a purpose, for a justification of interest (as a legitimate expression of consumer preferences) that nonetheless agrees with Cambridge critics that interest is not a productivity return.

The point of all this is that we cannot, surely, close our eyes to possible ideological implications of science. Our science may well be, perhaps, ideologically untainted and value-free (or, at any rate, honest efforts in this direction may be undertaken), but human beings are, as valuing citizens, vitally interested in the character of controversial phenomena. If one is asked: "What justifies interest?" it will simply not do to defend it as reward for productivity, if analysis shows that that is not what it *is*. Note that for ideological (i.e., for normative, evaluative) purposes, methodological essentialism is highly relevant. One can hardly arrive at a judgment concerning the defensibility of interest income by showing that its size depends upon physical productivity. A "theory of hospitals" that fails to identify hospitals in terms of the essentiality of their medical character is likely to be less than helpful for the purposes of normative evaluation by citizens. Citizens asked to vote to support hospitals seen as sleep-in restaurants may respond differently than when hospitals are correctly seen as institutions fighting to contain dread diseases. There is every reason for science to take note of the non-scientific purposes for which scientific results may be helpfully consulted. From this perspective, the methodologically essentialist aspects of PTPT may be considered valuable features of it, rather than as obfuscating metaphysics.

CONCLUSION

Our defense of PTPT against modern "bewilderment" has dealt primarily with its apparently astounding assertion that physical productivity has *nothing* essentially to do with the phenomenon of interest. Our discussion has: (a) made it clear that PTPT does not necessarily deny a role for physical productivity in interest rate determination; (b) emphasized that what PTPT addresses is a question that is *different* from that of interest rate determination; (c) identified the problem dealt with by PTPT as the interest problem addressed by Böhm-Bawerk, viz., what accounts for the phenomenon of net *value*-productivity (in the face of market competition that might be expected to squeeze it out of existence); (d) shown that PTPT refusal to recognize any physical productivity role in the explanation for the existence of interest income, rests on (the admittedly arbitrary) view that time and waiting are not to be seen as productive agents; (e) recognized the methodologically essentialist aspects of PTPT, and argued for their relevance, especially in the context of the Cambridge Capital Controversy, for citizens' normative understanding of interest income; (f) made it clear how numerous stylized examples (sheep, rice, Crusonia, etc.) designed to demonstrate the essential role played by physical productivity in interest income generation, in fact concern a phenomenon quite different from that upon which the Böhm-Bawerkian discussion focused. Regardless of one's opinion of the significance of income generated by physical productivity, we have emphasized the legitimacy of distinguishing between that income and the quite different income concept identified by Böhm-Bawerk, and addressed by PTPT.

The upshot of the discussion, then, is that PTPT affirms the phenomenon of pure value-productivity, that is, the phenomenon in which a source of value at a given date generates a flow of values during subsequent periods that exceeds, in total, the value of the source. PTPT accounts for this phenomenon by reference to widespread (possibly universal) preference for the earlier, rather than later, achievement of goals. Market rates of interest, and market interest income, are expressions of this underlying phenomenon of value productivity (and of its PTPT roots).

It is not my purpose here to offer a concise Austrian theory of capital. Rather I shall present an Austrian perspective on several concepts fundamental to modern capital theory. I shall show how this perspective enables us to fit certain characteristically Austrian ideas about capital into the more comprehensive Austrian view of the way in which the market system operates. To clarify what constitutes the uniquely Austrian way of thinking about capital, I shall begin with a critical interpretation of a 1974 paper by Sir John Hicks. My use of Hicks's work as a springboard also helps to explain why Hicks considered his book on capital theory to be "neo-Austrian" in character.[1]

HICKS, MATERIALISTS, AND FUNDISTS

Hicks grouped the numerous views on capital that have been expounded throughout the history of economic thought under two broad headings.[2] By means of this classification Hicks called attention to the two basic ways economists conceptualize the notion of a stock of capital goods existing in the economy at a given moment in time. One is to see the stock as a collection of physical goods; by this approach aggregation into a stock provides us with a measure of the "volume of capital." An important implication of this view is that "as between two economies which have capital stocks that are physically identical [the] Volume of Capital must be the same."[3] Those who share this view of the aggregate stock of capital, Hicks called "materialists." The alternative view conceives of the aggregate stock of capital goods, not as a volume of physical capital, but as a "sum of values which may conveniently be described as a Fund"—something evidently quite different from the physical goods themselves—with the values derived

---

"The Theory of Capital" is new to the Liberty Fund edition. It was originally published in Edwin G. Dolan, ed., *The Foundations of Modern Austrian Economics* (Kansas City: Sheed and Ward, 1976). The article was not part of *Essays on Capital and Interest*, published by Edward Elgar in 1996, and thus, for continuity, the heading "Essay 5" has been added.

1. John R. Hicks, *Capital and Time: A Neo-Austrian Theory* (Oxford: Clarendon Press, 1973).

2. John R. Hicks, "Capital Controversies: Ancient and Modern," *American Economic Review* 64 (May 1974): 307–16.

3. Ibid., p. 308.

from the expected future output flows. Those holding this view, Hicks called "fundists."[4]

This fundist-materialist dichotomy is an elaboration (and partial revision) of a comment that Hicks made in the 1963 edition of his *Theory of Wages*.[5] In that discussion Hicks identified "the two basic ways in which economists have regarded the capital stock of an economy" as involving, first, a "physical concept," which treats capital "as consisting of actual capital goods," and, second, a "fund concept," which reduces capital to the "consumption goods that are foregone to get it."[6] These are the same two concepts Hicks identified in his 1974 paper, except that there he preferred an interpretation of the fund view in terms of future outputs rather than in terms of opportunity cost.

FUNDISTS: A TERMINOLOGICAL PUZZLE

Now Hicks's use of the label *fund* to identify that notion of capital *not* viewed as physical goods is puzzling and could cause much confusion about the meaning of his discussion. Hicks declared that he "of course" borrowed the term *fund* from the history of economic thought; it is here that the confusion begins. The notion of capital as a fund is well known in the history of capital theory. It was carefully developed by John Bates Clark[7] and repeatedly expounded by Frank H. Knight.[8] Those who objected most vigorously to this view of capital were Eugen von Böhm-Bawerk in the first decade of the century and Friedrich A. Hayek in the fourth decade. Böhm-Bawerk declared that Clark's concept of capital was mystical, and he insisted that to measure a stock of capital in value units in no way

---

4. Ibid., p. 309.

5. John R. Hicks, *The Theory of Wages*, 2d ed. (London: Macmillan, 1963), pp. 342–48.

6. Ibid.

7. John Bates Clark, *The Distribution of Wealth* (1899; reprint ed., New York: Kelley & Millman, 1956), p. 117; Friedrich A. Hayek, *The Pure Theory of Capital* (London: Routledge & Kegan Paul, 1941), p. 93; George J. Stigler, *Production and Distribution Theories: The Formative Period* (New York: Macmillan, 1941), pp. 308–10.

8. See Frank H. Knight, "Capital, Time, and the Interest Rate," *Economica* 1 (August 1934): 259; idem, "The Theory of Investment Once More: Mr. Boulding and the Austrians," *Quarterly Journal of Economics* 50 (November 1935): 57; and idem, "The Ricardian Theory of Production and Distribution," in *On the History and Method of Economics*, ed. Frank H. Knight (Chicago: University of Chicago Press, 1956), p. 47; see also Hayek, *Pure Theory*, pp. 93–94.

implies that what is being measured is an abstract quantity apart from the physical goods themselves.[9] Hayek, in his debate with Knight, argued against the notion of capital as a fund of value, that is, a quantity apart from the particular goods making up the capital stock.[10] Thus Hicks's list of fundists must include Clark and Knight, and Böhm-Bawerk and Hayek must be on his list of materialists (certainly not on the list of fundists).

However, this was not the way Hicks classified these economists. J. B. Clark was "clearly" a materialist, and Hayek "of course, was a fundist."[11] Also, Böhm-Bawerk "kept the fundist flag flying"![12] A basic familiarity with the history of capital theory leaves one puzzled, if not startled, by Hicks's choice of terminology. Let us look more closely at how he employs his definitions.

HICKSIAN FUNDISM

To Hicks, the term *fund* apparently denotes a concept entirely different from that Clark and Knight had in mind when they used it. Knight's capital-as-a-fund notion refers to a special way of viewing capital goods— as the temporary embodiment of a permanent store, or "fund," of value. Hicks's declaration that the Austrians are fundists has to do with their treatment of capital goods as essentially forward-looking components of multiperiod plans.[13] The Clark-Knight view of capital as something other than the capital goods themselves is quite different from Hicks's fundists' view. Hicks himself—now a "neo-Austrian"—is on the side of his brand of fundists—the forward-looking kind. Without denying the propriety of a materialist, or backward-looking, perspective on capital, Hicks endorsed a "sophisticated" fundism in which the forward-looking character of capital goods is repeatedly emphasized. This made it easier for Hicks to recognize the importance of expectations in capital theory—a characteristically Austrian point of view.

Hicks apparently was inspired in his novel use of the term *fund* by

---

9. Eugen von Böhm-Bawerk, *Positive Theory of Capital*, vol. 2, *Capital and Interest*, trans. George D. Huncke and Hans F. Sennholz (South Holland, Ill.: Libertarian Press, 1959), pp. 60–66, 282; see also Israel M. Kirzner, *An Essay on Capital* (New York: Augustus M. Kelley, 1966), p. 123 (present edition, pp. 117–18).

10. See particularly Friedrich A. Hayek, "The Mythology of Capital," *Quarterly Journal of Economics* 50 (February 1936): 199–228.

11. Hicks, "Capital Controversies," p. 309.

12. Ibid., p. 315.

13. This refers to the 1973 rather than the 1963 classification that Hicks presented.

Böhm-Bawerk's notion of a subsistence fund.[14] Despite my criticism of Hicks's usage of the term *fund*, I must agree that Böhm-Bawerk did set a precedent for using it in this way. Moreover, by insisting that the notion of a subsistence fund is characteristic of Böhm-Bawerk's approach, Hicks preserved what we must consider to be the essentially pure Austrian element in Böhm-Bawerk's theory. Some effort has been made in recent work to ignore the forward-looking, multiperiod-planning aspect of Böhm-Bawerk's theory. The productivity side of his system has been emphasized, and the time-preference aspect has been either suppressed altogether or treated as an inessential encumbrance.[15] However, as Hicks recognized, the notion of a subsistence fund is an essential element of Böhm-Bawerk's thinking about capital. This notion embodies the insight that, in choosing between processes of production of different durations, men appraise the prospective sacrifices these processes call for in terms of abstaining from more immediate consumption. Crucial to such appraisals is the size of the available capital stock, because it influences the prospective disutility associated with each of the alternatively required periods of waiting. Not only is this notion of a subsistence fund central to Böhm-Bawerk's theory of capital, but it also is—in spite of his disconcerting concessions to the productivity-interest theorists[16]—the essentially "Austrian" element in his thought. In the subsistence-fund concept is encapsulated Böhm-Bawerk's concern for forward-looking, multiperiod human decision making; here the influence of subjective comparative evaluation of alternative future streams of income makes itself felt; and here there is room for a discussion of expectations and uncertainty. Hicks recognized all this when he identified the Austrians as fundists. Not only does the notion of the subsistence fund qualify Böhm-Bawerk as a Hicksian fundist, but it also, as Hicks implied, epitomizes what is "Austrian" in Böhm-Bawerk's theory. I heartily agree with all this. At the same time, to emphasize the differences between the fund notion as used by Hicks and as usually associated with Clark and Knight, we may recall Hayek's powerful criticisms of the subsistence-fund idea.[17] Hayek's extreme op-

14. Hicks, *Theory of Wages*, p. 343.

15. See, for example, Robert Dorfman, "A Graphical Exposition of Böhm-Bawerk's Interest Theory," *Review of Economic Studies* 26 (February 1959): 153–58; Kirzner, *Essay on Capital*, pp. 84–86 (present edition, also pp. 84–86).

16. See Frank A. Fetter's remarks in "The 'Roundabout Process' in the Interest Theory," *Quarterly Journal of Economics* 17 (November 1902): 177.

17. Hayek, "Mythology," pp. 204–10; idem, *Pure Theory*, pp. 93, 146–53, 189–92.

position to the Clark-Knight notion of a fund led him to point out some difficulties in Böhm-Bawerk's original presentation of the subsistence-fund idea. While we can understand why Hicks labeled Böhm-Bawerk a fundist, we must still decide whether Hicks was correct in naming Hayek and modern-day Austrians fundists as well.

AUSTRIANS, MATERIALISTS, AND FUNDISTS

Where indeed does modern Austrianism stand in relation to the Hicksian materialist-fundist dichotomy? I contend that—whatever validity Hicks's view of the Austrians has in terms of the older Austrian writers—Austrianism today does not at all fit this classification. Austrian economists occupy a position that is neither fundist nor materialist; they dismiss the basic question to which the fundists and materialists have traditionally addressed themselves as being unhelpful and completely irrelevant.

Austrians reject the fundist-materialist dichotomy because of their special understanding of the role individual plans play in the market process. A capital good is *not* merely a produced factor of production. Rather it is a good produced as part of a multiperiod plan in which it has been assigned a specific function in a projected process of production. A capital good is thus a physical good with an assigned productive purpose. To treat the stock of capital goods as a Hicksian materialist would is out of the question, for as Hicks recognized, this approach ignores the future streams of output that these capital goods are designed to help produce. But to treat the stock of capital goods as a Hicksian fundist might is also unacceptable, for it submerges the individualities of the various capital goods into a stock and replaces them with the sum of values supposed to represent the aggregate expected future value of the output imputed to these goods. To treat the stock of capital goods this way ignores the problem of the degree of consistency that prevails among the purposes assigned to each of the goods composing the capital stock. It also ignores questions of complementarity among goods, as well as the possibility that the productive purpose assigned by one producer to a particular capital good is unrealizable in the light of the plans of other producers or potential users of other capital goods. But all this is precisely what, to an Austrian economist, cannot be ignored.

In somewhat different terms, the Hicksian materialist-fundist classification is objectionable not so much for these alternative formulations as for the incompatibility of the task they attempt to carry out with the Austrian approach. That task is to arrive at a single value aggregate to represent the *size* of the stock of capital goods in an economy. It is this very attempt to collapse the multidimensional collection of capital goods into a single number that Austrian economists find unacceptable. If one wishes to talk about the total stock of all capital goods in an economy at a particular moment in time, one must not overlook the roles assigned to the various goods by individuals; in other words, one must treat the stock as consisting at all times of essentially heterogeneous items that defy aggregation. They defy aggregation not only because of physical heterogeneity but also, more important, because of the diversity of the purposes to which these goods have been assigned. Mises emphatically dismissed the very notion of an aggregate of physical capital goods as empty and useless. The "totality of the produced factors of production," Mises wrote, "is merely an enumeration of physical quantities of thousands and thousands of various goods. Such an inventory is of no use to acting. It is a description of a part of the universe in terms of technology and topography and has no reference whatever to the problems raised by the endeavors to improve human well-being."[18]

ON MEASURING CAPITAL: THE INDIVIDUAL

Other economists as well as the Austrians see the serious theoretical difficulties that face all attempts to measure real capital. It seems useful to review briefly where these difficulties lie, both in the attempt to measure a single individual's stock of capital goods and the attempt to measure society's stock of capital goods.[19]

Consider a list of all the physical items that make up a single individual's stock of capital goods. Their physical heterogeneity prohibits "adding them up"—there is no natural unit of measurement. Instead one may try to devise an index number that will permit the heterogeneous items to be treated as one dimensional. But if the measure thus obtained is to be interpreted as representing the quantity of physical goods in the stock, the attempt hardly seems worthwhile. Not only is the advantage in replacing a list by a number unclear, but such a replacement obviously hides an

18. Ludwig von Mises, *Human Action: A Treatise on Economics* (New Haven: Yale University Press, 1949), p. 264; for Mises's views on capital and interest, see Israel M. Kirzner, "Ludwig von Mises and the Theory of Capital and Interest," in *The Economics of Ludwig von Mises: Toward a Critical Reappraisal*, ed. Laurence S. Moss (Kansas City: Sheed & Ward, 1976). (Essay 3, above, pp. 134–46.)

19. See Kirzner, *Essay on Capital*, pp. 103–41 (present edition, pp. 101–33).

important aspect of economic reality. A man's future plans depend not only on the aggregate size of his capital stock but also very crucially upon the particular properties of the various goods making up the stock. Goods that can be used in a complementary relationship permit certain plans that a purely physical measure necessarily suppresses.

Instead of seeking to measure the quantity of physical goods as physical goods, one may seek to measure one's capital stock in terms of the amount of past sacrifice undertaken to achieve the present stock. This would be a backward-looking measure. For such a measure, the heterogeneity of the goods making up the capital stock would present no difficulty. While one may question the usefulness of measuring past sacrifice, it is at least a task that does not lack meaning. On the other hand, measuring the size of the capital stock in terms of past sacrifice raises heterogeneity problems of a different kind. Past sacrifices are unlikely to have been homogeneous in character. And even if market values, say, are employed to express past sacrifices, there remains a very special "heterogeneity" difficulty arising from the circumstance that past sacrifices were undertaken at different dates in the past. These difficulties must necessarily render the search for a backward-looking measure unsuccessful.

A far more popular alternative is to measure the size of stocks of capital goods in terms of expected contribution to future streams of output. Attempts to arrive at so-called forward-looking measures of capital are, of course, the essence of Hicksian fundism. It is misleading to talk of a particular resource as being unambiguously associated with a definite stream of forthcoming output, in the sense that such an output stream flows automatically from the resource itself. Decisions must be made as to how a resource is to be deployed before one can talk of its future contribution to output. Because there are alternative uses for a resource and alternative clusters of complementary inputs with which a resource may be used, it is confusing to see a resource as representing a definite future output flow before the necessary decisions on its behalf have been made.

Nonetheless, recognizing all these difficulties, it cannot be denied, in the last analysis, that forward-looking measures of the size of capital stocks are being made all the time. Individuals do measure the potential contributions of particular capital goods to future output. They do so whenever these goods are bought and sold, and whenever owners of such goods refrain from selling them at going market prices. What cannot be "objectively" measured by the outsider turns out to be evaluated subjectively by the relevant decision maker.

MEASURING CAPITAL: THE ECONOMY

The difficulties involved in measuring the size of an individual's stock of capital goods become exaggerated when it is the size of an entire nation's stock of capital goods that one is measuring. The theoretical difficulties involved in aggregating physical items present formidable obstacles to thoroughgoing, "aggregative," Hicksian materialism. As Hicks correctly pointed out, Austrian economists have little sympathy with such an approach. But measuring the size of the capital stock in economic rather than in physical terms is hardly more promising. We may dismiss backward-looking measures as having failed, even at the individual level. Forward-looking measures of an individual's capital stock are impossible to achieve in an objective way but are being made all the time in the private dealings of individual agents. In considering forward-looking measures of a nation's stock of capital goods—that is, Hicks's fundism in the 1973 version—the possibility of subjective evaluation loses virtually all meaning (except in a sense to be discussed in the subsequent section); the problems that prevent objective measurement at the level of the individual are intensely reinforced by additional problems. One difficulty is relating a given item (in the inventory of the social stock of capital goods) to its prospective output before the preliminary decisions, necessary for the identification of that output, have been made; another is that the prospective output associated with a capital good owned by Jones may be inconsistent with a capital good owned by Smith. A forward-looking measure of Jones's capital stock and also of Smith's must presume plans on the part of Jones and of Smith, but Jones's plan and Smith's plan may be, in whole or in part, mutually exclusive. Perhaps Jones expects rain and builds a factory to produce umbrellas, whereas Smith expects fine weather and builds a factory to produce tennis racquets. That one of the two has overestimated the possible output of his factory (and thus will, in the future, be seen to have incorrectly measured the size of his capital stock) is not significant. What is significant is that it is already *now* meaningless to add a valuation of Jones's factory to a valuation of Smith's factory when each valuation depends on the expectation of one that the expectation of the other will prove erroneous. We are, therefore, forced as Austrian economists to decline Hicks's invitation to join the fundist club. To view the aggregate capital stock as a fund requires us in the end to give up our concern with individual plans upon which forward-looking measures ultimately depend for their very meaning! By refusing to surrender our Austrian interest in individual plans, however, we face another difficulty.

ON THE NOTION OF THE QUANTITY OF CAPITAL PER HEAD

We have seen that attempts to measure the quantity of capital goods in an economy must fail on theoretical grounds. Yet it is virtually impossible to avoid making statements in which such measurement is implied. In the writing of Mises, for example, we find frequent reference to the consequences of the fact that one country possesses a greater quantity of capital (or a greater quantity of capital per worker) than a second country.[20] Such statements imply the possibility that aggregate capital measurement has a rough meaningfulness. Yet how do we reconcile our theoretical rejection of aggregative capital measurement with a willingness to make statements of this kind?

The answer to this difficulty lies in the possibility, mentioned above, of subjective evaluation by an *individual* of the aggregate worth of his own stock of capital goods. Individual forward-looking measurement is both possible and feasible, because the problem of possibly inconsistent plans does not arise. An individual evaluates each component of his capital stock in terms of the plans he has in mind; *he* may have to take care to avoid possible inconsistencies, but in appraising his measurement of his capital we may assume that he *has* successfully integrated his own plans. What cannot, except in the state of general equilibrium, be assumed for an economy as a whole is assumed as a matter of course for the individual.

Underlying statements that compare the quantity of capital in one country with that in another is a convenient and relatively harmless fiction. One imagines that one has complete control over all the items in a nation's capital stock—that one is, in effect, the economic czar of a socialist economy. One is then in exactly the same position in relation to the nation's stock of capital as an individual is in relation to his own stock. By the use of this fiction, problems of inconsistent plans have been simply imagined away.

In sidestepping in this way the theoretical difficulties that frustrate attempts to arrive at aggregate measures of capital, we have, it may be argued, endorsed Hicksian fundism after all. But this is by no means the case. In the context of a market economy the fiction that all inconsisten-

20. Mises, *Human Action*, pp. 495–99, 611.

cies among plans may be ignored is, for most purposes, highly hazardous and misleading. Although there are instances in which needed reference to the aggregate quantity of capital can be supported in the way described, to use this fiction to construct a general treatment of aggregated capital is entirely unacceptable to Austrian economists. It is the market process that has the property of discovering inconsistencies among plans and of offering incentives for their elimination. To introduce capital into the analysis of the market process in a way that assumes that plan inconsistencies do not exist is to espouse decidedly non-Austrian assumptions and to become enmeshed in those insoluble contradictions characterizing orthodox microeconomic theory, the escape from which provides the strongest case for a return (or an advance) to the Austrian position.

REFERENCES

Andersen, E. (1965) "The Measurement of Capital," *Nationalokonomisk Tidsskrift*, vol. 102, nos. 3–4 (1964). Page number referred to is in the abstract in *Journal of Economic Abstracts*, January 1965.

Baird, Charles W. (1982) *Prices and Markets: Intermediate Microeconomics*, 2nd ed. (St. Paul, Minn.: West Publishing).

Barna, T. (1961) "On Measuring Capital," in *The Theory of Capital*, ed. F. A. Lutz and D. C. Hague (New York: St. Martin's Press).

Barzel, Y. (1964) "The Production Function and Technical Change in the Steam-Power Industry," *Journal of Political Economy*, vol. 72, April, pp. 133–50.

Baumol, W. (1959) *Economic Dynamics: An Introduction* (New York: Macmillan).

Bien, Bettina [Greaves] (1969) *The Works of Ludwig von Mises* (Irvington-on-Hudson, N.Y.: Foundation for Economic Education).

Blaug, M. (1962) *Economic Theory in Retrospect* (Homewood, Ill.: R. D. Irwin).

———. (1974) *The Cambridge Revolution: Success or Failure?* (London: Institute for Economic Affairs).

Blyth, C. A. (1960) "Towards a More General Theory of Capital," *Economica*, new series, vol. 27, May, pp. 120–36.

Böhm-Bawerk, Eugen von (1895) "The Positive Theory of Capital and Its Critics," *Quarterly Journal of Economics*, vol. 9, January, pp. 113–31.

———. (1907) "Capital and Interest Once More. II: A Relapse to the Productivity Theory," *Quarterly Journal of Economics*, vol. 21, February, pp. 242–82.

———. (1959a) *Capital and Interest*, vol. 1: *History and Critique of Interest Theories*, trans. George D. Huncke and Hans F. Sennholz (South Holland, Ill.: Libertarian Press).

———. (1959b) *Capital and Interest*, vol. 2: *The Positive Theory of Interest*, trans. George D. Huncke and Hans F. Sennholz (South Holland, Ill.: Libertarian Press).

———. (1959c) *Capital and Interest*, vol. 3: *Further Essays on Capital and Interest*, trans. George D. Huncke and Hans F. Sennholz (South Holland, Ill.: Libertarian Press).

Bostaph, S. (1978) "The Methodological Debate between Carl Menger and the German Historicists," *Atlantic Economic Journal*, vol. 6, no. 3, pp. 3–16.

Boulding, K. (1950) *A Reconstruction of Economics* (New York: John Wiley).

Brems, H. (1959) *Output, Employment, Capital and Growth* (New York: Harper).

Brown, H. G. (1914) "The Discount versus the Cost-of-Production Theory of Capital Valuation," *American Economic Review*, vol. 4, June, pp. 340–49.

———. (1926) *Economic Science and the Common Welfare*, 3rd ed. (Columbia, Mo.: Lucas Brothers).

Clark, J. B. (1899) *The Distribution of Wealth* (reprinted, New York: Kelley and Millman, 1956).

Clower, R. W. (1954) "An Investigation into the Dynamics of Investment," *American Economic Review*, vol. 44, March, pp. 64–81.

Conard, J. W. (1959) *An Introduction to the Theory of Interest* (Berkeley and Los Angeles: University of California Press).

Denison, E. F. (1957) "Theoretical Aspects of Quality Change, Capital Consumption and New Capital Formation," in *Problems of Capital Formation* (National Bureau of Economic Research Studies in Income and Wealth, vol. 19) (Princeton, N.J.: NBER).

Dewey, D. (1963) "The Geometry of Capital and Interest," *American Economic Review*, vol. 53, March, pp. 134–9.

———. (1965) *Modern Capital Theory* (New York and London: Columbia University Press).

Domar, E. (1961) "Discussion" [of paper by Richard Ruggles and Nancy Ruggles], in *Output, Input and Productivity Measurement* (National Bureau of Economic Research Studies in Income and Wealth, vol. 25) (Princeton, N.J.: NBER).

Dorfman, R. (1959a) "A Graphical Exposition of Böhm-Bawerk's Interest Theory," *Review of Economic Studies*, vol. 26, February, pp. 153–8.

———. (1959b) "Waiting and the Period of Production," *Quarterly Journal of Economics*, vol. 73, August, pp. 351–72.

Enke, S. (1962) "Production Functions and Capital Depreciation," *Journal of Political Economy*, vol. 70, August, pp. 368–79.

Faber, M. (ed.) (1986) *Studies in Austrian Capital Theory, Investment and Time* (Berlin, Heidelberg, and New York: Springer-Verlag).

Ferguson, C. E. (1969) *The Neoclassical Theory of Production and Distribution* (Cambridge: Cambridge University Press).

Fetter, Frank A. (1902) "The 'Roundabout Process' in the Interest Theory," *Quarterly Journal of Economics*, vol. 17, November; reprinted in Rothbard (1977).

———. (1914) "Capitalization versus Productivity: Rejoinder," *American Economic Review*, December; reprinted in Rothbard (1977).

Fisher, Irving (1906) *The Nature of Capital and Income* (reprinted New York: A. M. Kelley, 1965).

———. (1930) *The Theory of Interest* (New York: Macmillan).

Fraser, L. M. (1937) *Economic Thought and Language: A Critique of Some Fundamental Economic Concepts* (London: A. & C. Black).

Garrison, Roger W. (1985) "A Subjectivist Theory of a Capital-Using Economy," in Gerald P. O'Driscoll and Mario J. Rizzo (eds.), *The Economics of Time and Ignorance* (Oxford: Basil Blackwell).

Green, H. A. John (1964) *Aggregation in Economic Analysis: An Introductory Survey* (Princeton, N.J.: Princeton University Press).

Griliches, Z. (1961) "Discussion" [of papers presented in session on "Capital Theory"], *American Economic Review*, vol. 51, May, pp. 121–30.

————. (1963) "Capital Stock in Investment Functions: Some Problems of Concept and Measurement," in C. Christ et al., *Measurement in Economics* (Stanford, Calif.: Stanford University Press).

Haavelmo, T. (1960) *A Study in the Theory of Investment* (Chicago, Ill.: University of Chicago Press).

Hahn, F. H., and Matthews, R. C. O. (1964) "The Theory of Economic Growth: A Survey," *Economic Journal*, vol. 74, December, pp. 779–902.

Hammer, F. S. (1964) *The Demand for Physical Capital: Application of a Wealth Model* (Englewood Cliffs, N.J.: Prentice-Hall).

Harcourt, G. C. (1972) *Some Cambridge Controversies in the Theory of Capital* (Cambridge: Cambridge University Press).

Harcourt, G. C., and N. F. Laing, eds. (1971) *Capital and Growth* (Harmondsworth, U.K.: Penguin Books).

Hausman, Daniel M. (1981) *Capital, Profits and Prices* (New York: Columbia University Press).

Hayek, Friedrich A. (1934) "Carl Menger," in *Grundsätze der Volkswirtschaftslehre*, Scarce Tracts in Economic and Political Science (London: London School of Economics and Political Science).

————. (1935) "Maintenance of Capital," *Economica*, new series, vol. 2, August, pp. 241–76.

————. (1936) "The Mythology of Capital," *Quarterly Journal of Economics*, February. Page numbers cited refer to the reprint in American Economic Association, *Readings in the Theory of Income Distribution* (Philadelphia, Pa., and Toronto: Blakiston, 1946).

————. (1941) *The Pure Theory of Capital* (London: Macmillan).

————. (1945) "Time-Preference and Productivity: A Reconsideration," *Economica*, new series, vol. 12, February, pp. 22–5.

————. (1949) *Individualism and Economic Order* (London: Routledge & Kegan Paul).

————. (1955) *The Counter-revolution of Science: Studies in the Abuse of Reason* (Glencoe, Ill.: Free Press).

Hazlitt, H. (1959) *The Failure of the "New Economics"* (Princeton, N.J.: Van Nostrand).

Hicks, J. R. (1939) *Value and Capital* (Oxford: Clarendon Press).

————. (1961) "The Measurement of Capital in Relation to the Measurement of Other Economic Aggregates," in F. A. Lutz and D. C. Hague (eds.), *The Theory of Capital* (New York: St. Martin's Press).

————. (1963) *The Theory of Wages*, 2nd ed. (London: Macmillan).

————. (1973) *Capital and Time: A Neo-Austrian Theory* (Oxford: Clarendon Press).

————. (1974) "Capital Controversies: Ancient and Modern," *American Economic Review*, vol. 64, May, pp. 307–16.

Hutchison, Terence W. (1953) *A Review of Economic Doctrines, 1870–1929* (Oxford: Clarendon Press).

Kaldor, N. (1937) "The Controversy on the Theory of Capital," *Econometrica*, July. Page numbers cited refer to the reprint in N. Kaldor, *Essays on Value and Distribution* (London: Allen & Unwin, 1960).

———. (1955) *An Expenditure Tax* (London: Allen & Unwin).

Kauder, Emil (1965) *A History of Marginal Utility Theory* (Princeton, N.J.: Princeton University Press).

Kendrick, J. W. (1961) "Some Theoretical Aspects of Capital Measurement," *American Economic Review*, vol. 51, May, pp. 102–11.

Kennedy, C. (1955) "The Valuation of Net Investment," *Oxford Economic Papers*, new series, vol. 7, February, pp. 36–46.

Kirzner, I. M. (1960) *The Economic Point of View* (Princeton, N.J.: Van Nostrand).

———. (1963) *Market Theory and the Price System* (Princeton, N.J.: Van Nostrand).

———. (1966) *An Essay on Capital* (New York: Augustus M. Kelley).

———. (1976) "Ludwig von Mises and the Theory of Capital and Interest," in L. S. Moss, ed., *The Economics of Ludwig von Mises: Toward a Critical Reappraisal* (Kansas City: Sheed and Ward).

Knight, F. H. (1931) "Professor Fisher's Interest Theory: A Case in Point," *Journal of Political Economy*, vol. 39, April, pp. 176–212.

———. (1934) "Capital, Time, and the Interest Rate," *Economica*, vol. 1, no. 3, August, pp. 257–86.

———. (1935) "The Theory of Investment Once More: Mr. Boulding and the Austrians," *Quarterly Journal of Economics*, vol. 50, November, pp. 36–67.

———. (1936) "The Quantity of Capital and the Rate of Interest: I," *Journal of Political Economy*, vol. 44, August, pp. 433–63.

———. (1941) "Professor Mises and the Theory of Capital," *Economica*, new series, vol. 8, November, pp. 409–27.

———. (1944) "Diminishing Returns from Investment," *Journal of Political Economy*, vol. 52, March, pp. 26–47.

———. (1946) "Capital and Interest," in *Encyclopedia Brittanica*, vol. 4, 1946. Pages cited refer to reprint in American Economic Association, *Readings in the Theory of Income Distribution* (Philadelphia, Pa., and Toronto: Blakiston).

———. (1950) "Introduction," in Carl Menger, *Principles of Economics*, trans. James Dingwall and Bert F. Hoselitz (Glencoe, Ill.: Free Press).

———. (1956) *On the History and Method of Economics* (Chicago, Ill.: University of Chicago Press).

Kuenne, R. E. (1962a) "The Technological Superiority of Present Goods," *Zeitschrift für Nationalökonomie*, vol. 22, October, pp. 271–7.

———. (1962b) "The Stationary State and the Technological Superiority of Present Goods," *Quarterly Journal of Economics*, vol. 76, November, pp. 648–52.

Kuznets, S. (1957) Comment on paper by E. F. Denison, in *Problems of Capital Formation* (National Bureau of Economic Research Studies in Income and Wealth, vol. 19) (Princeton, N.J.: NBER).

Lachmann, L. M. (1956) *Capital and Its Structure* (London: G. Bell).

———. (1958) "Mrs. Robinson on the Accumulation of Capital," *South African Journal of Economics*, vol. 26, June, pp. 87–100.

———. (1973a) *Macro-economic Thinking and the Market Economy* (London: Institute of Economic Affairs).

———. (1973b) "Sir John Hicks as a Neo-Austrian," *South African Journal of Economics*, vol. 41, September, pp. 54–62.

Lerner, A. P. (1944) *The Economics of Control* (New York: Macmillan).

———. (1953) "On the Marginal Product of Capital and the Marginal Efficiency of Investment," *Journal of Political Economy*, February. Pages cited refer to the reprint in *Landmarks in Political Economy*, Earl J. Hamilton, Albert Rees, Harry G. Johnson, eds. (Chicago, Ill.: University of Chicago Press, 1962).

Lindahl, E. (1939) *Studies in the Theory of Money and Capital* (London: Farrar & Rinehart).

———. (1961) "Discussion of Professor Lutz's Paper," in F. A. Lutz and D. C. Hague (eds.), *The Theory of Capital* (New York: St. Martin's Press).

Little, I. M. D. (1950) *A Critique of Welfare Economics* (Oxford: Clarendon Press).

Lutz, F. (1961) "The Essentials of Capital Theory," in F. A. Lutz and D. C. Hague (eds.), *The Theory of Capital* (New York: St. Martin's Press)

Lutz, F., and V. Lutz (1951) *The Theory of Investment of the Firm* (Princeton, N.J.: Princeton University Press).

Malinvaud, E. (1961a) "The Analogy between Atemporal and Intertemporal Theories of Resource Allocation," *Review of Economic Studies*, vol. 28, June, pp. 143–60.

———. (1961b) Contribution to "The Discussion of Professor Hicks' Paper," in F. A. Lutz and D. C. Hague (eds.), *The Theory of Capital* (New York: St. Martin's Press).

Menger, Carl (1888) "Zur Theorie des Kapitals," in (Conrad's) *Jahrbücher für Nationalökonomie und Statistik*, neue folge, vol. 17, pp. 1–49.

———. (1950) *Principles of Economics*, translation of first German edition of *Grundsätze der Volkswirthschaftslehre* (1871), by James Dingwall and Bert F. Hoselitz (Glencoe, Ill.: Free Press).

Metzler, L. (1950) "The Rate of Interest and the Marginal Product of Capital," *Journal of Political Economy*, vol. 58, August, pp. 289–306.

Mises, Ludwig von (1931) "Das Festangelegte Kapital," in *Economische Opstelen: Aangeboden aan Prof. Dr. C. A. Verrijn Stuart* (Haarlem: De Erven F. Bohn N.V.); translated in Mises (1960).

———. (1940) *Nationalökonomie: Theorie des Handelns und Wirtschaftens* (Geneva: Editions Union).

———. (1949) *Human Action* (New Haven, Conn.: Yale University Press).

―――. (1953) *The Theory of Money and Credit* (New Haven, Conn.: Yale University Press), translation of the 2nd German ed. (1924); 1st ed. (1912).

―――. (1959) *Socialism: An Economic and Sociological Analysis* (New Haven, Conn.: Yale University Press).

―――. (1960) *Epistemological Problems of Economics,* trans. George Reisman (Princeton, N.J.: Van Nostrand), translation from German edition of *Grundprobleme der Nationalökonomie,* 1933.

―――. (1963) *Human Action: A Treatise on Economics,* 2nd rev. ed. (New Haven, Conn.: Yale University Press).

Neuberger, E. (1960) "Waiting and the Period of Production: Comment," *Quarterly Journal of Economics,* vol. 74, February, pp. 150–53.

Pellengahr, Ingo (1986a) "Austrians versus Austrians. I: A Subjectivist View of Interest," in Faber (1986).

―――. (1986b) "Austrians versus Austrians. II: Functionalist versus Essentialist Theories of Interest," in Faber (1986).

Ramsay, F. R. (1928) "A Mathematical Theory of Saving," *Economic Journal,* vol. 38, December, pp. 543–59.

Robinson, Joan (1954) "The Production Function and the Theory of Capital," *Review of Economic Studies,* February. Pages cited refer to the reprint in J. Robinson, *Collected Economic Papers,* vol. 2 (Oxford: Basil Blackwell).

―――. (1956) *The Accumulation of Capital* (London: Macmillan).

―――. (1962) *Economic Philosophy* (Chicago, Ill.: Aldine).

Rolph, E. (1939) "The Discounted Marginal Productivity Doctrine," *Journal of Political Economy,* August. Pages cited refer to the reprint in American Economic Association, *Readings in the Theory of Income Distribution* (Philadelphia, Pa., and Toronto: Blakiston).

Rothbard, M. (1962) *Man, Economy, and State* (Princeton, N.J.: Van Nostrand).

―――. (ed.) (1977) *Capital, Interest, and Rent: Essays in the Theory of Distribution,* by Frank A. Fetter (Kansas City: Sheed Andrews & McMeel).

Rothenberg, J. (1961) *The Measurement of Social Welfare* (Englewood Cliffs, N.J.: Prentice-Hall).

Ruggles, R., and Ruggles, N. (1961) "Concepts of Real Capital Stocks and Services," in *Output, Input and Productivity Measurement* (National Bureau of Economic Research, Studies in Income and Wealth, vol. 25) (Princeton, N.J.: NBER).

Samuelson, P. A. (1961) "The Evaluation of 'Social Income': Capital Formation and Wealth," in F. A. Lutz and D. C. Hague (eds.), *The Theory of Capital* (New York: St. Martin's Press).

―――. (1962) "Parable and Realism in Capital Theory: The Surrogate Production Function," *Review of Economic Studies,* vol. 29, June, pp. 193–206.

―――. (1966) "Paradoxes in Capital Theory: A Symposium. A Summing Up," *Quarterly Journal of Economics,* vol. 80, November, pp. 568–83.

———. (1981) "Schumpeter as an Economic Theorist," in H. Frisch (ed.), *Schumpeterian Economics* (New York: Praeger).

Saulnier, R. (1938) *Contemporary Monetary Theory* (New York: Columbia University Press).

Schumpeter, Joseph A. (1934) *The Theory of Economic Development* (Cambridge, Mass.: Harvard University Press), translated from the German original of 1912.

———. (1954) *History of Economic Analysis* (New York: Oxford University Press).

Sen, A. K. (1960) *Choice of Techniques: An Aspect of the Theory of Planned Economic Development* (reprinted New York: Augustus M. Kelley, 1968).

Smith, V. L. (1961) *Investment and Production: A Study in the Theory of Capital-Using Enterprise* (Cambridge, Mass.: Harvard University Press).

———. (1962) "The Theory of Capital," *American Economic Review*, vol. 52, June, pp. 481–91.

Solow, R. M. (1956) "The Production Function and the Theory of Capital," *Review of Economic Studies*, vol. 23, no. 2, pp. 101–8.

———. (1962) "Technical Progress, Capital Formation and Economic Growth," *American Economic Review*, vol. 52, May, pp. 76–86.

———. (1963) *Capital Theory and the Rate of Return* (Chicago, Ill.: Rand-McNally).

———. (1975) "Cambridge and the Real World," *The Times Literary Supplement*, 14 March.

Sraffa, Piero (1960) *The Production of Commodities by Means of Commodities: A Prelude to a Critique of Economic Theory* (Cambridge: Cambridge University Press).

Stigler, G. J. (1941) *Production and Distribution Theories: The Formative Period* (New York: Macmillan).

———. (1961) "Economic Problems in Measuring Changes in Productivity," in *Output, Input and Productivity Measurement* (National Bureau of Economic Research Studies in Income and Wealth, vol. 25) (Princeton, N.J.: NBER).

Streissler, Erich (1973) "The Menger Tradition," in J. R. Hicks and W. Weber, *Carl Menger and the Austrian School of Economics* (Oxford: Clarendon Press).

Thalberg, B. (1961) "An Analysis of a Market for Investment Goods," in F. A. Lutz and D. C. Hague (eds.), *The Theory of Capital* (New York: St. Martin's Press).

Uhr, C. G. (1960) *The Economic Doctrines of Knut Wicksell* (Berkeley and Los Angeles: University of California Press).

Usher, D. (1965) "Traditional Capital Theory," *Review of Economic Studies*, vol. 32, April, pp. 169–86.

Weckstein, R. (1962) "Welfare Criteria and Changing Tastes," *American Economic Review*, vol. 52, March, pp. 133–53.

Weston, J. F. (1951) "Some Perspectives on Capital Theory," *American Economic Review*, vol. 41, May, pp. 129–44.

Whately, R. (1826) "On Certain Terms which Are Peculiarly Liable to Be Used Ambiguously in Political Economy." Reprinted as an appendix to N. Senior, *An Outline of the Science of Political Economy* (New York: A. M. Kelley, 1951).

Wicksell, K. (1934) *Lectures on Political Economy* (London: Routledge).

Witte, J. G. Jr. (1963) "The Microfoundations of the Social Investment Function," *Journal of Political Economy*, vol. 71, October, pp. 441–56.

Yeager, Leland B. (1976) "Toward Understanding Some Paradoxes in Capital Theory," *Economic Inquiry*, vol. 14, September, pp. 313–46.

———. (1979) "Capital Paradoxes and the Concept of Waiting," in M. Rizzo (ed.), *Time, Uncertainty, and Disequilibrium* (Lexington, Mass.: D. C. Heath).

This book is set in Scala and Scala Sans, created by the
Dutch designer Martin Majoor in the 1990s.

Printed on paper that is acid-free and meets the
requirements of the American National Standard for
Permanence of Paper for Printed Library Materials,
z39.48-1992. ∞

Book design by Richard Hendel, Chapel Hill, North Carolina
Typography by Newgen, Austin, Texas
Printed and bound by Worzalla Publishing Company,
Stevens Point, Wisconsin